Field Guide to Leadership and Supervision for Nonprofit Staff

Second Edition

By Carter McNamara, MBA, PhD

AUTHENTICITY CONSULTING, LLC
MINNEAPOLIS, MN USA

For reprint permission, more information on Authenticity Consulting, LLC, or to order additional copies of this or any of our other publications, please contact:

Authenticity Consulting, LLC
4008 Lake Drive Avenue North
Minneapolis, MN 55422-1508 USA

800.971.2250 toll-free
763.971.8890 direct

http://www.authenticityconsulting.com

Trademarks

Authenticity Circles, Free Management Library, Free Nonprofit Micro-eMBA and Free Micro-eMBA are service marks of Authenticity Consulting, LLC, Minneapolis, Minnesota. "Leveraging the Power of Peers" is a registered mark of Authenticity Consulting, LLC, Minneapolis, Minnesota. "Policy Governance" is a registered trademark of Carver Governance Design, Inc.

Credits

Cover design and illustrations by Erin Scott/Wylde Hare Creative, Woodbury, Minnesota.
Photographs © 2005 JupiterImages Corporation/Comstock.com, primary cover photo;
   © Teri McNamara/Impressions & Expressions and © Erin Scott/Wylde Hare Creative,
   secondary cover photos.
Clip art by Nova Development Corporation Art Explosion 750,000 Images.
Printed by Graphic & Printing Services, Big Lake, Minnesota.

Manufactured in the United States of America
First Edition July 2003
Second Edition November 2008

Waiver of Responsibility

Various Web addresses are referenced in this book. The author and publisher have no legal responsibility or liability for the currency or accuracy of these Web addresses or the content at these addresses.

Publisher's Cataloging in Publication Data

McNamara, Carter, 1953 -

   Field Guide to Leadership and Supervision for Nonprofit Staff / by Carter McNamara
   ISBN 13: 978-1-933719-07-8
   ISBN 10: 1-933719-07-9

1. Leadership development. 2. Supervision. 3. Nonprofits. I. Title

Table of Contents

Table of Tables

Introduction

About This Guide

Focus of Guide: All Areas of Leadership and Supervision

Simply put, leading is setting direction and influencing to follow that direction. You can lead yourself, others, groups and the organization. This Field Guide is useful for leading all of these areas of focus. Supervision is overseeing the productivity and progress of employees who report to you, that is, leading those employees – this guide is for supervisors, too.

Note that this Field Guide does not address specifics of conducting certain management functions, such as financial management, program management, fundraising and administration. You can gain a large amount of that type of management information by referencing our Free Management Library^{SM}, one of the world's largest collections of well-organized, free resources about personal, professional and organizational development. The Library is described in Appendix B of this guide.

Nature of Guide: Highly Practical Tips, Tools and Techniques

This guide is written in a highly practical, how-to style that is immediately useful to nonprofit organizations, especially those that have very limited resources and, many times, burned-out staff. The guide includes tips, tools and techniques, rather than general discussions, concepts and analyses. Thus, this guide is customized particularly to the real world of the extremely busy Chief Executive Officer and other nonprofit leaders among the staff.

Usually there are many approaches that can be used to address a particular challenge, for example, approaches for successful time and stress management. This author strongly believes that nonprofit leaders can benefit most from consistently applying almost any one of these approaches, rather than gathering more and more of them. Consequently, this guide provides one set of time-tested and useful tools, rather than many.

Audiences

This Field Guide is written for you if you are a:

- Founder or Chief Executive Officer of a nonprofit

- Nonprofit manager or supervisor

- Member of a Board of Directors

- Consultant to nonprofits

The guide also includes occasional references to USA-specific and Canadian-specific information, which are marked as such. There are differences between various countries regarding employment laws and those laws are highly relevant to the practices of leadership and supervision of staff. Therefore, you are advised to establish an up-to-date set of personnel policies with the guidance of an expert in local regulations and norms. Guidelines to do this are on page 202.

How to Use This Guide

Leaders of small to medium-sized nonprofits rarely have sufficient funds for professional development. However, in our firm's experience, that is not the biggest issue in developing nonprofit leaders. The biggest issue is that nonprofit leaders seldom seek help and, when they do, they rarely can use that help to its fullest advantage because the help is not customized to the nature and needs of small- to medium-sized nonprofits. This guide is customized to those needs.

Do not be concerned about the large size of this guide. It is designed to be a reference manual for you. Refer to each topic in the guide as you need that topic in the day-to-day activities of leading in your organization. Each topic includes references to Web addresses that provide additional free information.

Here are some suggestions for the best way to use this guide:

1. Ensure that each nonprofit staff leader and manager has a copy of the guide. This is usually much cheaper than hiring an expert to conduct one-shot training sessions – sessions that often result in unused materials, left to collect dust on shelves.

2. Schedule one hour a week to read the guide until it has been read cover to cover. As you go through the guide, complete a calendar of the activities that you plan to conduct from referencing the guide. Reference "Typical Timing of Nonprofit CEO's Tasks" on page 49.

3. Refer to the guide whenever the nonprofit organization is engaged in an activity that is addressed in this guidebook. Post a copy of this guide's Table of Contents on the side of your desk or somewhere accessible for easy reference.

4. Schedule half an hour per month to discuss a topic in this guide with the rest of your management staff or with a group of peers in other organizations.

5. Be sure that you have mastered use of the guidelines in PART III, "How to Lead and Manage Yourself!" Those are the skills that are most important in being an effective leader, yet those are the skills that are most frequently forgotten.

Frequently Used Terms in Guidebook

The following terms are used frequently in this guide and with the following definitions:

Clients

The people or groups of people who directly benefit from the programs and services of a nonprofit.

Board of Directors

The group of people who are legally charged to govern the corporation, whether for-profit or nonprofit.

The term "Director" is not used in this Field Guide as it is in many other books about Boards. The term can be confusing because it can apply to members of a Board of Directors or to the Executive Director. The guide instead refers to "Board members" or "members of the Board."

Chief Executive Officer (or CEO, Chief Executive or Executive Director)

The CEO position is the singular organization-wide, staff position that is primarily responsible to carry out the strategic plans and policies established by the Board of Directors (sometimes the Board and CEO work in a "strategic partnership" in which the Board does not direct the CEO in such a top-down, hierarchical manner). The CEO (in nonprofits, commonly referred to as the Executive Director) reports to the Board of Directors. Not all nonprofits have staff members, including a CEO. Particularly in small or new nonprofits, the Board members and Executive Director often seem to work in partnership to oversee and manage the nonprofit's operations, even though the Board has the ultimate authority. This guide uses the phrases Chief Executive Officer (or Chief Executive), Executive Director and CEO interchangeably.

Leader

This is a role that has significant responsibility for setting direction for oneself, another individual, group or the entire organization, and ensuring that direction is followed.

Nonprofit

A nonprofit organization is formed to meet a public need – and should be held accountable to prove that it is meeting that need (ensuring that accountability is one of the Board's most important jobs). An organization that is chartered with the appropriate government agency to be a corporation; thus, requiring a Board of Directors. It can also be tax-exempt and/or charitable in status. The guide often refers to "nonprofit" to mean the overall organization, including members of its Board and staff.

Stakeholders

These are people or groups of people who "have a stake," or strong, vested interest in the operations of the organization, for example: Board members, staff members, clients, funders, collaborators, community leaders and government agencies. The most important stakeholder of the nonprofit is the group of clients whose needs the nonprofit is aiming to meet.

Supervisor

This is a position that is responsible for the progress and productivity for people who report directly to the position. The role of supervisor is a leadership role.

 The Glossary on page 253 also provides definitions of these and other key terms.

Frequent References to Useful Resources

The guide includes numerous references to useful resources, internal and external to the book. Each reference is marked with a handy symbol for ease of recognition. The following symbols are used.

 References to other sections of the guide that you may want to look at more closely.

 References to related content available in external resources, such as other books.

 References to related content available on the web, such as tools and sample documents.

1. Numbered lists suggest guidelines and the order in which they should be applied. They also indicate that there are a specific number of items in the list.

- Bulleted lists provide information that can be considered in any order and may not be all-inclusive.

About the Author

Carter McNamara, MBA, PhD, is a partner in Authenticity Consulting, LLC. He started working with nonprofit Boards in 1978 and has worked with and for a variety of organizations since then – for-profit, nonprofit, government, small and large. He has strong experience in leadership and supervision from working his way along the "ladder" from individual contributor to director. He has consulted in a wide array of services to for-profit and nonprofit organizations. He is founder and developer of the Authenticity Circles^{SM} peer coaching group models, Free Management Library^{SM}, and Free Micro-eMBA^{SM} and Nonprofit Micro-eMBA^{SM}. He has extensive training and experience in training and coaching, including Action Learning and peer coaching. He is confident of the ability of learners to recognize their own development needs and direct their own learning.

Dr. McNamara holds a BA in Social and Behavioral Sciences, a BS in Computer Science, an MBA from the University of St. Thomas, and a PhD in Human and Organization Development from The Union Institute in Cincinnati, Ohio.

About Authenticity Consulting, LLC

Authenticity Consulting, LLC, publisher of this guidebook, is a Minneapolis-based consulting firm specializing in development of nonprofit organizations, management and programs. While many firms specialize in one or a few specific services to nonprofits, Authenticity brings a highly comprehensive and integrated approach with focus on building the capacity of the entire organization, including its governance, management and staffing, programs, marketing, finances, fundraising and evaluation. We provide services in nonprofit:

- Board development and governance

- Strategic planning and strategic management

- Leadership and management development

- Program development and evaluation

- Overall organizational change

We also provide powerful, practical peer learning programs for networking, training, problem solving and support – either free-standing or to enrich other programs – through Authenticity Circles peer coaching group models. Our unique Action Learning-based group coaching process ensures ongoing support and accountability among participants during the organizational change process – few change models recognize and build in processes to ensure these two critical elements of any change process. We also include ongoing, frequent one-on-one coaching sessions with key leaders in client organizations.

 We can be reached at 800.971.2250 or +1.763.971.8890.

 You can see our website at http://www.authenticityconsulting.com .

PART I:

TO LEAD NONPROFITS,

FIRST UNDERSTAND

THEM

Nonprofits – What They Are and How They Work

To lead nonprofits, you should understand them – their purpose, how they work, how they typically are designed, what nonprofit programs are and are not, and the nature of a typical nonprofit. This section provides all of that information to you.

How Nonprofits Differ From For-Profits – and How They Are the Same

Perhaps the best way to explain the purpose and designs of nonprofit corporations is to compare them to for-profit corporations, a form with which most of us are quite familiar. Table I:1 depicts differences between both types of organizations.

Table I:1 – Comparison Between For-profit and Nonprofit Corporations

For-Profit Corporations	Nonprofit Corporations
Owned by stockholders	Owned by the public
Generate money for the owners	Serve the public
Success is making sizeable profit	Success is meeting needs of public
Board members are usually paid	Board members are usually unpaid volunteers
Members can make very sizeable income	Members should make reasonable, not excessive, income
Money earned over and above that needed to pay expenses is kept as profit and distributed to owners	Money earned over and above that needed to pay expenses is retained as surplus and should be spent soon on meeting the public need (the nonprofit can earn profit from activities not directly related to the nonprofit's mission; however the nonprofit often has to pay taxes over a certain amount)
Chief Executive Officer is often on the Board of Directors, and sometimes is the President of the Board	Conventional wisdom suggests that the Chief Executive Officer (often called the "Executive Director") not be on the Board
Usually not exempt from paying federal, state/provincial, and local taxes	Can often be exempt from federal taxes, and some state/provincial and local taxes, if the nonprofit was granted tax-exempt status from the appropriate governmental agency
Money invested in the for-profit usually cannot be deducted from the investor's personal tax liability	Money donated to the nonprofit can be deducted from the donor's personal tax liability if the nonprofit was granted charitable status from the appropriate government agency

Although Table I:1 depicts distinct differences between for-profit and nonprofit corporations, there is much more similarity between them than many people often realize. Both types of organizations must have effective governance, leadership, robust planning, quality services to constituents, competent and committed personnel, and cost-effective operations.

Also, the types of issues that can occur in small nonprofits are very similar to the types of issues that can occur in small for-profits, including the constant struggle to obtain funding and good people, reacting to the changing day-to-day demands in the workplace, ensuring that customers are always satisfied, and managing time and stress to avoid burnout. In many ways, a small nonprofit is much more like a small for-profit in nature than a large nonprofit. Similarly, a large nonprofit is much more like a large for-profit in nature than a small nonprofit.

There Is More Than One Type of Nonprofit Organization

1. **Informal nonprofits**
    The purpose of this type of nonprofit is to address an occasional, and not critical, need in your community. For example, if you want to gather some people together for a short time in order to clean up your neighborhood, then you probably do not need to file to be a nonprofit corporation (see below). Instead, you can form a rather informal nonprofit just by getting together with some neighbors for a seasonal project.

2. **Formal nonprofit corporations ("chartered" and incorporated)**
    If the purpose of the nonprofit is to meet a current, major, ongoing need in your community, then you probably want to incorporate the nonprofit organization as a separate legal entity. In the United States of America (USA), you form a corporation by filing papers (usually Articles of Incorporation) in your state, usually by contacting your Secretary of State's office. In Canada, you can form a nonprofit corporation either at the provincial or federal levels, and you might be able to form under a variety of regulations, for example, a provincial Societies Act or Companies Act, or the federal Canada Corporations Act. In Canada, it is necessary to be incorporated in order to become a charity. That is not always true in the USA, for example, private foundations formed as trusts can get tax-exemption without incorporation.

    Depending on the country in which you live, benefits of incorporation might be that the nonprofit corporation can own property and its own bank account, enter into contracts, continue operations as a legal entity after you are gone, be eligible to conduct tax-exempt activities (see below), be eligible for tax-deductible donations (see below), and conduct operations for which you are personally not liable (in most cases).

3. **Tax-exempt nonprofits**
    If you want the nonprofit to be exempt (and if you think the nonprofit deserves to be exempt) from paying federal and possibly other taxes, then you should file with the appropriate government agency to gain tax-exempt status. For example, in Canada, you can get tax-exempt status at the provincial or federal level. In the USA, you would have to file with the Internal Revenue Service (IRS) to get tax-exempt status, usually after first gaining corporate status. To qualify for tax-exempt status in the USA, the nonprofit must serve a need that is religious, educational, charitable, scientific or literary in nature. If the IRS grants 501(c)(3) status (often referred to as "charitable" status) to the nonprofit, it will send you a determination letter. Be sure to keep and safely protect this letter. Tax-exempt nonprofits sometimes do not have to pay certain state and local property taxes. Note that all nonprofits still must pay employment taxes.

4.   **Tax-deductible (charitable nonprofits, or charities)**
     Depending on the nature of the mission of the nonprofit corporation, it might also be granted tax-deductible (or charitable) status, for example, from the IRS in the USA or the Canada Revenue Agency in Canada. Being tax-exempt is not the same as being tax-deductible. Tax-deductible means that donors can deduct their contributions to your organization during their federal and (sometimes) state, or provincial, tax computations. Tax-deductible status is granted usually to nonprofits that meet certain types of public needs (see the next section).

     In the USA, the IRS does not grant tax-deductible status to all nonprofits, nor does the Canada Revenue Agency in Canada. For example, the IRS does not grant tax-deductible status to social welfare nonprofits, 501(c)(4)'s, that exist primarily to lobby, or to associations, 501(c)(6)'s, that exist primarily to support networking and development of their members. IRS Publication 526 lists the types of organizations to which donations are deductible.

Different Types of Public Needs Met by Nonprofits

Nonprofit corporations get special tax benefits from their governmental agencies (for example, tax-exempt and/or charitable status from the Internal Revenue Service in the USA) for providing services primarily to meet certain kinds of public needs, usually including:

- Arts
- Charitable needs
- Civic affairs
- Education
- Environment

- Health
- Literary
- Religion
- Scientific
- Social services (or human services)

Three Most Important Levels Within Nonprofits

Boards and Governance

Because the nonprofit organization is incorporated, it requires a Board of Directors. The Board is responsible to provide governance in the form of overall strategic direction, guidance and controls. This does not mean that Board members only focus inward – they are responsible to ensure, even to verify, that the nonprofit is indeed meeting the needs of the community. Many people are coming to consider governance as a function carried out by the Board, top management and even by affiliated organizations. Effective governance depends to a great extent on the working relationship between Board and top management (if the nonprofit has staff members as management – not all of them do).

Central Administration

Central administration includes the staff and facilities that are common to running all programs and services. This usually includes at least the Chief Executive Officer (Executive Director) and office personnel, such as finance staff or executive assistants. If there are no paid staff members, then Board members might conduct the central administrative duties themselves. Nonprofits usually strive to keep costs of central administration low in proportion to the cost of running programs.

Programs

Nonprofit programs are services conducted to meet community needs by achieving outcomes among clients in that community. Evaluations ensure that the outcomes are achieved and that the program is a good investment. People often confuse programs with a random set of activities aimed to help people. Instead, programs are much more organized than that (see the following reference).

Consider "Nonprofit Programs – What They Are and What They Are Not" on page 7.

Most Important Roles People Play in Nonprofits

Clients

Everything in a nonprofit is ultimately directed to serving clients. Clients are the "consumers" or "customers" of the nonprofit. Services can be in the form of tangible or intangible products, and are often provided in the form of nonprofit programs. Some people refer to "primary clients" as those who directly benefit from the program and "secondary clients" as those who indirectly benefit. This Field Guide refers to clients as being the primary clients.

Board Members

Law and theory dictate that the Board is in charge and that its members are directly accountable for the overall direction and policies of the organization. Powers are given to the Board by its governing documents, for example, Articles of Incorporation, Articles of Association or its Constitution. The Board can configure itself and the nonprofit in whatever structure it prefers to best work toward the organization's mission, and usually does so via specifications in the By-Laws (more information about By-Laws is provided in the next section about starting a nonprofit). Members of nonprofit Boards are generally motivated by a desire to serve the community, their own professional development, and personal satisfaction of volunteering. Usually, nonprofit Board members do not receive direct monetary compensation for serving on the Board. Board members have authority only when acting as a body of all members – each member cannot officially act for the entire Board.

Board Chair

The Board Chair's role is central to facilitating and coordinating the work of the Board and Board committees, if the nonprofit chooses to use committees. The Chair's role is specified in the By-Laws, and usually includes authority to appoint Chairs and members of Board committees. Members of the Board do not work for the Board Chair, they work for the entire Board. The power of the Board Chair is through persuasion and general leadership ability.

Committees or Task Forces

The Board might choose to carry out its operations and oversight function by using a variety of Board committees. (Some nonprofits choose not to use committees and instead to use temporary "task forces" to address a certain function or priority.) Committees often are matched to the strategic priorities of the nonprofit (for example, to expanding markets or building a facility) or to oversight of common management functions. Examples of common committees are the Executive Committee,

Finance Committee, Fundraising Committee, Marketing Committee, Programs Committee and Personnel Committee.

Chief Executive Officer (CEO, Executive Director)

The Board might choose to retain a Chief Executive Officer role in the nonprofit organization. If so, the Board typically chooses to have this role be ultimately responsible to carry out the wishes of the Board. Usually, the Chief Executive Officer is directly accountable for the work of the staff and supports the work of the Board committees. The Board members and Chief Executive often work together in the nature of a "strategic partnership." The Chief Executive Officer is a member of the staff. This might be a volunteer role in a small nonprofit.

Staff

Staff members (if the nonprofit has staff members) other than the Chief Executive usually report to the Chief Executive and may support the work of Board committees at the request of the CEO (if the nonprofit chooses to use committees). As mentioned above, the role of Chief Executive is a staff role. Staff, in this context, might refer to program directors / managers, accountants, executive or administrative assistants, or people who provide direct services to clients. Some nonprofits might not have any paid staff members; they might have only volunteer staff members.

Volunteers

Volunteers are unpaid personnel who serve as staff members or assist staff members. In many nonprofits, the volunteers are every bit as valuable to the organization as paid staff members. In well-managed nonprofits, volunteers are supervised as carefully as staff members, including careful selection, orienting and training, organizing and evaluation. Board members of nonprofits are themselves volunteers.

Nonprofit Programs – What They Are and What They Are Not

True Programs Versus Loosely Organized Activities

Activities

Activities are not the same as programs. Experienced nonprofit leaders recognize the difference. Activities are a set of events that, although they are seemingly beneficial to the community, are so loosely or informally conducted that it is difficult to readily ascertain if the events are truly needed by the community and/or are making any substantive difference in the community.

There are many types of activities that can be useful to a community, even someone standing on a corner and handing out food to whomever happens to walk by. On first impression, that event might seem beneficial to the community. However, without knowing whether the food is safe, whether those walking by really need the food or not, and whether handing out the food on the corner is the best means to provide the food, it is difficult to ascertain whether the event deserves the ongoing investment of resources from the community.

Programs

The typical nonprofit organizational structure is built around programs. A nonprofit program is an integrated set of services conducted to meet specific, verified community needs by achieving certain specific benefits and changes (outcomes) among specific groups of clients in that community. Services include ongoing systematic evaluations, as much as possible, to ensure that the specific outcomes are indeed being achieved and that the community's resources are best invested in that particular program. Nonprofit leaders should always be asking if those outcomes are being achieved.

Community needs are verified to exist by some means of market research (formal or informal research). The methods or programs to meet those needs are also researched to verify that they are likely to meet those needs in the community. During delivery of the programs, program activities are evaluated to ensure they remain high-quality. Outcomes from programs are evaluated, with strong feedback from clients, to be sure the program is indeed meeting the needs in the community.

In essence, a well-designed program is similar to a well-designed research project from which a community can benefit and a great deal can be learned. Common examples of nonprofit programs are food-shelf programs, transportation programs, training programs, health services programs and arts programs.

Nonprofits often define their programs during strategic planning. Programs become major methods, or strategies, to reach strategic goals. For example, a nonprofit might have a mission to "Enhance the quality of life for young adults by promoting literacy." Major strategies, or programs, to work toward that mission might be a High School Equivalency Training Program and a Transportation Program to get the young adults to the Training Program.

To clearly understand the nature of well-developed programs, it helps to think of them in terms of inputs, processes, outputs and outcomes.

- Inputs are the various resources needed to run the program, such as money, facilities, clients and program staff.

- Processes are how the program is carried out, for example, clients are counseled, children are cared for, art is created, and association members are supported.

- Outputs are the units of service, for example, number of clients counseled, children cared for, artistic pieces produced, or members in the association.

- Outcomes are the impacts on the clients from participating in the nonprofit's services, for example, increased mental health, safe and secure development, richer artistic appreciation and perspectives in life, and increased effectiveness among members.

How to Understand Overall System of Programs

It is very important that Board and staff members truly understand the nature and structure of nonprofit programs – programs are the most important tools by which nonprofits meet the needs of their communities. One of the best ways to get a clear impression of what occurs in a program is to develop a logic model. A logic model is a top-level depiction of the inputs, processes, outputs and outcomes of a program. Constructing a logic model helps program planners and evaluators answer the following questions:

- What outcomes does the program want to help its participants to achieve, including short-term, intermediate and long-term outcomes?

- What activities, or processes, need to occur in the program for those outcomes to be achieved?

- What resources are needed to be able to conduct the processes?

Table I:2 depicts a logic model for a fictitious program called the Self-Directed Learning Center (SDLC). This example is intended to portray the scope and level of detail in a program's logic model.

Table I:2 – Logic Model for Nonprofit Program "Self-Directed Learning Center (SDLC)"

This logic model depicts a program called the Self-Directed Learning Center (SDLC). The mission, or purpose, of the program is to enhance the quality of life for low-income adults by providing free, online training materials and programs and by helping them help each other to learn. Feedback from the environment is from inputs, environmental scanning, market research and program evaluations. Feedback to the environment is principally from public relations, advertising and promotions, outputs and outcomes.

Inputs	Processes	Outputs	Short-Term Outcomes	Intermediate Outcomes	Long-Term Outcomes
• Collaborators	• Provide peer-assistance models in which learners support each other	• 30 groups that used peer models	• High-school diploma for graduates	• Full-time employment for learners in jobs that require high-school education	• Improved attitude toward self and society for graduates, e.g., studies social issues to be a more well informed voter
• Computers	• Provide free, online training programs	• 100 learners finished training programs	• Participants sign up for advanced schooling	• Independent living for learners, e.g., from using salary to rent housing	• Improved family life for families of graduates, e.g., uses strong conflict management skills
• Free articles and other publications on the Web	• Provide free, online training program: Basics of Self-Directed Learning	• 900 learners who finished Basics of Self-Directed Learning		• Strong basic life skills for learners, e.g., can use a budget and balance check book	• Increased reliability and improved judgment of learners, e.g., stops using self-destructive habits
• Funders					
• Self-directed learners	• Provide free, online training program: Basic Life Skills	• 900 learners who finished Basic Life Skills			
• Supplies					
• Volunteers	• Provide free, online training program: Passing Your GED Exam	• 900 learners who finished Passing Your GED Exam			
• Web					

How You Can Build Your Programs (Five Approaches)

There are at least five different common approaches to developing a new nonprofit program. Each of the approaches is described in the rest of this topic. Some approaches seem to start out slow and soon stop altogether. Other approaches start out fast and then end in a flurry of confusion. Still, other approaches start out carefully and go on to make a huge difference for their clients. The approach you use depends on various factors.

Note that sometimes the approach to development of a new nonprofit organization is essentially the same as the approach to development of its new program, particularly if the organization is new or only has one program. In that case, it might be difficult to detect any difference between the approaches to developing the overall organization and its new program. Whether it is a new organization or a new program, the development process depends on several factors.

1. **The nature and complexity of the organization's programs and services**
   For example, the process to develop a program that provides mental health services would probably be more complex than the process to develop a program that provides a food shelf for low-income families.

2. **The resources and stability of the overall organization**
   For example, if the organization has been in operation for several years and its current programs have been using the same processes and procedures over those years, the organization probably has more accurate and reliable processes from which to design new or related programs. On the other hand, if the organization is relatively new, it likely has limited expertise and resources from which to design programs.

3. **The extent of program development expertise in the organization**
   It is not surprising to find that many nonprofit leaders have little, if any, formal training in developing programs. There have been few comprehensive resources in this regard. Many nonprofits have resorted simply to doing whatever seems reasonable for the day, while collecting as many resources as possible and hoping that they will be useful.

 Consider the guidebook, *Field Guide to Nonprofit Program Design, Marketing and Evaluation,* from Authenticity Consulting, LLC. Go to the "Publications" link at http://www.authenticityconsulting.com .

Following are descriptions of five common approaches to developing nonprofit programs. The nature of the approaches can overlap somewhat.

"Build It and They Will Come" Approach

This approach is common in new nonprofit organizations. It is most likely to occur if the founder is rather inexperienced in program development, in conducting marketing analysis, and/or has a strong passion – even an obsession – about meeting a perceived need in the community. In these situations, the founder believes that there is an unmet need in the community. He bases his belief almost entirely on his own perception, even though there is sometimes no verified evidence of a strong unmet need. In this approach, the founder:

1. On his own, designs a method (often a roughly designed program) to meet the need that he perceives in the community.

2. Applies for funding to a donation source (individuals, corporations, foundations or the government) and is turned down due to lack of evidence that the perceived unmet need really exists.

3. Advertises the program to the community, usually through word-of-mouth, flyers, brochures and direct mailings.

4. Experiences a great deal of frustration that most of the people having the perceived unmet need do not flock to the program.

5. Substantially increases the advertising throughout the community.

6. Continues to experience frustration that most of the people having the unmet need do not flock to the program.

7. Either abandons the effort or, if the unmet need really does exist, persists and accomplishes the seat-of-the-pants approach to program development. The program, however, often suffers from Founder's Syndrome, where the nonprofit is operated according to the personality of someone in the organization (usually the founder), rather than according to the mission of the organization.

Seat-of-the-Pants Approach

This approach is common to many new nonprofit organizations, especially if their founders are rather inexperienced in organizational development and management. In these situations, the nonprofit organization and its primary program are so highly integrated that it is difficult to discern what resources go directly into providing services to clients versus those resources needed to run the entire organization. The seat-of-the-pants program development process usually parallels the development of the organization itself, and might best be described to include the following steps:

1. A person realizes a major, unmet need in the community. The person starts doing whatever he/she can to meet the need, mostly through his/her own efforts.

2. The person realizes that he/she cannot do it all, and/or others start to chip in and help the person. Over time, all the people involved start to agree on who is going to do what to be more efficient. At this point in the program, all the participants are often still volunteers.

3. Over time, some or all of the people realize that they need more help, including money, to continue to meet the community need. To get funding, they usually start to form a nonprofit corporation by filing Articles of Incorporation, usually with the Secretary of State's office in their state. Filing for incorporation requires that the nonprofit have a Board of Directors. They are soon granted the status of nonprofit corporation. Next, they often seek tax-exempt status from the Internal Revenue Service so they do not have to pay federal taxes. So they apply for tax-exempt status and may eventually get tax-deductible/charitable status, too.

4. They continue to work to meet the major need in the community, while they continue to organize themselves, usually by having a volunteer Chief Executive Officer and other volunteers.

5.   Organizations, like people, go through life cycles. Nonprofit organizations and/or programs rarely get through the first life cycle until they have established the necessary processes and structures to sustain continued growth. Hopefully, the nonprofit realizes that they need yet more planning and organization of resources to meet the community need in a more effective and efficient fashion. If they do not achieve this realization, they can succumb to Founder's Syndrome.

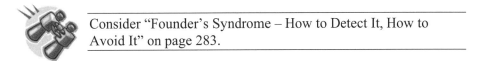

Consider "Founder's Syndrome – How to Detect It, How to Avoid It" on page 283.

6.   At this point, whether the nonprofit achieves more organization of its resources or not, it has developed a program geared to meet the unmet need of the community. The program development approach was somewhat seat-of-the-pants in nature – people scraped the program together by doing whatever they had to and whenever they had to do it. The program just kind of came together.

While this seat-of-the-pants approach often works when first developing a nonprofit organization, it certainly is not the best way to go forward or to add other programs.

Incremental Planning Approach

People can probably develop a new program without having to resort to the high-risk, seat-of-the-pants approach or to a more comprehensive, in-depth process if:

1.   They know their client needs well. (They should be careful about assuming that they do!)

2.   They plan to meet those needs by using program methods with which they are familiar.

3.   The cost and risk of starting the new program are quite low.

If the above conditions are true, they can develop their new program with a straightforward plan that specifies:

1.   Outcomes and/or goals for the new program to achieve.

2.   Program methods or activities to accomplish those goals.

3.   Any minor changes that must be made to current programs in order to implement the new program methods.

4.   Who is responsible to implement the program methods and make the minor changes.

5.   Timelines for achievement of the goals.

6.   Budget that lists the funds necessary to obtain the resources required to achieve the goals.

Business Planning Approach

There are a variety of views, formats and content regarding business plans. Usually, a business plan includes careful analyses of:

1. A major unmet need in the community.

2. Program method(s) to meet the need.

3. How the community and nonprofit can engage in a productive, ongoing relationship where the nonprofit program continues to meet the community need and the community, in turn, returns sufficient value to the nonprofit.

4. How the program methods can be implemented and managed.

5. What the costs are to build and implement the program methods.

Usually, the business plan includes contents that are organized into several other subordinate (or smaller) plans, including a marketing plan, management plan and financial plan.

You might have recognized that a business plan is essentially the same as a well-written fundraising proposal; thus, it might be said that the more you use a business-planning approach in your program development, the more probable it is that you will get funds from donors.

Particularly in the for-profit world, bankers and other investors often require a business plan because the plan includes a careful look at all aspects of a project. Business planning is often conducted when:

- Expanding a current organization, product or service.

- Starting a new organization, product or service.

- Buying an organization, product or service.

- Working to improve the management of a current organization, product or service.

People should do a business plan for a nonprofit program if any of the following conditions exist:

1. The nature of the program is new to the organization.

2. They will need funding to develop and operate the program.

3. They are not familiar with the program's clients and their needs.

4. They are not completely sure how to meet their needs.

Business Development Approach

"Nonprofits have to recognize that they are businesses, not just causes. There is a way to combine the very best of the not-for-profit, philanthropic world with the very best of the for-profit, enterprising world. This hybrid is the wave of the future for both profit and nonprofit companies."

From *Genius at Work*, an interview with Bill Strickland, CEO
of Manchester Craftsmen's Guide and the Bidwell Training Center

A new trend in nonprofit program planning is focus on nonprofit business development, which might take program planning to an even higher level of quality than that done in business planning. Note that nonprofit business development includes the business planning process so, technically, it is not a completely different alternative to business planning. However, business development usually includes more upfront, rigorous examination for numerous opportunities to provide products and services among a variety of stakeholders to generate revenue and still work toward the mission of the organization. Business development often helps groups of clients identify new needs that they did not even realize, whereas processes that start right away with business planning are based on one currently known, particular need among clients without rigorous analysis for many other opportunities. Business development is quite market-driven, whereas business planning can be quite program-driven. Andy Horsnell, co-founder of Authenticity Consulting, LLC, describes the main phases in the business development process, including:

1.   Clarifying the current, overall situation of the nonprofit and its external environment, particularly to ensure a solid base from which to develop current or new programs.

2.   Inventorying the assets and capabilities of the nonprofit, particularly those that can contribute toward developing current or new programs.

3.   Brainstorming, screening and selecting a short list of opportunities in which to sell products or services, particularly those that might be used to deliver more of current programs to current clients, new programs to current clients, current programs to new clients, and new programs to new clients.

4.   Researching the short list for feasibility and selecting the most appropriate opportunities, including careful consideration to likely sales and profitability, business models, payers and competitors, processes and materials required to develop each idea, and the influence of laws and regulations.

5.   Strategizing and planning to implement the selected opportunities, including developing a business plan.

6.   Implementing the plan and adjusting it to reality.

Program Building Approaches Compared to Good Program Management

The business planning and business development approaches are usually much more comprehensive and in-depth than the "build it and they will come" and seat-of-the-pants approaches to program development. The business planning and business development approaches form the foundation for good program management because the approaches are likely to ensure:

- More accurate understanding of community needs.

- Higher quality of service by focusing on what you do best.

- More effective and efficient operations in your organization.

- Increased financial resources, notably through increased mission-related earned income.

- Better use of financial resources.

- More freedom and choices of resources to meet community needs.

- Improved coordination between Board and staff.

- Better relationships with clients and other external stakeholders.

- Enhanced credibility with clients and funders.

So, rather than thinking of business planning or business development as processes to develop programs, you might benefit best from thinking of the business planning and business development processes as activities required for good program management.

Some Common Structures of Nonprofits

An organization chart is a handy tool for depicting the structure of an organization, including its various roles and programs and also how those roles and programs relate to each other. The charts on the following pages depict the typical designs of new and small nonprofit organizations. Keep in mind that, although there are distinct lines between the boxes (the roles) on the following images, there are seldom such distinct and rigid differences in application. Instead, people in various roles often share responsibilities and their responsibilities are often changing.

Organization Chart of Typical Start-Up Nonprofit Organization

It is common that a startup nonprofit organization has one major program that is carried out by a hands-on group of volunteers, some of whom act as the Board of Directors and perhaps others who act as staff. Both groups might be involved in providing services to clients. A new nonprofit often does not include the role of Chief Executive. It is important to remember that the Board of Directors, regardless of the Board model preferred by the nonprofit, works for the public.

Table I:3 – Organization Chart of Typical Start-Up Nonprofit

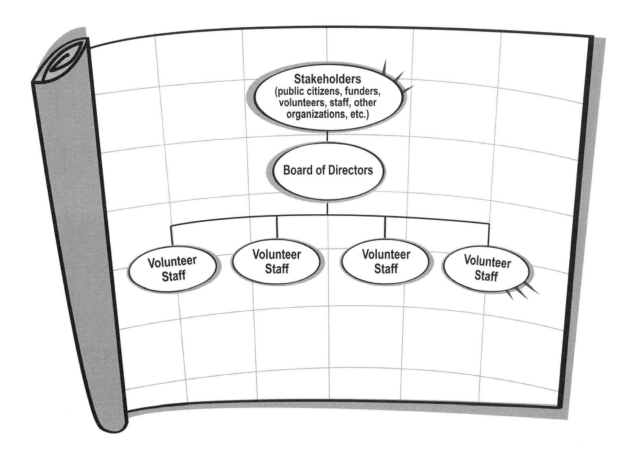

Organization Chart of Typical Small Nonprofit with CEO

A small nonprofit might have a part-time or full-time Chief Executive Officer (CEO) in a paid or volunteer position. Officially, the Chief Executive Officer reports to a Board of Directors (who are themselves volunteers). The Board members are expected to supervise the CEO, including selection, delegation and evaluation.

If the nonprofit has staff other than the CEO, then the CEO usually is expected to supervise the other staff members, who also might be part-time or full-time and in paid or volunteer positions.

The degree of formality of supervision between Board and CEO and between CEO and staff depends on its culture. Some nonprofits prefer a top-down, formal level of supervision, while others prefer a more team-based, egalitarian approach.

Table I:4 – Organization Chart of Typical Small Nonprofit

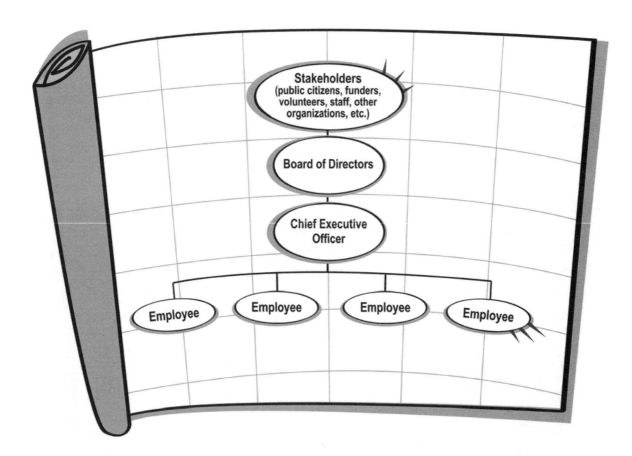

Organization Chart of Typical Medium-Sized Nonprofit

This design might be called a medium-sized nonprofit, although there really is no standard delineation of size for nonprofits. An organization like this usually has a paid Chief Executive, often on a full-time basis, who supervises various staff members. Staff members might be paid on a full-time or part-time basis, and can include volunteers. The Chief Executive reports to a Board of Directors (comprised of volunteers).

This size of nonprofit often has more than one program, each of which has a manager and is staffed by employees or volunteers.

Again, the degree of formality of supervision between Board and CEO and between CEO and staff depends on its culture. Supervision can range from a top-down, formal approach to more of a team-based, egalitarian approach.

Table I:5 – Organization Chart for Typical Medium-Sized Nonprofit

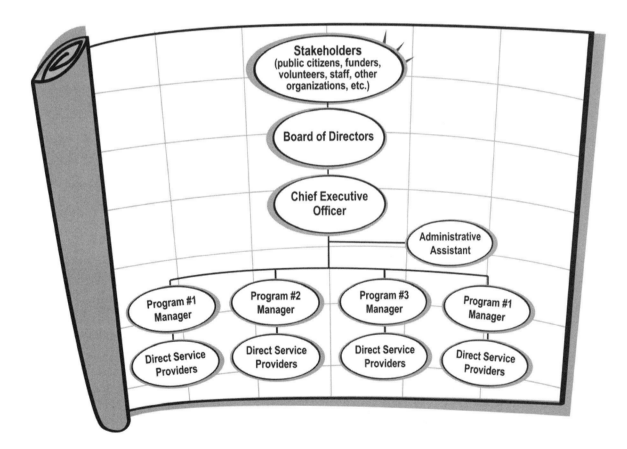

Typical Culture of a Small Nonprofit

It is very important for nonprofit leaders to really understand the nature of a small nonprofit, so they have realistic expectations and do not become overly frustrated when things do not always get done on time for them. The culture of a small nonprofit tends to be a rather tight-knit group of people, each of whom is very dedicated to the mission of the organization. They will chip in to help wherever and whenever they can. Often, they are like a small family. This tends to change as the organization goes through various life cycles.

(Adapted with permission from Sandra Larson, previous Executive Director of The Management Assistance Program for Nonprofits, St. Paul.)

- **The heart of the matter is leadership and management.**
  At the heart of any successful nonprofit is an effective Chief Executive and Board of Directors, assuming the organization is big enough to warrant having a Chief Executive. These leaders must work as a team with vision, skill and sufficient resources to accomplish the organization's mission. The Chief Executive must have strong skills in both leadership and management. The Board must be sufficiently skilled in leadership and management to assess the work of this Chief Executive and assist in strategic decision-making.

- **Values are the bottom line.**
  Values are the driving force in a nonprofit. The bottom line is the realization of a social mission, not profits. This poses complex problems for the leadership team. How are programs agreed upon, progress monitored and success measured? How are priorities set and consensus reached? How is staff rewarded and what control systems are applicable? Skilled consultants may be needed from time to time to assist the team in answering these qualitative, value-laden questions and focus on appropriate management systems.

- **Nonprofit personnel are often highly diverse.**
  Diversity is reflected, not only by different races and ethnic groups, but also by different values and perspectives. This strong diversity is a major benefit to the nonprofit because input from a wide variety of perspectives usually ensures complete consideration of situations and new ideas. However, nonprofit personnel must ensure they cultivate and remain open to the various values and perspectives.

- **Problems are especially complex for the small nonprofit.**
  The majority of nonprofits have small staffs and small budgets (less than $500,000) which compounds the leadership and management problems they face, especially given their charters and the magnitude of community needs with which they deal. Those new to nonprofits may assume that, because nonprofits tend to be small in size, issues in nonprofits should be simple in nature. On the contrary, the vast majority of organizations (regardless of size) experience similar issues: challenges in planning, organizing, motivating and guiding. However, when these issues are focused in a small organization, the nature of the organization becomes very dynamic and complex.

- **Sufficient resources to pay leadership may be lacking.**
  With lack of sufficient money, attracting and retaining paid management also can be problematic. Hard work with little career development opportunity encourages turnover of Chief Executives and staff. This can stall the organization's work. Expertise that is brought in to advise the management may be lost once that leadership leaves.

- **Lack of managerial training is problematic for the small nonprofit.**
  Many nonprofit managers have been promoted primarily for their technical or program expertise and may not have the managerial skills that are needed to run a nonprofit organization. Training and consultation can do much to help these new leaders and managers to gain the skills they seek and help them up the myriad of learning curves that rainbow out in front of them.

- **Chief Executives wear too many hats.**
  A nonprofit Chief Executive has to be a current expert in planning, marketing, information management, telecommunications, property management, personnel, finance, systems design, fundraising and program evaluation. Obviously this is not possible, regardless of the size of the organization. A larger organization may be able to hire some internal experts, but this is certainly not the case for the smaller organization. Furthermore, the technology of management today progresses too rapidly for the non-specialist to keep abreast of new thinking and expertise, whatever the size. Outside expertise therefore is often a must for both the large and small organization.

- **Nonprofit is too small to justify or pay for expensive outside advice.**
  Most nonprofits, even larger ones, often hesitate to spend money on administrative "overhead" such as consultants or other outside experts. This is seen as diverting valuable dollars from direct service. Of course, most nonprofits have no choice. They do not have enough money to even consider hiring consultants at for-profit rates. Low-cost, volunteer-based assistance often is an appropriate solution.

- **One-shot assistance often is not enough.**
  While most consultant organizations want to teach managers "how to fish," rather than give them a "fish," "fishing" (management skills) is not something that often can be learned in one consultation. Learning comes while grappling with an issue or management problem over a period of time, whether in a technical area, such as computerization, or in a leadership area, such as delegation. Building internal management capacity takes more time than a one-shot consultation. Repeat help therefore is not a sign of failure but of growth – a new need to know has surfaced.

- **Networks are lacking.**
  Many people outside the nonprofit sector observe, "Why don't those Chief Executives get together more often and help each other?" There are many reasons. First of all, running a successful organization (delivering the quality service that fulfills the organization's mission) is not enough. Most nonprofit Chief Executives run a second business – raising money to support the first. Both are complex and very time-consuming activities, especially when the Chief Executive wears all the management hats. Second, developing networks or researching joint ventures is time-consuming, expensive and risky.

- **Nonprofits usually have little time and money.**
  Funders do not seem to think research and development activity justifies new expenditures; at least many are hesitant to fund what might not succeed. While nonprofits may be more entrepreneurial than funders, they have little capital to risk. Collaborative planning will be enhanced by computerization and telecommunications, but these investments also are difficult to fund. In some ways, affordable consultants can substitute for expensive, up-front research and development costs, at least at the feasibility level. In many cases, they can carry an organization through the needed planning to actually develop a new system of collaboration, merger, or automation.

- **Nonprofits need low-cost management and technical assistance.**
  Nonprofits are valuable community assets that must be effectively managed. The need to provide affordable, accessible management and technical assistance to these organizations is clear for all the reasons stated above: the complexity of the task, the lack of Board and internal expertise, the lack of time and money, changing needs, the learning curve, and the importance of the results to the community. What is well done is based on what is well run.

- **Typical nature of planning in nonprofits is on current issues.**
  Many nonprofits do not have a lot of time, money, or resources for sophisticated, comprehensive strategic planning. The focus is usually on the major issues facing the nonprofit and quickly addressing them. Typical major challenges for the facilitator are: basic training of personnel concerning planning concepts and processes; helping the nonprofit to focus and sustain its limited resources on planning; ensuring that strategies really are strategic rather than operational or efficiency measures; and helping design small and focused planning meetings which produce realistic plans that become implemented.

Removing the Mystique from Management and Leadership

In the previous major section, you learned about the world of organizations, particularly nonprofit corporations. Now, we will expand your learning by looking at what goes on in the world of management, leadership and supervision.

Whether you are a Chief Executive Officer, program manager or other supervisor (and these roles overlap) in the nonprofit organization, you will benefit from "getting back to the basics" about your understanding of the major functions of management and leadership. This section provides a basic overview of the roles of management, leadership and supervision and breaks through the myths that many have about the role of manager.

Myths about Management

Many people aspire to be a manager, yet when they get to that role, they often find themselves completely overwhelmed and confused. They believed that the role of manager involved making decisions and plans according to a consistent set of rules. They believed that they would be "managing – whatever that means." Here are some of the most common myths about management.

Myth #1: Management is a science, a set of established rules and regulations.
In an ideal world this would be true, but in reality, management is rarely any kind of science. Managers are constantly making new decisions in new situations. They often rely on seat-of-the-pants judgment – which is why it is so important to get a lot of management experience under your belt.

Myth #2: Managers know what their people are doing and are experts at what their people do.
Not necessarily. Many managers do not have the expertise to carry out the roles and responsibilities of the people who work for them. Good managers know how to trust their people and know how to delegate.

 Consider "How to Delegate for Growth and Performance of Your Employees" on page 221.

Myth #3: Managers are the "bosses" and are highly respected at all times.
Wrong! In today's rapidly changing world, many times managers cannot make decisions by themselves – and should not. Usually they should include advice and feedback from their employees and their customers. Many times, managers are not liked for the decisions that they make – management is not a popularity contest. It is usually better to be respected than liked.

Myth #4: Employees are adults and should be able to do their jobs on their own.
Watch out! If you treat an employee like a some kind of tool that should just go away and "get the job done," then more than likely the "tool" will go away and not come back! It can be very costly to continually have to find and train new employees. Managers need to give a lot of attention to ensuring that their employees have all the resources that they need to get the job done, including occasional guidance and praise about a job well done.

What is "Management"?

What is "Management"?

There are a variety of interpretations of this term. A classic definition is that "Leaders do the right thing and managers do things right." Another common definition is that management is getting things done through other people.

Traditionally, the term "management" refers to the set of activities, and often the group of people, involved in four general functions: planning, organizing, leading and coordinating activities. Note that the four functions recur throughout the organization and are highly integrated.

Some writers, teachers and practitioners assert that the traditional view is rather outmoded and that management needs to focus more on leadership skills, including establishing vision and goals, communicating the vision and goals, and guiding others to accomplish them. Other people assert that this view of leadership really is not a change in the traditional functions of management; rather it is re-emphasizing certain aspects of management.

Yet another view, quite apart from the traditional view, asserts that the job of management is to support employee's efforts to be fully productive members of the organizations and citizens of the community.

To most employees, the term "management" probably means the group of people, including executives and other managers, who are primarily responsible for making decisions in the organization. Therefore, in a nonprofit organization, the term "management" might refer to all or any of the activities of the Board, Chief Executive Officer and/or program directors.

This Field Guide refers to "management" as the Chief Executive Officer and others who are responsible for a major function or group of people among the nonprofit.

What Do Managers Do?

The traditional view of management is that it includes four major functions, including:

1. **Planning**
    This includes identifying goals, objectives, methods, resources needed to carry out methods, responsibilities and dates for completion of tasks. Examples of planning are strategic planning, business planning, project planning, staffing planning, advertising and promotions planning, etc.

2. **Organizing**
    Resources are organized to achieve the nonprofit's goals in an optimum fashion. Examples are organizing new departments, human resources, office and file systems, re-organizing businesses, staffing, budgeting, etc.

3. **Leading**
    Leading includes setting direction for the organization, groups and individuals as well as influencing people to follow that direction. Examples are establishing strategic direction (vision, values, mission and/or goals) and championing methods of organizational performance management to pursue that direction.

4. **Controlling, or coordinating**
    All of the resources have to be coordinated or controlled to effectively and efficiently reach goals and objectives. This includes ongoing collection of feedback, and monitoring and adjustment of systems, processes and structures accordingly. Examples include use of financial controls, policies and procedures, performance management processes, measures to avoid risks etc.

Levels of Management

In a traditional sense, large organizations may have different levels of managers, including top managers, middle managers and first-line managers. Top-level, or executive, managers are responsible for overseeing the entire organization or some major function in the organization. These managers engage in more strategic and conceptual matters, with less attention to day-to-day detail. The top executive in a nonprofit is often called Chief Executive Officer (or Executive Director) and reports to the Board of Directors, if the nonprofit is big enough to warrant having a top executive. The Board of Directors is the group of people who are legally charged to oversee, or govern, the nonprofit corporation (this is true for for-profit corporations, as well).

In large organizations, top-level managers often have middle managers working for them. Mid-level managers are in charge of a major function or department. Middle managers may have first-line supervisors working for them. First-line supervisors are usually responsible to manage the day-to-day activities of a group of workers. In nonprofits, middle managers, and sometimes first-line supervisors, are often called program directors or program managers.

Note that you can also have different types of managers across the same levels in the organization. A project manager is in charge of developing a certain project, for example, development of a new building. A functional manager is in charge of a major function, such as a department in the organization, for example, marketing, sales, engineering, finance, etc. A product manager is in charge of a product or service. Similarly, a product line manager is in charge of a group of closely related products. In a nonprofit, the functional manager or product manager might be a program manager.

What is "Leadership"?

The topic of leadership has become dominant in management literature. People have very strong perceptions and feelings about leadership, including widely differing definitions of the concept. In this guide, leading is establishing direction and influencing to follow that direction. You can lead yourself, other individuals, groups or the entire organization. Each area of focus might require different skills in leadership.

Some people believe that leading is one of the four major functions of management, along with planning, organizing and controlling resources. Others strongly assert that leading and managing are different. Among the traditional, four major functions of management (planning, organizing, leading, controlling), leading is focused, more than any other function, on conducting activities with other people. Any adult has a lot of experience in working with other people, so most adults also have very strong feelings about what comprises good leadership.

The term "leadership" can be used to refer to the role, or positions, in an organization, for example, the CEO or Program Director. The term can also apply to the nature of activities included in setting direction and influencing others to follow it, whether those activities are conducted by Chief Executive Officers or clerical secretaries.

No matter what definitions or perceptions that people have about leadership, it is critical for managers and supervisors to have good skills in leadership. This guide provides guidelines for many areas of leadership, for example: planning, delegating, managing meetings, organizing staff, building teams, setting goals, cultivating motivation among yourself and employees, giving feedback, etc.

What is "Supervision"?

There are several interpretations of the term "supervision," but typically supervision includes the activities carried out by supervisors to oversee the productivity and progress of employees who report directly to the supervisors. For example, first-level supervisors supervise entry-level employees. Depending on the size of the organization, middle managers supervise first-level supervisors, and Chief Executive Officers supervise middle managers (for example, program managers), etc. Supervision is a management activity and supervisors have a management role in the organization.

The role of supervision is a leadership role – leading other individuals. Therefore, the roles of supervisors and leaders are very similar and often overlap a great deal.

Supervision of a group of employees often includes:

1. Conducting basic management skills (decision making, problem solving, planning, delegation and meeting management).

2. Organizing department and teams.

3. Noticing the need for and designing new job roles in the group.

4. Hiring new employees.

5. Training new employees.

6. Employee performance management (setting goals, observing and giving feedback, addressing performance issues, firing employees, etc.).

7. Conforming to personnel policies and other internal regulations.

PART II:

ROLES OF BOARD,

CHIEF EXECUTIVE

OFFICER

AND STAFF

Nonprofit Board – What It Is and How It Works

You *do not* have to be an expert on nonprofit Boards of Directors to be a leader on the staff. However, because the Board of Directors is ultimately responsible to set the purpose and direction for the nonprofit, it is critical to understand the basic purpose and nature of your Board of Directors. Likewise, it is critical for the Chief Executive Officer to have a very strong working relationship with the Board. Therefore, this section about Boards is included in this guide for nonprofit leaders on the staff.

What is a Board of Directors?

Before you review the various kinds of Boards, you should first understand what a Board of Directors is.

All incorporated organizations (nonprofit or for-profit) must have a Board.
An incorporated organization is an organization that has filed with the appropriate government agency to formally organize as its own official, legal entity (or corporation). This is usually done by filing a legal description, for example, Articles of Incorporation, with the appropriate government agency. (Note that not all nonprofits are incorporated. Some nonprofits are less formal, for example, a group of citizens gathered to address a community need, such as picking up garbage.)

Consider "There is More Than One Type of Nonprofit Organization" on page 4.

Board is legally charged to govern a corporation, whether nonprofit or for-profit.
In a for-profit corporation, the Board is responsible to the stockholders who purchased stock in the corporation. In a nonprofit corporation, the Board is responsible to the public, particularly the communities that the nonprofit serves, because the public owns the nonprofit. A more progressive perspective is that both types of Boards are responsible to stakeholders, that is, to everyone who is interested and/or can be affected by their corporations.

It is very important for founders of nonprofits to realize that they do not own the nonprofit; the public owns the nonprofit. It also is very important for founders to realize that, ultimately, they work for the Board of Directors, not the other way around.

The power of a Board is vested in all Board members, not individual Board members.
Individual Board members do not have formal authority. The Board as a body of members must approve the nonprofit's plans and procedures. Boards have policies and procedures (By-Laws and Board policies) that determine how the Board acts as a body to make plans and procedures.

In theory, Board establishes top-level policies, staff implements. (Reality might be different.)
Boards are responsible to establish top-level plans and policies that define the purpose and direction for a nonprofit. The Chief Executive (if the Board chooses to have a CEO in the organization) is responsible to manage the nonprofit's resources in an effective and efficient manner according to the plans and policies of the nonprofit. Staff, or personnel who work for the Chief Executive, (if the nonprofit has a CEO) are responsible to implement the plans according to the policies of the nonprofit and the management practices of the CEO. How this all occurs in a nonprofit depends very much on the structure of the Board. In some nonprofits, there is no CEO and the Board

members do much of the work that staff members typically would do. In other nonprofits, Board and staff members prefer that they work much more in an egalitarian fashion where Board members are involved in governance and management.

Roles and Responsibilities of Nonprofit Board Members

Fiduciary (Legal) Duties

Board members have fiduciary, or legal, duties as established in corporate law. These are the duty of care and duty of loyalty. The nature of the two duties can overlap as described below.

Examples of performing the duty of care include clearly making a reasonable and good-faith effort to, for example:

- Be aware of the nonprofit's mission, plans and policies, and be sure that they indeed serve the needs of the community that the Board members represent.

- Be sure that all nonprofit activities are in according with the mission, plans and policies, in addition to accordance to rules and regulations of the society and community. (Some people refer to these activities as being in accordance with a duty of obedience.)

- Fully participate in Board meetings, deliberations and decisions.

- Read, evaluate and ensure accuracy of all reports, including minutes, financial and evaluations.

- Ensure the organization has sufficient resources, including people, funding and other assets.

Examples of performing the duty of loyalty include clearly making a reasonable and good-faith effort, when acting as a Board or staff member, to:

- Always be thinking about, and focusing on, priorities of the nonprofit, and not that of yourself or another organization.

- Share ideas, opinions and advice to forward the progress of the nonprofit.

- Represent the nonprofit in a favorable light.

More clarity will come from considering more specific types of activities conducted by Board members. There are many resources that suggest roles and responsibilities of nonprofit Boards. Therefore, more than one perspective is included in this guide.

Overall Responsibilities

BoardSource (formerly the National Center for Nonprofit Boards), in its booklet *Ten Basic Responsibilities of Nonprofit Boards*, itemizes the following 10 responsibilities for nonprofit Boards.

1.   Determine the organization's mission and purpose.

2.   Select the Chief Executive.

3.   Support the Chief Executive and review his or her performance.

4.   Ensure effective organizational planning.

5.   Ensure adequate resources.

6.   Manage resources effectively. (Appointing a Chief Executive to manage the organization often does this.)

7.   Determine and monitor the organization's programs and services.

8.   Enhance the organization's public image.

9.   Serve as a court of appeal.

10.   Assess its own performance.

Brenda Hanlon (2001, www.ncnb.org) suggests the following duties from *In Boards We Trust*.

1.   **Provide continuity for the organization.**
      This is done by setting up a corporation or legal existence, represent the organization's point of view through interpretation of its products and services, and establish advocacy for them.

2.   **Select, appoint and evaluate a Chief Executive Officer.**
      The CEO is the person to whom responsibility for the administration of the organization is delegated. The Board's activities include:

      a.   To review and evaluate his/her performance regularly on the basis of a specific job description including the Chief Executive's relations with the Board and leadership in the organization, in program planning and implementation, and in management of the organization and its personnel.

      b.   To offer administrative guidance and determine whether to retain or dismiss the Chief Executive.

3.   **Govern the organization by broad policies and objectives.**
      These are formulated and agreed upon by the Chief Executive and employees, including assigning priorities and ensuring the organization's capacity to carry out programs by continually reviewing its work.

4.   **Acquire sufficient resources for the organization's operations.**
      This includes more than getting finances. It includes ensuring sufficient personnel, expertise, facilities and other assets.

5.   **Account to the public for the products and services of the organization.**
      This is true especially for the organization's expenditures and conformance to rules and regulations, for example:

      a.   To provide for fiscal accountability, approve the budget, and formulate policies related to contracts from public or private resources.

b. To accept responsibility for all conditions and policies attached to new, innovative, or experimental programs.

Types of Decisions Made by Board Members

The specific types of decisions made by Board members depend on the level of involvement of Board members in the management of the nonprofit. Members of working Boards and collective Boards (both are types of governing Boards) might be very involved in day-to-day affairs. In contrast, members of Policy Governance® and policy Boards are not very likely to be involved in those affairs.

However, there are some decisions that major stakeholders, such as funders, expect Board members to make – and to formally approve, regardless of the form of Board structure or involvement used by the Board.

1. Add or remove Board member(s).

2. Hire and terminate the Chief Executive Officer.

3. Approve the strategic plan.

4. Approve major organizational changes, for example, new program or a merger.

5. Approve the annual budget.

6. Approve personnel policies.

7. Approve expenditures above a certain limit (the limit is often specified in the By-Laws).

8. Approve contracts with expenditures over a certain limit.

Certainly, there are other decisions that a nonprofit might wish that Board members attend to (again, depending on the structure used by the Board), such as modifying compensation and benefits to the Chief Executive, selecting major vendors for certain services and when to conduct major fundraising activities.

Common Types of Board Models / Structures

Board members can proactively and planfully decide the model (the roles and structures) they use to work together, or that model can emerge over time as members conduct their business. The model also depicts, or directs, the level of members' involvement in policy-making and managerial affairs. Therefore, it is useful for you to have some basic understanding of some of the various models that your Board members might choose to operate (common models are described later on below). The various models are differentiated from each other usually based on:

- Their structure, for example, a top-down, hierarchical and directive style of governance versus a more egalitarian and team-based approach.

- Whether they have governing powers or not, for example, an Advisory Board which does not have governing authority.

- Their primary focus, for example, a Fundraising Board (which can be a governing or Advisory Board, with members primarily responsible for fundraising).

- Commercial and proprietary design, for example, the Policy Governance® Board.

A Board can have features of several different types of models, for example, a governing Board that focuses on fundraising and uses committees. Keep in mind that there is no one perfect model that all Board members should use all of the time for every nonprofit everywhere. Three common different governing Board models (based on different structures) are described below, including the policy governing Board, the working governing Board and the collective governing Board.

Consider "How Much Should Your Board Be Involved in Management?" on page 73.

Policy (Traditional) Governing Board

In this model, Board members attend primarily to strategic matters, such as developing top-level plans and policies, while staff members attend primarily to managerial matters (implementing those plans and policies). Often, the definitive characteristic of a policy Board is the presence of a variety of Board committees and a Chief Executive who reports to the Board. Many people refer to this structure as a "traditional" Board because of its rather top-down, committee-driven nature. (The policy governing Board is not to be confused with the Policy Governance® Board.)

The extent to which the structure is strictly implemented depends on the nature of the nonprofit (see the above reference to factors that influence members' involvement and to matching the Board's priorities to the life cycle of the nonprofit). Also, the distinction between the roles of the Board and Chief Executive depends on the nature of the nonprofit as well.

When the Board's structure, including its various committees, is designed to be in close accordance and involvement with common management functions (for example, with staffing, programs, marketing, finances and fundraising), this type of Board is sometimes referred to as a "management Board." This type of Board might have staff or none at all – the management functions might be done by the Board members themselves in their various committees.

Working Governing Board (Administrative Governing Board)

In a "working" Board, Board members attend to the top-level strategic matters of the organization in addition to attending to day-to-day matters. This structure usually arises when the nonprofit is just getting started and so it has no paid staff members, or it prefers to operate completely on a volunteer basis. The nature of this Board structure is usually rather flexible and informal. A working Board might utilize committees or not. Many times there is no Chief Executive role in the organization.

A "policy" governing Board is often viewed as more "mature," having passed through the "working" Board stage. This view is not fair because many nonprofits prefer to remain as working Boards because they do not want to hire staff, or because they benefit from Board and staff members successfully working together.

Ideally, Board members remember that they are responsible for the governance of the organization, and so they ensure that top-level plans and policies are established in addition to attending to whatever day-to-day tasks need to be done. They might conduct Board operations in the form of Board committees.

Sometimes people mistakenly refer to a working Board as a Board where members are actively working. The distinction is what the members are working on, not whether members are active or no. In a working-Board model, members are working on strategic and managerial tasks.

Collective Governing Board Model

In a collective, or co-operative, Board, the Board and staff members always prefer to share equal responsibility in all matters. The collective Board is the epitome of a democratic and team effort. This type of Board is often popular among cultures that highly value equality and power sharing. A collective Board might utilize committees or not. In this type of Board structure, it could be difficult to discern who is a Board member or a staff member – all members are considered as Board members and staff members.

Corporate law requires that specific persons be in the official positions as Board members – the fiduciary, or legal, responsibilities cannot be continually shared, changed and ultimately diffused with others who are not themselves Board members. While this structure is highly flexible and adaptable, it could be very difficult to efficiently identify any ultimate, personal responsibilities and accountabilities for fiduciary responsibilities. So it is important in this model that Board members can individually be identified if necessary.

For another useful overview, go to Mel Gill's information at http://www.synergyassociates.ca/publications/OverviewGovernanceModels.htm .

Also, see Nathan Garber's information at http://garberconsulting.com/governance%20models%20what's%20right.htm .

Finally, see David Renz's typology of Board types at http://www.nonprofitquarterly.org/content/view/69/28/ .

Table II:1 – Comparison of Common Board Models (Based on Structure)

Activity	Policy Governing [1]	Working Governing	Collective Governing
Has ultimate authority	Board	Board	Per law: Board members Per the Board: shared
Hires / fires Chief Executive	Board (usually has CEO role)	Board (if CEO role exists)	Joint (probably does not have CEO role)
Delegates to Chief Executive	Board (although Board and CEO might work as "strategic partners")	Board and CEO might share duties	Joint
Staffing	Board approves Personnel Policies; distinct Board-staff hierarchy	Board approves Personnel Policies; might not have staff; loosely defined hierarchy	One team
Drive strategic planning	Board	Board and / or joint	Joint
Strategic planning	Board does mission, vision, values, and overall goals	Joint	Joint
Approves strategic plan	Board	Board	Joint
Fundraising	Board approves Fundraising Plan (heavily engaged)	Board approves Fundraising Plan (joint fundraising)	Joint
Financial planning and controls	Board approves budget, fiscal policies and procedures (Treasurer and Finance Committee take lead role)	Board approves budget, fiscal policies and procedures (Board and staff share other responsibilities)	Joint
Financial reporting and decisions	Board reviews statements, makes decisions (Treasurer and Finance Committee take lead role)	(Board and staff share responsibilities)	Joint
Program delivery	Board approves programs	Joint	Joint
Public / community relations	Board heavily engaged	Joint	Joint

Note 1: A policy governing Board is not the same as a Policy Governance® Board, which is a commercial Board design and a registered trademark of Carver Governance Design, Inc.

What Nonprofit Boards Typically Do and When

This section about how Board members do their work includes descriptions of many of the most important activities conducted by a Board of Directors. Board members conduct those activities at certain times of the year. Often, the By-Laws and/or Board policies specify when certain activities will be conducted and when. Activities include: conducting regular Board meetings (every month, two months, etc.), conducting the Board self-evaluation, evaluating the Chief Executive, reviewing and updating Board and personnel policies, conducting strategic planning, recruiting new members, holding an annual meeting, reviewing and authorizing the yearly budget, conducting fundraising, etc.

One of the ways that Board members remember to do those activities is by continually referencing a Board Calendar. Therefore, one of the most important Board policies is the calendar of activities. If Board members used only one policy, this is the policy that might produce the most benefit because the calendar would continually remind members to do all of the important activities required in strong governance. Therefore, one of the first policies, in addition to the By-Laws, that Board members should develop and adopt is the Board Calendar.

Table II:2 – Sample Annual Calendar of Board Activities

	Yearly Board Activity	Suggested Timing
1.	Fiscal year begins (assumes fiscal year beginning January 1)	January (fiscal-year timing is often specified in the By-Laws and fiscal policies)
2.	Conduct Board Self-Evaluation (do once a year and in preparation for first Board retreat , might be twice per year)	February-March (do shortly before evaluating Chief Executive)
3.	Evaluate Chief Executive (reference his or her progress towards last fiscal year's goals and job description)	March-April (do shortly after completion of last fiscal year)
4.	Review and update By-Laws, Board policies, insurances, personnel policies and Board staffing policies	March-May (do concurrent to Board and chief evaluations)
5.	Conduct first Board retreat (team building, address Board self-evaluation results, begin strategic planning, etc.)	April
6.	Begin recruiting new Board members	April-May (in time for June/July elections)
7.	Conduct strategic planning to produce organizational goals and resources need to reach goals	May-June-July (start planning in time for setting mission, vision, values, issues, goals, strategies, resource needs, funding needs, and getting funds before start of next fiscal year)
8.	Develop slate for potential new Board members	June-July (per By-Laws)
9.	Establish Chief Executive's goals for next year (as produced from strategic planning)	August (as organizational goals are realized from planning)
10.	Hold annual meeting and elect new Board members	July (per By-Laws)
11.	Draft next year's budget (based on resources needed to reach new strategic goals)	July-August-September
12.	Develop fundraising plan (with primary goals to get funds needed for budget)	July-August-September
13.	Conduct second Board retreat (address Board orientation/training, review Board/staff roles, re-organize or form new committees based on strategic goals, develop committee work plans, update Board operations calendar, review planning status, etc.)	August (in time to orient new Board members soon after they join the Board)
14.	Conduct fundraising plan (primarily to meet fundraising goals)	August-December
15.	Implement strategic plan, including to achieve goals and objectives according to deadlines in the action plans of the overall strategic plan	Ongoing

What Does a Healthy Board Look Like?

There has been an extensive amount of research and sharing of opinions about what makes for a highly effective Board. Asking what a healthy Board looks like is akin to asking what a healthy person looks like or how much a car costs. It all depends. Yet for the sake of furthering your understanding of Boards, it might be useful to consider at least one description. One of the most useful, yet not constricting descriptions, is offered in the book *The Executive Director's Survival Guide* (Mim Carlson and Margaret Donohoe, John Wiley and Sons, 2005, p. 95). The authors assert that the attributes of an effective Board include:

- Focus on, and passion for, the mission, and a commitment to setting and achieving vision. Board members realize that one of their most important jobs is to verify that their nonprofit is indeed meeting the community need that their nonprofit was formed to meet.

- Clear responsibilities that refrain Board members from micro-managing. [Micro-managing is when members are so involved in the details of management that they 1) damage operations because staff are continually updating members with trivial information, and 2) do not sufficiently attend to strategic matters of top-level policies and plans.]

- Desire of Board members to work together, listen to diverse views, and build consensus.

- Flexible structure that changes to fit the nonprofit's life cycle and priorities.

- An understanding of, and ability to shape, the organization's culture.

- An interest in knowing the good, bad and uncertain about the nonprofit, and commitment to resolving its issues.

- Commitment to self-reflection and evaluation, with clear expectations and each member's accountability to meet them.

Others mention overall features of a high-performing Board, for example:

- Governance – Board members employing very effective practices to establish the nonprofit's purpose and priorities in the community, and ensuring they are effectively and efficiently addressed for maximum benefit of stakeholders (clients, funders, collaborators, government agencies, etc.).

- Diligence – All Board members consistently attending to their duties of care and loyalty, with full attention, participation and responsibilities in all deliberations, decisions and interactions with stakeholders.

- Transparency – Board members always providing full disclosure and explanation of the nonprofit's governance, finances and effects on communities, and willingly supporting stakeholders' efforts to understand that information.

- Accountability – Board members continually making their nonprofits and themselves responsible to meet the expectations of stakeholders, and continually verifying with those stakeholders that their expectations are indeed being met.

Strategic Questions for Your Board Members to Always Ask

Board members must not be afraid to ask the hard questions of the Chief Executive and each other. That is always better than just "numbing out" and only focusing on whatever is put in front of them during Board meetings. To make strategic impact, Board members and other nonprofit leaders should always be asking the questions listed in Table III:3. This page could be in front of the Board members during their meetings to encourage strategic questioning.

Table II:3 – Strategic Questions for Board Meetings

Programs and Services

1. What are the different programs? Who does each serve? How? For what desired results?
2. How do we know who really needs our programs? Have we verified our impressions?
3. Who are our collaborators? Who might be? Have we reached out to them? Should we?
4. What are the results of each program? How do we know? Are those results acceptable?
5. Are programs results really meeting the community need that we were formed to meet?

Board Operations and Meetings

1. Do all Board members know their roles? How do we know?
2. Are all Board members participating actively in Board operations?
3. Are the topics on the agenda the ones that we should be addressing? How do we know?
4. Are all pertinent topics being addressed effectively? How do we know?
5. Are all Board members attending meetings?
6. Are all members actively taking part in deliberations and actions?
7. Are meetings very effective? How do we know?
8. Are we doing our job to verify that the nonprofit is meeting a specific community need?

Personnel (Chief Executive Officer, Paid Staff and Volunteers)

1. Do we have the best people for the jobs? How do we know?
2. Are they doing their jobs well? How do we know?
3. Are all personnel policies up-to-date and adhered to? How do we know?
4. What if the CEO suddenly left the organization? What would we really do?

Fundraising

1. How much money do we need from fundraising? How do we know?
2. Have we identified all of the possible sources of funding from individuals, foundations, corporations and the government? How did we do that?
3. What are the best sources for funding? What is the best way to approach the sources? How do we know? Are all the sources being approached effectively?
4. Is the Board involved? Are all Board members making a contribution to the organization? How do we know?

Promotions and Public Relations

1. What different groups of stakeholders do we have? Clients? Funders? Collaborators?
2. What image do we want each to have about our nonprofit? Do they have it? Really?
3. Are we clearly conveying the benefits of each of our programs to its clients? Really?

Finances, Rules and Regulations

1. What are the most recent highlights, trends and issues depicted by recent financial reports?
2. Are the financial numbers really accurate? How do we know?
3. Are all taxes being paid? How do we know?
4. Are all rules, regulations and fiscal policies being followed? How do we know?

If Your Gut Tells You "Something Is Not Right," Then SAY SO Now!

What Board Committees Typically Do (If Used, At All)

Depending on the particular Board structure preferred by Board members, Boards often organize their members into various committees, or small working groups. If your structure does not highly value committees then your Board might instead use task forces, or small groups of people who work together to conduct some current activity and then disband when the activity has been carried out. This Field Guide will refer to the term "committees." Your Board also might have non-Board members on certain committees, for example, on Programs, Marketing and Fundraising.

When starting your Board, it is useful to have some basic sense about typical Board committees. You will get a good sense for what committees your Board will need after you have done some basic strategic planning. There is more about strategic planning later on in this guidebook.

About Committees

The following points are in reference to small, working groups of the overall number of Board members. Whether the Board chooses to call them "committees" or not is up to the Board members.

1. **Committees are useful to take full advantage of Board members' resources.**
    This includes members' expertise, time, commitment and diversity of opinions. These resources are more fully utilized if focused into a small group of members in a committee.

2. **Establish committees when issues are too complex or numerous for quick response.**
    Each of the major functions required to manage a nonprofit requires a complicated range of activities, for example, planning and oversight of financial management, fundraising, personnel management, programs and marketing. All Board members cannot be deeply involved in the planning and oversight of each. Thus, Boards often choose to associate a committee with each function.

3. **Use standing (permanent) and ad hoc (temporary) committees.**
    One of the biggest frustrations of Board members is having a committee for the sake of having a committee. Members of those committees usually struggle to find any purpose in the organization. Have standing committees only for the most important, current priorities; otherwise, terminate the committee. Temporary priorities, such as building a facility or coordinating an event, might need an ad hoc committee.

4. **Committees recommend policy for approval by the entire Board.**
    Be clear that the role of a Board Committee is not to act for the entire Board. Committees should not be making decisions for all Board members. Committees should make recommendations to the full Board for full Board deliberation and approval. (The full Board might delegate to the Executive Committee the ability to make certain types of Board decisions when it is impractical to gather all Board members together. However, all Board members are still responsible for the decisions made by the Executive Committee.)

5. **Frequency of committee meetings depends on urgency and complexity of priorities.**
    The more urgent and complex the issues facing the organization, the more frequent might be the meetings of the committees. For example, a Fundraising Committees might meet at least monthly if the planned amount of donations is down dramatically. Likewise, a Programs Committee might meet monthly if the nonprofit has the opportunity to add several new programs to meet the needs in the community.

6.   **Minutes should be recorded and approved for all committee meetings.**
Boards often forget to do this and, as a result, the full Board often is not aware of the
activities and results of meetings of the committees. Minutes are documentation usually of
the meeting attendance, discussions, decisions and results.

Potential Standing (Permanent) Committees

Table II:4 portrays the various functions often conducted by standing Board committees, or
committees that exist year round. Note that this list is not intended to suggest that all of these
committees should exist; it is ultimately up to the organization to determine which committees
should exist and what they should do. You likely will need only three or four of these standing
committees during your first years of operation. The list of standing committees often is specified in
the By-Laws.

Potential Ad Hoc (Temporary) Board committees

Table II:5 describes the various functions often conducted by ad hoc Board committees, that is,
committees that exist to accomplish a goal and then cease to exist. This list is not intended to
suggest that all of these committees should exist or that these are the only ad hoc committees that
might be used; it is ultimately up to the organization to determine which committees should exist and
what they should do.

Table II:4 – Potential Standing Committees

Committee Name	Their Typical Roles
Board Development - sometimes called Governance, with Nominating Committee	Ensure effective Board processes, structures and roles, including retreat planning, committee development, and Board evaluation; sometimes includes role of Nominating Committee, such as keeping list of potential Board members, orientation and training.
Evaluation	Ensures sound evaluation of products/services/programs, including, for example, outcomes, goals, data, analysis and resulting adjustments.
Executive	Oversee operations of the Board; often acts on behalf of the Board during on-demand activities that occur between meetings, and these acts are later presented for full Board review; comprised of Board Chair, other officers and/or committee Chairs (or sometimes just the officers, although this might be too small); often performs evaluation of Chief Executive.
Finance	Oversees development of the budget; ensures accurate tracking/monitoring/accountability for funds; ensures adequate financial controls; often led by the Board Treasurer; reviews major grants and associated terms.
Fundraising	Oversees development and implementation of the Fundraising Plan; with all Board members, identifies and solicits funds from external sources of support, working with the Development Officer if available; sometimes called Development Committee.
Marketing	Oversees development and implementation of the Marketing Plan, including identifying potential markets, their needs, how to meet those needs with products/services/programs, and how to promote/sell the programs.
Personnel	Guides development, review and authorization of personnel policies and procedures; sometimes leads evaluation of the chief Executive; sometimes assists Chief Executive with leadership and management matters.
Programs	Guides development of service delivery mechanisms; may include evaluation of the services; link between the Board and the staff on program's activities.
Promotions and Sales	Promotes organization's services to the community, including generating fees for those services.
Public Relations	Represents the organization to the community; enhances the organization's image, including communications with the press.

Table II:5 – Potential Ad Hoc Committees

Committee Names	Their Typical Roles
Audit	Plans and supports audit of major functions, for example, finances, programs or organization.
Campaign	Plans and coordinates major fundraising event; sometimes a subcommittee of the Fundraising Committee.
Compensation	Conducts analysis to determine and recommend appropriate compensation for staff, particularly the Chief Executive, to the Board for approval.
Ethics	Develops and applies guidelines for ensuring ethical behavior and resolving ethical conflicts.
Events	Plans and coordinates major events, such as fundraising, team building or planning; sometimes a subcommittee of the Fundraising Committee.
Nominations	Identifies needed Board member skills, suggests potential members and orients new members; sometimes a subcommittee of the Board Development Committee.
Research	Conducts specific research and/or data gathering to make decisions about a current major function in the organization.

Leadership Role of Your Board Chair

The role of Board Chair is critical to the effectiveness of a nonprofit Board of Directors. Leadership on the Board starts with the role of Board Chair. (The other important aspect of Board leadership is the Executive Committee.) Therefore, it is important to understand the role and how it is carried out. Here are some observations about what makes for a highly effective Board Chair.

General Guidelines for Board Chair Effectiveness

In addition to the specific activities listed in the Board Chair job description included above, the Board Chair should:

1. Clearly understand the roles and responsibilities of the nonprofit Board of Directors. (The Board Chair should have this guide!)

2. Clearly understand the roles and responsibilities of the Board Chair position.

3. Maintain clear focus on the organization's plans, particularly its mission, when guiding Board operations. The Chair should be very familiar with the strategic plan.

4. Focus as much as possible on Board processes and not personalities.

5. Model strong participation and team building required for a highly effective Board.

6.   Highly value a strong, working relationship with the Chief Executive.

Consider "How Your Board Chair and CEO Can Work Well Together" on page 53.

7.   Highly value the participation and opinions of Board members.

8.   Possess good decision making and problem solving skills. Have strong facilitation skills during Board meetings, particularly regarding reaching consensus and time management.

For basic guidelines for decision making and problem solving, go to http://www.managementhelp.org/misc/mtgmgmnt.htm .

9.   Play a leading role in fundraising activities, including visiting funders with the Chief Executive, co-authoring solicitations to funders, etc.

10.   Not be reluctant to ask for help.

11.   Understand the basic principles of effective delegation.

For basic guidelines about delegation, go to http://www.managementhelp.org/guiding/delegate/basics.htm .

12.   Have basic understanding of parliamentary procedure.

For basic guidelines about Robert's Rules, go to http://www.managementhelp.org/boards/boards.htm#anchor1463640 .

Nonprofit CEO –
How Your CEO and Board Can Work Together

Role of Typical Nonprofit Chief Executive Officer (CEO)

It is the Board's responsibility to hire and supervise the Chief Executive, though the Board and CEO often work together in a "strategic partnership", as discussed in the next major section. (Not all nonprofits choose to have a Chief Executive in their nonprofit organization. When they do, the Chief Executive reports to the Board of Directors and is often referred to as the "Executive Director.") The Chief Executive is the major "player" in the nonprofit, the person who often knows the most about the nonprofit's services and clientele. The first Chief Executive of the nonprofit is also commonly the founder of the nonprofit. Therefore, the Chief Executive plays a major role in first organizing the Board and helping members to do their job as Board members. Here is an overview of the CEO's role. Note that the description is provided in the context of a policy governing Board structure.

Consider "How Your Board and CEO Can Work in Strategic Partnership" on page 48.

Board Administration and Support

Theory and law asserts that the Board oversees and governs the nonprofit organization. Many experts assert that it is the CEO who actually facilitates the Board to perform those roles. The CEO often knows much more about the nonprofit organization than does the members of the Board. Consequently, the CEO must continually update Board members about the nonprofit organization, often by providing written reports to Board members that are reviewed during Board meetings. An effective Board hires the CEO and regularly evaluates the CEO's performance. The CEO often helps with Board development and administration, often in a Board Development Committee.

Program, Product and Service Delivery

The CEO is an expert on the nonprofit's programs and the needs of the nonprofit's clientele, including who they are, what their needs are and how those needs should be met. The CEO oversees design of programs to ensure that the organization continually meets the needs of clients in a highly effective fashion. Programs must be advertised and promoted to community stakeholders, particularly clientele and funders. The CEO works with the Board in this regard, often in a Programs Committee, to ensure Board members are up-to-date about programs and their effectiveness.

Financial, Tax, Risk and Facilities Management

The CEO works with the Board Treasurer, or with a Finance Committee, to develop the yearly budget. The budget should be derived from results of the Board's yearly strategic planning. Once the budget is established, the CEO must operate the nonprofit in accordance with the strategic plan, and in a manner that is consistent with various laws and regulations, and also the policies of the Board. This includes ensuring that all relevant taxes are paid. It also includes managing the facilities of the organization in an efficient and safe fashion. The CEO works with the Board in this regard, often in a Finance Committee.

Human Resource Management

The CEO leads the effort to design organizational roles and responsibilities among staff. These roles and responsibilities should be derived directly from results of yearly strategic planning. The CEO oversees staffing, training and supervision of personnel. These activities must closely conform to up-to-date personnel policies and procedures that are reviewed on a regular basis by an employment law expert and also approved by the Board. The CEO works with the Board in this regard, often in a Personnel Committee.

Community and Public Relations

The CEO often takes the lead in ensuring that the community continues to have a strong positive image about the nonprofit and its services. It is often most effective if the CEO works from a comprehensive marketing plan that is developed in conjunction with a Board Marketing Committee and approved by the Board in general.

Fundraising

One of the primary responsibilities of a nonprofit Board of Directors is to actively participate in fundraising activities. Unfortunately, many Board members do not assume this full responsibility. In any event, the CEO usually leads the fundraising efforts including: clarifying the amounts of monies needed to reach strategic goals, where to go to appeal for those monies, how to make those appeals, and making the appeals themselves. Fundraising is often most effective if the CEO works from a comprehensive fundraising plan that is developed in conjunction with a Board Fundraising Committee and approved by the Board in general.

What Title Should Be Used for This Position?

New nonprofits might wonder what title to use to refer to its most senior staff position. Here are the most frequently considered titles:

Executive Director?

This is the traditional title and it is still used widely. It is clear to most people when they encounter the title that it refers to the "boss" of all of the staff members in a nonprofit. So it usually is not confusing to people who, for example, are referencing the title on salary surveys, searching for senior-level nonprofit jobs, or using it to send correspondence to nonprofits.

Chief Executive Officer?

The trend is for nonprofits to choose this title more frequently. Organizations might choose it because it somehow conveys more stature than "Executive Director" or because it is more consistent with the title in the for-profit business world. Large nonprofits seem to use the title more than smaller nonprofits. This title is used much more in for-profits than nonprofits.

President?

Use of this title seems to be increasing, probably to convey more stature in the position. However, it can be confusing because the role of Board Chair often is also referred to a "President." A related issue is that the title might somehow convey that the most senior staff position (President) is also a Board position (Board Chair) – many experts and stakeholders would rather not see the senior staff position also as a Board member.

Administrator?

This title is used particularly in hospitals. Similar to "President" it can be confusing because senior clerical staff or program staff are sometimes referred to as "administrators," as well.

How Your Board and CEO Can Work In Strategic Partnership

Although theory and law assert that the CEO works for the Board, the relationship and mutual support between the Board and CEO is critical to the success of a nonprofit. There might be an impression that the traditional structure of Boards, with its conventional job descriptions and committees, is somehow a rigid, top-down hierarchy, but this often is not the case. In many nonprofits, it is actually the CEO who facilitates and guides the Board members to do their jobs. Many nonprofits have staff members on certain committees. The CEO has strong input to the deliberations and decisions of Board members. Research suggests that a successful working relationship – a "strategic partnership" – between the Board members and CEO is one of the most important criteria for a high-performing nonprofit organization.

Descriptions of the traditional policy Board often portray the Board members as the "bosses" of CEOs, handing down directives and then "policing" the CEOs to ensure that those directives are followed. CEOs presented with that perspective often are confounded to understand why they must report to a group of people (Board members), many of whom do not seem to understand much, if anything at all, about the nonprofit and its programs. Consequently, these CEOs struggle to acknowledge the credibility and accept directions from Board members. New or struggling CEOs can even resent and disrespect Board members to the extent that the CEO ignores them altogether.

Many experts assert that one of the reasons that a Board might struggle to be effective is because the CEO really does not want an effective Board and, therefore, does not help members to realize their roles and does not provide needed information to the Board members. Seasoned CEOs have learned that their jobs can be enhanced considerably with the additional guidance and resources from a highly effective Board of Directors – but the CEOs realize they must help the Board members to be that effective. CEOs can support the development of a Board when they:

- **Help Board members to understand their roles as members of a governing Board.**
  The CEO often has more interest and resources to fully understand the role of a nonprofit Board and, therefore, can be extremely helpful to Board members' learning their roles. The CEO can work with the Board Chair or Chair of a Board Development Committee to design and conduct the first several Board trainings.

- **Suggest people to recruit as Board members.**
  As much as possible, these people should be independent Board members – people who have no other strong, vested interest in the nonprofit, for example, people who are not staff members or very close and personal friends of the CEO.

- **Orient Board members about the nonprofit and its programs.**
  Frequently, members can serve on a Board for years and still not really know what programs are offered by the nonprofit. CEOs can significantly increase the effectiveness of Board members, and their contributions to the nonprofit, by orienting members about the nonprofit, including its history, programs, collaborators and successes.

- **Play a strong role in strategic planning discussions and decisions.**
  Boards that view members as attending primarily to top-level policy will sometimes make the mistake of determining mission, vision, values and top-level goals without input from the CEO and senior staff members. That is a mistake. The most useful strategic planning sessions often involve information, discussions and suggestions from staff members.

- **Participate in Board committees.**
  The CEO can provide great value to committees, especially Fundraising, Finance, Personnel (except when the Board is evaluating the CEO and determining his/her compensation), Programs and Marketing. A trend is for other staff members to be on some of the Board committees, as well.

- **Provide useful information to Board members in time for their review before meetings.**
  Some CEOs have learned that one of the best ways to incapacitate a Board is by giving them new materials during a Board meeting, so that members are quickly overwhelmed and confused. As a result, members end up listening and agreeing with whatever the CEO suggests. Seasoned and collaborative CEOs share materials well before Board meetings.

An excellent resource that researched and explained the value of this partnership is *Executive Leadership in Nonprofit Organizations: New Strategies for Shaping Executive-Board Dynamics* by R.D. Heimovics and R.D. Herman (Jossey-Bass, 1991).

Typical Timing of Nonprofit CEO's Tasks

There are certain activities that recur regularly during the calendar year for a Chief Executive Officer. The following sample should be modified according to the nature and needs of the nonprofit organization.

Table II:6 – Sample Annual Administrative Calendar

Yearly Activity	Suggested Timing
1. Fiscal year begins	January (fiscal-year timing is often specified in the By-Laws)
2. With the Board, be evaluated about progress towards last fiscal year's goals and job description	April-May (do shortly after completion of last fiscal year)
3. With the Board, review and update Board policies and personnel policies	April-June (do concurrent to Board and Chief Executive Officer evaluations)
4. Ensure programs are evaluated, or at least the most important programs, regarding process and outcomes	April-June (do concurrent to Board and Chief Executive Officer evaluations)
5. Support the Board to conduct first Board retreat (address Board self-evaluation results, team building, begin strategic planning, etc.)	April
6. With the Board, conduct strategic planning to produce organizational goals and resources need to reach goals	May-June-July (start planning in time for setting mission, vision, values, issues, goals, strategies, resource needs, funding needs, and time for getting funds before beginning of next fiscal year)
7. Support Board to hold annual meeting	July (per By-Laws)
8. Establish CEO's goals for next year (as produced from strategic planning)	August (as organizational goals are realized from planning)
9. With Board Treasurer, draft next year's budget (based on resources needed to reach new strategic goals)	July-August-September
10. Conduct staffing analysis to clarify expertise needed to achieve this year's strategic goals, and update staff job descriptions accordingly	July-August-September
11. Support Board to develop Fundraising Plan (with primary goals to get funds needed for budget)	July-August-September
12. Support Board to conduct second Board retreat (address Board orientation/training, re-organize or form new committees based on goals from strategic plan, develop work plans, update Board operations calendar, review planning status, etc.)	August (in time to orient new Board members soon after they join the Board)
13. Support Board to conduct fundraising planning (primarily to meet fundraising goals)	August-December
14. Conduct written yearly performance reviews for each staff member.	Per anniversary date of employees

Sample List of Monthly Activities

The Chief Executive Officer might conduct the following activities on a monthly basis.

1. **Staff-wide meetings**
    This would include meeting with all staff members to review the overall condition of the organization and review recent successes. Consider conducting "in service" training about the organization where employees take turns describing their roles to the rest of the staff. For clarity, focus and morale, be sure to use agendas and follow up with minutes. Consider bringing in a client to tell his/her story of how the organization helped them.

2. **Review of financial reports**
    Note that the particular financial statements and their titles depend on the locale of the nonprofit, for example, the following terms are common in the USA. Reports would include:

    a. Cash Flow (to be sure there are sufficient monies to pay the bills)

    b. Statement of Financial Activities (the income statement)

    c. Statement of Financial Position (the balance sheet; probably on quarterly basis)

3. **Write Director's Report to present to the Board, and briefly describe:**

    a. Status of programs

    b. Major accomplishments of the past month

    c. Expected major accomplishments of the coming month

    d. Any highlights, trends and/or issues that Board members should know about.

4. **Meet with any Board committees and officers as scheduled by the Board.**

5. **Meet with the Board in the regular (usually monthly) Board meetings.**

6. **Meet face-to-face, one-on-one with each direct report.**

Sample List of Weekly Activities

1. **Collect written weekly status reports from each direct report that include:**

    a. Accomplishments over the past week.

    b. Any current highlights, trends and issues

    c. Plans for next week

2. **Meet face-to-face with direct reports together.**
    This further cultivates cohesiveness and communications among staff members.

Should CEO Be Member of Your Board?

There is no clear consensus on this question. It is this author's belief that it is probably fine to have the Chief Executive on the Board for the first year or two, while the Board is developing itself and getting to know the new organization. However, after that first year or two, it is best if the Chief Executive leaves the Board as an official Board member. With that arrangement, Board members might provide more objective assessment and supervision of the Chief Executive. Additionally, Board members might develop more of their own "strategic identity" without the Chief Executive on their team. That is, Board members begin to see themselves as the primary strategic role in the organization, regardless of the input from the Chief Executive. That strategic role, after all, is the Board's job.

The Chief Executive can still attend Board regular meetings, of course (unless the Board is in Executive, or in camera, Session). The Chief Executive, when not attending as an official Board member, cannot vote in Board decisions.

How Your Board Members and CEO Can Work Well Together

Basic Practices to Ensure Effective Coordination

1. Board members must know their roles and responsibilities, including how they differ from those of the Chief Executive and staff. Board training should be conducted at least once a year to ensure all Board members and the Chief Executive clearly understand each other's roles and responsibilities.

2. The Chief Executive and other staff should be aware of the Board's roles and responsibilities, including how they differ from those of the Chief Executive and staff.

3. Board, Chief Executive and staff should engage in yearly strategic planning activities. Board and Chief Executive should be involved primarily in determining the organization's mission, vision, goals and strategies. Chief Executive Officer and staff might be involved primarily in defining action planning, including who will do what and by when in order to implement the strategies. The resulting strategic plan should be provided to everyone in the organization.

4. Board members should have regular Board meetings, usually once a month during the first several years of the organization's life. Thereafter, have Board meetings at least every two or three months, ideally with committee meetings between Board meetings that are every other month.

5. Chief Executive Officer and Board Chair design the agenda for Board meetings, and the agenda is sent to Board members at least one week before the Board meeting.

6. The Chief Executive Officer should provide regular, written reports to Board members, usually on a monthly basis.

7. The Chief Executive Officer and Board Chair should have a strong, ongoing, working relationship.

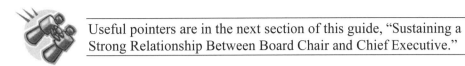

Useful pointers are in the next section of this guide, "Sustaining a Strong Relationship Between Board Chair and Chief Executive."

8. The Board should conduct regular, at least annual, formal evaluations of the Chief Executive Officer.

9. There should be clear Board policies regarding the roles and coordination of Board members and staff, including:

   a. Staff participation on Board committees.

   b. Ensuring that the Chief Executive Officer approves Board member contacts to staff (unless a current, major issue suggests the Chief Executive Officer should not be involved).

10. Board members and staff should meet each other at least once a year in a rather casual environment focused on celebrating the accomplishments of the organization.

11. Staff should be allowed to make occasional presentations at Board meetings regarding program activities and how they are carried out.

How Your Board Chair and CEO Can Work Well Together

Inherent Struggles Between Both Roles

Many experts assert that one of the most important ingredients to a successful corporation (nonprofit or for-profit) is a high-quality relationship between the Board Chair and the Chief Executive. However, this relationship has several inherent struggles to overcome. The Chief Executive was usually in the organization before the Chair was appointed and will be around after the Chair will be gone. In addition, the Chief Executive is also much closer to the day-to-day activities in the organization. Lastly, the Chief Executive usually knows far more about the organization's customers. Consequently, the Chief Executive may feel that he or she knows far much more about the organization than the Board Chair. Yet, the Board Chair is responsible to provide leadership to the Board to whom the Chief Executive is accountable. The Board Chair leads the Board, which evaluates the performance of the Chief Executive. Maintaining a high-quality relationship between the two roles requires a high level of maturity and understanding from both people filling those roles.

Practices That Can Minimize Destructive Conflict

Conflict is inherent in groups where diverse members are participating in deliberations and decisions about very important matters, in particular when each member is sharing his/her beliefs and opinions. Conflict itself is not bad – conflict becomes destructive when it is prolonged about the same issue or decision, involves members openly making judgments about a member's character or personality, or involves escalating emotions to the extent that some members are shouting or otherwise impeding the group process. The following suggestions are provided to help ensure a high-quality relationship between the Board Chair and the Chief Executive by establishing formal practices and procedures.

1. **Have clearly written and approved procedures for evaluating the Chief Executive.**
    Ensure the procedures include getting strong input from the Chief Executive.

2. **Have regular Board training sessions.**
    They should include overviews of the roles of Board Chair and Chief Executive.

3. **Board Chair and Chief Executive meet to discuss how they can work together.**
    They should share their preferences for how they like to communicate, plan and coordinate.

4. **Board Chair and Chief Executive jointly design Board meeting agendas.**
    This helps to ensure that all important matters of the Board and staff are included.

5. **Board Chair can consult with the Chief Executive when appointing Committee Chairs.**
    Many times, the Chief Executive has a clearer understanding of who knows what on Board.

6. **Have clearly written guidelines about the roles of staff.**
    This is especially important when staff provide ongoing support to Board committees.

7. **Get a new person in the Board Chair position at least every few years.**
    This helps to ensure new and fresh perspectives in the role.

8. **Consider developing Board Chairs by having Vice Chairs.**
    The Vice Chair gets a year to "shadow" the Chair to really learn the role.

9. **Have a Board discussion about meetings between the Chief Executive and Board Chair.**
    Get all Board member's ideas about when and why the Board Chair and Chief Executive should meet – do not make the meeting a matter of only those two people.

10. **Avoid frequent meetings that include only the Board Chair and Chief Executive.**
    Involve other Board members or other staff.

11. **Always write and share highlights of meetings of Chief Executive and Board Chair.**
    Otherwise, other Board members forget about these meetings.

12. **Ensure all Board members are trained about the role of the Board.**
    That way, all Board members know what to expect from the Board Chair and CEO roles.

13. **The Chief Executive and Board Chair should never conceal information.**
    CEO and Board Chair information is Board business – all members should know about it.

14.   **Celebrate accomplishments.**
        All Board members should recognize and appreciate the hard work of the Chair and CEO.

Personal Practices to Minimize Interpersonal Conflicts

In addition to formal practices to minimize conflicts as listed above, the two people in these two roles can follow certain practices themselves.

 Consider "How to Understand and Manage Conflict" on page 237.

If Worse Comes to Worst

Obviously, the course of action for a situation such as this depends to a great extent on the nature of the organization and the two people involved. If you are a Board Chair or Chief Executive who continues to feel conflict in working with the other person, then consider:

1.   **Approach the other person and ask for five minutes of uninterrupted time.**
        Explain your concern, what you see and hear that leads you to believe there is continued conflicts between both of you, what you would like to see or hear between both of you in the future, and why continued conflict can be so destructive to the organization.

2.   **If the other person says there is no conflict, then assert what you want from them.**
        They either will change their behaviors, in which case things should improve, or they will not. In that case, you can escalate the issue up the organization (for example, present the matter to entire board), if appropriate, or seek additional assistance about how you plan to handle the problem: avoid it, confront it further, negotiate further, etc.

3.   **If the problem persists, ask to have time with the Executive Committee.**
        At this point, it is critical to remember that any "badmouthing" or "conspiring" against the other person will only end up hurting the entire Board and organization. Therefore, talk with a friend or take careful time to reflect about what you want to say and how to say it to the other Board members. Explain the situation in terms of the behaviors in the issue, not the personality or character of the other person. Explain what you have done so far to address the issue. Describe your perception of the results of your efforts with the other person – note that it is your perception. Ask for specific advice to address the issue. At the end of the meeting, echo back what you hear them suggesting. Attempt to follow their advice. Commit to follow up with them about the results of your following their advice.

4.   **If the problem persists, you might consider getting outside help.**
        This may be more constructive than posing the problem to the entire Board where it may cause great confusion and unease with little or no clear course of action to resolve the issue.

How Your Board Can Evaluate Your CEO

Many Benefits of Formal Evaluation

Evaluating the Chief Executive Officer is a primary responsibility of the Board. There are several key benefits from this evaluation, including that the process:

1. Ensures the Board is meeting its duty to effectively lead the organization.

2. Ensures organizational goals are being met.

3. Ensures continued development of the Chief Executive to more effectively conduct his or her role.

4. Ensures a formal and documented evaluation process that meets standards of fairness and practicality.

5. Ensures the Chief Executive values his or her role, is benefiting from it and therefore is more likely to stay (finding good Chief Executives seems increasingly difficult).

6. Leaves written record of the Board's impression of the Chief Executive's performance in case this record is needed for future verification, for example, for salary increases, probationary activities, firing, etc.

Table II:7 – Sample Schedule to Evaluate Chief Executive

Activity	Approx. # of months before start of next fiscal year
Evaluate the Chief Executive, by referencing his or her progress towards last fiscal year's organizational goals and responsibilities on their job description	10
Conduct Board self-evaluation	9
Hold Board retreat to address results of Board self-evaluation, conduct any team building and begin strategic planning	7
Conduct strategic planning to produce organizational goals and identify resources needed to accomplish the goals	7
Establish Chief Executive's goals for the next fiscal year, by referencing goals produced from strategic planning	6
Establish next year's fundraising goals and budget by referencing resources needed to reach strategic goals	6
Conduct fundraising to meet fundraising goals	6
Fiscal year begins	0

General Guidelines When Evaluating Chief Executive

1.   Be sure the process is fully documented in a procedure so the process is well understood and carried out consistently year to year. The procedure should be in conformance with up-to-date, Board-approved personnel policies and procedures.

2.   If staff members are involved in evaluation of the Chief Executive, be sure this procedure is clearly specified and understood by the Chief Executive.

3.   A Board committee, not just one Board member, should manage the evaluation process, and all Board members should have input to the evaluation feedback to the Chief Executive. Committees might be the Executive Committee, a Personnel Committee or an ad hoc committee.

4.   If the Board perceives the Chief Executive to have performance issues, then Board members can initiate an evaluation. However, do not initiate evaluations only when there are perceived issues – this is abusive. Be sure that conclusions about performance issues are based on observed behaviors of the Chief Executive, rather than on interpretations or speculations about the Chief Executive's character or personality.

Sample Form to Evaluate Chief Executive: Guidelines

Table II:8 provides one sample set of guidelines and a form that might be used by the Board to evaluate the Chief Executive. This sample should be customized to the particular culture and purpose of the nonprofit by modifying the performance criteria in the left column as appropriate for the organization, updating those criteria in the table, and conducting the evaluation using the updated table.

1.   The Board should establish a policy for evaluating the Chief Executive and establish a current or ad hoc committee to carry out the evaluation.

2.   The Board, working with the Chief Executive, should establish performance criteria and insert them in the table below. Criteria should come from the Chief Executive's job description and any strategic goals from the most current strategic plan.

3.   The Board then assigns specific weighting factors for each of the major categories below. Factors depend on what the Board believes should be priorities for the Chief Executive during the evaluation period. The factors should total 100%. Example weightings might be finances 15%, revenue 20%, human resources 15%, products/programs 20%, facilities 10%, planning and governance 20%.

4.   Each Board member and the Chief Executive complete the table below about the Chief Executive's performance during the evaluation period. Each criteria is ranked from 1-5, with 1=unsatisfactory, 2 = partially within expectations, 3=meets expectations, 4=exceeds expectations, and 5= far exceeds expectations. This numerical ranking system tends to give clear perspective more than commentary. Rankings with commentary are ideal.

5.   Multiply each ranking by the category's weighting factor. Put the answer in the score column.

6.   On a separate sheet of paper, provide any commentary that addresses rankings lower than 3. Consider adding commentary for high ratings as well.

7.   Provide evaluation sheets and commentary to the Board member who is assigned to collate the sheets (usually the Board Chair).

8.   The Board may decide to provide the Chief Executive an average ranking for each category. Similarly, commentary can be summarized or each comment provided to the Chief Executive.

9.   The evaluation committee provides the evaluation report to the Chief Executive and schedules a meeting with him or her shortly thereafter.

10.   Ensure the meeting ends on a positive note.

11.   Ensure plans are made to address ratings below 3, including specific actions by specific dates.

Table II:8 – Sample Form to Evaluate Chief Executive

Name of Preparer	Ratings	Weight Factor	= Score
Planning and support of governance, consider: ▪ Provides relevant and meaningful information to support Board plans and policies ▪ Establishes appropriate plans and priorities, which are clearly described to staff members ▪ Ensures implementation of plans in a timely manner Comments:			
Finances, consider: ▪ Stays within budgets and/or gets approval for deviations ▪ Maintains needed cash flow to pay bills on time ▪ Receives a "clean" financial audit ▪ No loss of operating funds ▪ No prolonged legal difficulties Comments:			
Revenue, consider: ▪ Raises enough revenue through fundraising and fees for services to accomplish significant program goals ▪ Maintains a financial balance in keeping with organizational policy Comments:			
Programs and services, consider: ▪ Ensures high-quality operations in programs ▪ Verifies that each program is achieving its program goals and the desired outcomes among clients Comments:			
Human resources, consider: ▪ Maintains or increases productivity of staff ▪ Maintains sufficient and effective volunteer corps ▪ No undue staff turnover ▪ No ongoing personnel complaints Comments:			

How Your Board Can Ensure Smooth Succession to A New CEO When Needed

The Board is responsible to ensure that the nonprofit continually has high-quality operations. If the Board chooses to have a CEO or Executive Director role in the nonprofit, then it is extremely important that that role be filled reliably with a high-quality person. CEOs leave their jobs on an unplanned or a planned basis. Unplanned termination may occur because of sudden illnesses or death, or poor performance on the part of the CEO. Planned termination usually occurs because the CEO is making a career or life change.

Research indicates that most of the nonprofit CEOs will leave their jobs within the next five years. Also, demographic trends indicate that there are not sufficient numbers of next-generation leaders to replace retiring baby-boomers in nonprofits. Thus, succession management is an increasingly important priority for Board members. (Various phrases are used to refer to aspects of ensuring a complete and successful transition to a new CEO, for example, succession planning, succession management and transition management.)

For a very interesting report about nonprofit executives, and their intentions to stay in their jobs, see *Daring to Lead 2006* at http://www.compasspoint.org/assets/194_daringtolead06final.pdf .

Principles for Successful Succession Management

- **Do not wait until the CEO will be terminating employment. Start planning now.**
  Succession management is a matter of strong practices in ongoing governance and management, not a matter of sudden crisis management. Start attending to those practices now.

- **Focus on practices, not on personalities.**
  Succession management is re-filling a role, not replacing a certain person. Be sure the CEO position is defined well, then look to find the best person to fill the position. Do not look for someone who is just like, or a lot different than, the previous CEO.

- **Succession management is a responsibility of the Board and the CEO.**
  The best succession management results from 1) a working partnership of Board members working to understand and define and fill the CEO role, and 2) the CEO ensuring that Board members have the information and resources to refill the role.

- **Succession management is leadership transition, and staffing and risk management.**
  Leadership is ensuring clear direction and creating the environment so that others are motivated to follow that direction – that function must continue during a transition. The CEO is a staff role and, therefore, must be filled by using up-to-date personnel policies to ensure fair, equitable and legally compliant employment practices. Activities must minimize the risks from lapses in poor management and undue fears among stakeholders.

- **Quality in managing succession is often proportionate to the quality of the new CEO.**
  The more thorough and careful that Board members are during succession, the more likely that the nonprofit will get a new CEO who successfully fills the position for the long-term. The best way for Board members to convey their expectations of high quality in the CEO role now, is to have the CEO perceive a high-quality succession management process.

Key Governance and Management Practices in Succession Management

If Board members have already established strong practices in governance and in management, then succession management often is a matter of using current practices, rather than establishing many new ones. Key practices include having:

1. A strategic plan that clearly conveys the nonprofit's mission and current strategic priorities. Ideally, that plan also includes specific action plans that specify who is going to do what and by when in order to address each priority.

2. Up-to-date and Board-approved personnel policies about hiring, supervising and firing personnel in a fair and equitable manner that comply with employment laws.

3. An up-to-date job description for the Executive Director role that explains the general duties and responsibilities of the position.

4. Suitable compensation for the CEO role (very often this is a major challenge for nonprofits because they often have very limited resources).

5. An annual calendar of the CEO's most important activities, for example, when the CEO: evaluates personnel, does any staffing analysis, updates job descriptions, evaluates programs, participates in certain Board committees, etc.

6. Regular reports from CEO, in particular reports to Board members prior to or during Board meetings, and about the trends, highlights and issues regarding the CEO's activities.

7. Evaluation of the CEO on an annual basis, including in reference to the CEO's job description and any performance goals established for that role.

8. Arrangements with the CEO when he/she goes on vacation so Board members and staff have an opportunity to effectively replace the CEO if only for a temporary period of time.

9. A complete list of major stakeholders. Get a list of donors, including contact information, how each is approached and who does that (ideally, there is some form of Fundraising Committee or task force that has been heavily involved in fundraising with the CEO) in case that information is needed when/if the CEO leaves. Get a complete list of other stakeholders, including collaborators, suppliers, facilities management contacts, etc.

10. Fiscal policies and procedures to ensure strong Board oversight of finances, including that financial numbers are correct and tracked accurately, and also that there are sufficient funds to pay near-term expenses.

11. At least annual discussions with the CEO regarding succession management, including how management can be done effectively in the CEO's absence. (Be careful about raising this topic with the CEO so that he/she is not overly concerned that Board members somehow want a change now). This discussion can be opportunity to hear about the CEO's career plans and desires, too.

12. At least annual discussions, not only about succession of the CEO role, but of other critical positions in the staff, for example, program directors and development (fundraising) officers.

Replacing an Outgoing CEO

If the nonprofit has regularly been conducting succession planning with the current CEO, then it could be a straightforward matter to replace the CEO in a relatively low-risk and smooth manner. The following guidelines assume that the CEO has given sufficient notice that he/she is leaving soon. Some of the guidelines in the following section will need to be modified if the CEO is suddenly leaving, for example, was fired, seriously ill or deceased.

CEO's Notification to Board

1. **Typically, the Chief Executive will notify the Board Chair or other Board member.**
   The Chair should immediately notify the rest of the Board members prior to the next Board meeting.

2. **Ask the Chief Executive to document his/her decision in writing to the Board.**

3. **Attempt to negotiate a four-week-notice period from the Chief Executive.**
   It is not unlikely that there will be a period without a new Chief Executive. This procedure will minimize disruption through that period.

Maintaining Confidentiality During Transition

1. **All Board members should be apprised as soon as possible.**
   Occasionally, members believe that transitions should be handled so cautiously that even some Board members should not hear about the transition. This is the wrong approach. Each Board member is legally responsible for the leadership of the organization, and deserves to know about all matters when they occur.

2. **Discuss how to handle public relations.**
   The community will soon hear or read that the Chief Executive is leaving. Agree on how this message will be conveyed to the community. If the transition is expected to take over a month (they often do), consider sending a letter to the major stakeholders (advisors, suppliers, "peer" organizations, funders if in the case of a nonprofit, etc.) notifying them of the transition and assuring them that transition planning is being carried out thoroughly. Invite them to contact the Board Chair if they have any concerns or questions.

Board Activities During Transition

1. **Start activities to recruit and hire new CEO. Appoint an ad hoc Search Committee?**
   The Board might choose to form a Board Search Committee (or task force) now, in which case that Committee could handle the search activities, too. The Committee will manage the transition, including developing a transition plan. This Committee role could be assumed by the current Executive Committee or a Personnel Committee. Committee members should commit to availability over the next four to eight weeks. The Search Committee should focus on:

   a. Identifying desired skills of the new Chief Executive, if not already identified.

   b. Verifying the accuracy of the job description of the Chief Executive.

   c. Conducting the recruiting and selection activities itemized in this section.

2. **Develop a written transition plan and have the Board approve it.**
    The contents of this section about succession management could comprise much of the transition plan, but responsibilities and deadlines would need to be added to the plan.

3. **As soon as the transition plan is developed, promptly notify staff of the transition.**
    A Board member should attend the staff meeting where notification is given and the staff should be assured that the transition is being carefully planned and carried out. The plan might be reviewed in the staff meeting. A copy of the transition plan should be shared with all staff members.

4. **Identify any necessary funding for the transition.**
    For example, are any funds needed for a national search, to move the new candidate, for training the new candidate, for consultants on interim basis, etc.?

Administrative Activities During Transition Before New CEO Arrives

1. **Establish an interim staff structure.**
    Consider appointing an acting Chief Executive from staff reporting to the current Chief Executive. If this course is followed, ensure the job description is well understood by the acting Chief Executive and the acting arrangement is documented in a letter between the acting Chief Executive and the Board. Send a memo throughout the staff, indicating this interim appointment and how the acting Chief Executive will work with the staff until a permanent Chief Executive is identified. (Be very careful with this type of temporary arrangement as it can lull Board members into believing the transition is complete, which it is not. Also, it can foster the illusion that the Board members will always be delegating directly to staff.)

2. **Update the administrative calendar for the organization.**
    Ask the outgoing Chief Executive to make a schedule of all major recurring activities during the year, for example, of performance reviews, special events, staff meetings, one-on-one meetings, lease/contract expiration dates, when paychecks come out, etc. Be sure any deadlines for contracts are included in the schedule.

3. **Get a list of key stakeholders from the outgoing CEO.**
    Have the outgoing Chief Executive make or update a list of all community key stakeholders whom the new Chief Executive should know about, for example, funders, advisors (legal, accounting, real estate), "peer" organizations, etc.

4. **Review outgoing Chief Executive's office facilities.**
    Ask the outgoing Chief Executive to document the status of his/her office, for example, ensure there are labels on all documents and drawers. Appropriate staff and at least two Board members should meet with the Chief Executive to review where he/she keeps files and major documents. Staff should retain a key to the office and appropriate Board members should retain keys to the desk drawers and file cabinets.

5. **Review personnel status with the outgoing CEO.**
    Two or more Board members, ideally from the Personnel Committee, should meet with the outgoing Chief Executive to review personnel files, for example, are there any current personnel issues, for example, some personnel will be leaving/retiring or have performance issues.

6. **Outgoing CEO should complete performance reviews on all personnel.**
    This ensures that the outgoing Chief Executive's important feedback to personnel is collected before he/she goes, gives personnel a fair opportunity to reflect their past performance to the new Chief Executive, and gives the new Chief Executive the input he/she deserves about each employee to ensure effective supervision.

Interim Coordination Between Board and Staff During Transition

1. **Get emergency contact information for each of the staff members.**
    Staff should be given names and phone numbers of at least two Board members who can be contacted if needed. These two members should brief the entire Board on the nature of any emergency calls from staff, if calls were made.

2. **Have weekly meetings with staff until the new CEO arrives.**
    Depending on the size of the organization, have weekly meetings of full staff (if small) or all managers (if large) during the transition until a new Chief Executive is hired. Have a Board member attend the meetings. Have a staff member (acting Chief Executive, or the current top reports, or rotate among top reports) attend portions of the Board meetings.

3. **Come up to speed on outgoing CEO's current activities in the organization.**
    Have the current Chief Executive ask all staff members to update a "to do" list of their current major activities over the past month, planned activities over the coming two months and any major issues they are having now. These "to do" lists will serve to coordinate work details during the transition and help the new Chief Executive come up to speed.

4. **Develop any authorization lists.**
    Decide who will issue paychecks and sign off on them during the transition. Often, the Board Treasurer and/or Secretary will conduct this sign-off role.

5. **Board members should meet with the outgoing CEO once a week until he/she goes.**
    Review status of work activities, any current issues, etc.

How Your Board Can Determine Your CEO's Compensation

The position of CEO is one of the most critical assets in the nonprofit. It is very important that the CEO's compensation be sufficient to attract, keep and help motivate a highly competent CEO. Determination of compensation is one of the most important activities of the Board. Much of that activity should be done even before a new CEO is hired. Unfortunately, there is no specific procedure that accurately and reliably computes exactly what you should pay your CEO. Instead, the process is one of addressing certain general and specific considerations, referencing some salary surveys to identify suitable pay ranges for the CEO role in the nonprofit and locale, making a best estimate on what might be a reasonable salary and set of benefits. This section explains major considerations and suggests additional resources for salary and benefits information.

Board members' explanation of how they addressed each consideration can support and justify the CEO compensation and benefits to stakeholders (for example, the Internal Revenue Service in the USA). That explanation might be useful if, for example, the nonprofit was ever challenged about its compensation to the CEO. A team, or committee, of Board members, for example, a Personnel Committee, should address the considerations and make recommendations. However, the Board as a body (with at least a quorum) should approve the approach to determining compensation and benefits, and the resulting amount and benefits.

The following information is not offered as legal or tax advice. Nonprofits would benefit from consulting authorities in the related fields to gain the most up-to-date and thorough advice and materials. In addition to considering the information in this section, Board members would benefit from consulting a local specialist who has expertise in benefits and compensation for nonprofit executives. Any final compensation and benefits decisions should be carefully described in updated personnel policies.

Broad Considerations – Societal, Public and Community

1. **Consider the strength of the economy, local and national.**
    For example, a lower unemployment rate might be reason to offer a higher salary in order to be more competitive with other jobs that the CEO might be able to get. A weak economy, for example, a rate of slow spending or low confidence in the economy, might suggest reason to be conservative, offering a lower salary.

2. **Consider public perception.**
    The public believes that nonprofits should be dedicated to meeting the needs of the public, not to making certain people rich. The public already has strong distaste for the seemingly exorbitant salaries of for-profit CEOs. A trend is for some very large nonprofits to pay their CEOs very high salaries in order to attract highly experienced executives, but this can result in negative public perceptions. Consequently, nonprofit executive compensation is increasingly under public scrutiny.

3. **Consider pay for similar positions in local nonprofits with similar nature of services.**
    For example, if yours is a social service agency, then consider the salaries of other social service agencies in your area. This consideration is one of the strongest to address when determining salary. (This end of this section references a list of sources of salary surveys.)

Considerations – Organizational and Personal

1. **Consider the organization's personnel policies.**
   Personnel policies should have up-to-date guidelines about how to hire, manage and fire personnel in a fair, equitable and legally compliant manner. The guidelines should be reviewed annually by an expert on employment laws and then approved by the Board. Guidelines in the policies should be referenced in case they provide any direction about determining salaries.

2. **Consider the CEO's match to the job description.**
   This consideration is probably the strongest when determining the CEO's salary. The job description should specify the duties and responsibilities of the position, along with ideal and minimal requirements for the position. The closer the match between the CEO's expertise and the job description, the higher the salary that you would offer.

3. **Consider the match between the CEO's expertise and current strategic priorities.**
   For example, if the nonprofit has strategic goals to build a firm foundation for further growth by instilling strong management systems, then a CEO with that kind of experience would warrant a higher salary.

4. **Consider the culture and values of the nonprofit.**
   For example, if the culture highly values a highly inclusive and participatory management style, then a CEO with those values might warrant a higher salary. In contrast, some members of the Board and organization might strongly believe that nonprofits should always pay below-market rates because that is the duty of a nonprofit.

Nonprofits are strongly discouraged from expecting the CEO to spend a great deal of his/her time in continually raising the vast majority of funds needed to pay his/her salary during the year. The nonprofit should already have sufficient and somewhat stable revenue from fees for services and/or from regular fundraising to pay the salary – and all Board members should participate in fundraising, not just the CEO. CEOs should be paid as based on their expertise and performance, not primarily on the success of their fundraising.

Considerations – Some Restrictions and Limitations

1. **Consider expectations of donors and funders.**
   For example, some foundations prefer that administrative costs (costs that are not specific to one program, such as the CEO's salary, facilities costs and general supplies) be under a certain threshold. The higher the CEO's salary, the greater the likelihood that the nonprofit will exceed that threshold.

2. **Consider concerns of governmental agencies.**
   Compensation should be "reasonable" and approved by the Board of Directors. For example, the Internal Revenue Service (IRS) in the USA poses excise taxes on tax-exempt nonprofits whose Board and staff members receive "excess benefit" from the nonprofit. Reasonable compensation might be determined by using salary surveys that depict salaries for similar positions in similar types of nonprofits in the locale. The Board's approach to determining compensation for staff should be explained in the personnel policies, which also should be approved by the Board. Board members' deliberations and decisions about the compensation should be fully described in the minutes of the Board meeting. If a Board

member has a conflict of interest in the consideration, then he/she should abstain from that matter.

 There is more information about the IRS's concerns at http://www.irs.gov/newsroom/article/0,,id=128328,00.html .

3.   **Consider requirements for fair and ethical treatment.**
Compensation should not be based on the CEO's personal features, including age, race, gender, sexual orientation or physical disability. Compensation should be based on the person's expertise and match to the job requirements.

Forms of Compensation and Benefits

Payments

1.   **Salary**
This is the most common form of compensation. Executives in the USA usually are classified by the government as "exempt" (rather than "non-exempt"), meaning they usually should be paid a certain amount (a salary), regardless of the hours worked (within reason). Non-exempt personnel usually are paid by the hour (wages). Salary surveys are extremely useful when determining salary. There is more information about surveys at the end of this section.

2.   **Incentive-based compensation (bonuses)**
Bonuses seem to be used increasingly as means to reward CEOs for his/her, or the organization's, performance. Ideally, the performance is measured in reference to pre-established and specific goals that were discussed with the CEO before this form of compensation is determined and issued.

3.   **Salary adjustments**
These are sometimes used when nonprofits do not have funds to pay all of a salary payment. Instead, the nonprofit might issue a payment near the end of the year in order to make up for the amount that was not afforded and paid earlier. Sometimes these are paid as means to compensate a CEO who wanted other forms of benefits, such as a certain form of insurance, which the organization was not able to provide. These should not be a regular form of payment, but should be used only on rare occasions when funds for the full salary were not available.

Benefits

1.   **Insurances**
The most common forms of insurance in benefits include life insurance, medical insurance, disability insurance and dental insurance. In the USA, costs of insurance have increased dramatically, resulting in organizations dropping forms of insurance from benefits or expecting employees to pay an increasing percentage of the costs of their insurance.

2.   **Pensions and individual retirement plans (deferred compensation)**
Pensions are not as important as they were decades ago when an employee expected to remain with an organization through his/her entire career. There are a variety of individual retirement options for individuals, such as 401(k) and Roth IRA plans, to which

organizations can contribute amounts. Sometimes the organizations provide a "matching" amount, meaning they contribute a certain percentage of the amount contributed by the employee on a regular basis.

Other Forms of Reward

1. **Professional development (and/or tuition reimbursements)**
   This is one of the most important forms of providing value to the CEO because it helps him/her, not only to enhance competence and credibility, but also to provide more value and performance to the organization. Many would argue that professional development should not be means of compensation and benefits, but rather should be a right for the CEO within an organization.

2. **Flexible time or compensation time**
   This might be particularly valuable to a CEO who has worked a large number of hours in a certain month or who needs a particular flexible schedule for personal needs, such as family responsibilities.

3. **Lodging and meals**
   This would apply especially to nonprofits that have facilities, for example, churches and camps. Many times, lodging and meals are extremely important to the CEO because related costs can be quite high. Yet, lodging and meals might be a much lower cost for the nonprofit. The nonprofit should have careful policies about the amounts of payment for lodging and meals because these expenses to the nonprofit can quickly become much higher than expected. The employee or staff member should be careful to specify on his/her personal tax forms whether lodging and meals are a form of compensation.

Using Salary Surveys

It is extremely useful to reference salary surveys when determining salaries. The surveys lend tremendous credibility and fairness to the process of determining compensation. Be sure that surveys are somewhat current. Reference them to find the salaries for the job roles that are the closest match to your CEOs. Unfortunately, many surveys use job classifications only, for example, they might refer to "Chief Executive" in the category of "Nonprofit". Ideally, the classifications also are matched to the nature of the nonprofit (for example, "social services") and its locale. Note that some types of nonprofits tend to have higher-than-usual CEO compensation, including educational institutions and hospitals. The closer you can match your CEO role to the type of services, locale and job title, the more useful the survey is likely to be to you, especially if the survey was generated in the past five years or less.

The following reference is to a list of nonprofit surveys. You might also contact your local United Way or nonprofits similar to yours to ask them for references to specific surveys.

Idealist.org has a list of nonprofit salary surveys at
http://www.idealist.org/en/career/salarysurvey.html .

How Your Board Can Use an Employment Contract With Your CEO

Before hiring a new CEO, it is useful to consider how to retain the person in that role. Many organizations directly hire the CEO as an employee. However, some organizations are now considering use of an employment contract instead.

Rather than the standard employee-nonprofit relationship that is usually entered into when an employee accepts of letter of offer, an employment contract is like hiring a contractor to do the job of CEO. However the nonprofit might still withhold payroll taxes – consult a tax specialist about this specific matter because the appropriate governmental tax agency (for example, the Internal Revenue Service in the USA) might be particularly concerned about organizations hiring contractors to avoid paying payroll taxes. The terms of the contract supercede standard personnel requirements as specified in personnel policies and any state laws about "at will" employment. Contracts can bring an extra level of specificity, clarity, credibility and focus to the agreement between the CEO and the nonprofit. Contracts might decrease the likelihood of lawsuits about unfair employee termination because contracts can specify specific start and stop dates of service, so Board members can simply choose not to renew the contract as a means to remove the CEO.

An employment contract might include the following (the following is not offered as legal advice):

- Name of the organization
- Name of the CEO
- Date the contract went into effect
- Date service starts and stops
- Duties and responsibilities to be met (for example, those in a job description)
- Performance goals
- Contractor's conformance to mission, vision, values, plans and policies

- Non-compete and confidentiality requirements
- Specification of compensation and benefits
- Specification of termination (with cause, without cause)
- How the contract can be amended
- Terms of mediation, if needed
- Signatures of all parties

 Consider "How to Hire and Work With Consultants" on page 173.

How Your Board and Staff Can Work Together

Organization Chart of Typical Board and Staff Relationships

The drawing in Table II:9 depicts the typical arrangement in a policy (traditional) Board structure. The solid lines indicate formal lines of authority – authority that is official to the position. For example, corporate law asserts that the Board of Directors is legally responsible for the nonprofit corporation. Therefore, the Executive Director formally reports to the Board of Directors. The official authority of the Executive Director position is derived from the Board's specification for the position, for example, in the By-Laws and/or Board-approved job description of the Executive Director.

The power of the Board is vested in the Board as an entirety of all of its members – no one member has the full authority of the Board. Therefore, the Board Chair (a single Board member) formally reports to the full Board. Committees formally report to the Board Chair or the full Board, depending on the official specification in the By-Laws. Staff members, other than the Executive Director, typically report to the Executive Director, as specified in the By-Laws and/or Board-approved job description of the Executive Director.

Table II:9 – Organization Chart of Typical Board and Staff Relationships

(Used with permission of Greater Twin Cities United Way)

Your Board and Staff – How Their Roles Might Compare

The following table is adapted from James M. Hardy, *Developing Dynamic Boards* (Essex Press, Erwin, Tennessee, 1990). The nature of the extent of separation between Board and staff, if at all, depends very much on the particular Board model that members prefer.

Table II:10 – Comparison of Board and Staff Roles

Activities	Primary Responsibility
Organizational Planning	
Drive the process of strategic and organizational planning	Board
Provide input to mission and long range goals	Joint
Approve mission and long range, strategic goals	Board
Develop action plans (who does what and when) to achieve long-range goals	Staff
Approve action plans (for example, in an annual Operating Plan)	Board
Implement action plans to achieve long-range goals (Board via committee work plans)	Joint
Follow-up to insure achievement of major goals and objectives	Board
Board of Directors	
Select new Board members	Board
Orient, train and organize members into committees	Board
Promote attendance at Board/committee meetings	Board
Plan agenda for Board meetings (joint with Board Chair and Exec. Dir.)	Joint
Take minutes at Board meetings (Board Secretary)	Board
Programs	
Assess stakeholder (customers, community, member, etc.) needs	Joint
Suggest program clients, outcomes, goals, etc.	Joint
Approve program outcomes and goals	Board
Ensure evaluation of products, services and programs	Board
Evaluate products, services and programs	Staff
Maintain program records; prepare program reports	Staff
Financial management	
Prepare preliminary annual budget	Staff
Finalize and approve annual budget	Board
Approve major expenditures outside authorized budget	Board
Ensure annual audit of organization accounts	Board
Ensure that expenditures are within budget during the year	Joint
Fundraising	
Establish fundraising goals (amounts / goals to be raised)	Board
Solicit contributions in fundraising campaigns	Joint
Organize fundraising campaigns	Joint
Manage grants (reporting, etc.)	Staff
Personnel Activities (staff and volunteers)	
Employ and supervise Chief Executive (Exec. Dir.)	Board
Decision to add general staff roles and / or volunteer roles	Staff
Select / train general staff and / or volunteers	Staff
Direct work of the general staff and /or volunteers	Staff
Public / Community Relations Activities	
Present / describe organization to community	Joint
Write descriptions of organization (newsletters, web, etc.)	Staff

How Much Should Your Board Be Involved in Management?

Policy-Making Versus Management Activities?

Experts often frame the question in terms of how much Board members should be attending to establishing top-level plans and policies versus how much Board members should be involved in management, that is, in actually implementing those plans and policies.

First, it is helpful to recognize that there are different levels of policies in organizations, as listed below. A policy is a set of guidelines that can guide the behaviors of others in a certain area or practice, including for them to generate more detailed policies, or procedures.

1. **Strategic (top-level) policies**
    These affect the entire organization and how it is integrated with other organizations, for example, the organization's mission, vision, values and strategic goals. Strategic policies direct and guide the management activities in the organization.

2. **Management / functional policies**
    These guide the activities in major functions and operations, for example, Boards, strategic planning, staffing, programs, finances, fundraising and evaluations.

3. **Program policies**
    These guide how programs operate, for example, how clients first come into the program, how they receive services and how services are evaluated.

4. **Day-to-day policies and procedures**
    These are detailed sets of directions, for example, what to do in case of fire, how to ensure that there is always a sufficient amount of office supplies, etc.

Factors That Influence Focus of Board Members' Involvement

Experts on nonprofits often have very strong beliefs and feelings about what should be the extent of involvement of Board members in developing top-level policies versus actually implementing those policies in the day-to-day affairs of the nonprofit. Many experts would assert that Board members should attend primarily to top-level policies. However, various factors influence how involved Board members are in policy making versus "management," that is, in implementing the policies.

- New and small nonprofits often have hands-on Board members who are heavily involved in day-to-day activities because the nonprofits have no staff or very little in staff resources.

- Larger, established nonprofits usually have members who attend primarily to top-level planning and policies because those nonprofits have adequate resources in staffing to effectively implement top-level policies.

- If Board members have little confidence in the CEO, there have been frequent operational problems, or the CEO is leaving the organization, then Board members often are highly involved in management affairs, at least temporarily.

- Very autocratic cultures usually place strong value on respecting the role of top-level leaders, in which case Board members would be perceived as being on a rather superior level and probably not involved in management affairs.

- Very egalitarian cultures that value equal treatment, value and participation of people might perceive Board members and the clients of the nonprofit to have equal influence in the affairs of the nonprofit, in which case members and others would have similar roles.

- If a nonprofit has been struggling to work toward clear mission and priorities, then Board members (who had previously been focused primarily on the activities of management) should probably focus much more on policy making – thereby ensuring more clear mission and priorities that can be conveyed to all members of the organization.

Regardless of the model chosen by the Board, the nonprofit has to be sure that certain strategic decisions are always made and certain questions are always addressed.

Consider "Roles and Responsibilities of Nonprofit Board Members" on page 30.

Should Your Staff Members Be On Your Board?

This Field Guide explains that there are several different types of Board models, for example, a working Board, policy Board, collective Board, etc. It is probably more common to have staff members on a working or collective Board than on a policy Board.

Many experts assert that staff should not be on the Board because it is an inherent conflict of interest. Board members who are also staff might struggle when trying to govern for the best interests of the organization as a whole. This happens when they encounter the opportunity to make decisions that might benefit themselves personally, such as deliberation over staff salaries. Also, it might be a major challenge for Board members to remain effective when attending to their staff roles.

As with membership of the Chief Executive to the Board (mentioned above), it is probably best if staff members are not Board members. This is for some of the same reasons that the Chief Executive eventually should not be a member of the Board. Staff can attend Board meetings (unless the Board is in Executive Session) to make presentations, be acquainted with Board members, etc. Staff, when not attending as official Board members, cannot vote in Board decisions.

How Your Staff Members Might Participate In Various Board Committees

As with many other aspects of Board design, whether staff members are on Board committees or not depends on the nature of the nonprofit and the Board model that it chooses to use. The following graph depicts what might be a typical arrangement for staff membership on committees. Terms of whether staff can be on committees should be specified somehow, for example, in the By-Laws and/or in the charter document that describes the purpose of the committee.

Table II:11 – Staffing of Board Committees

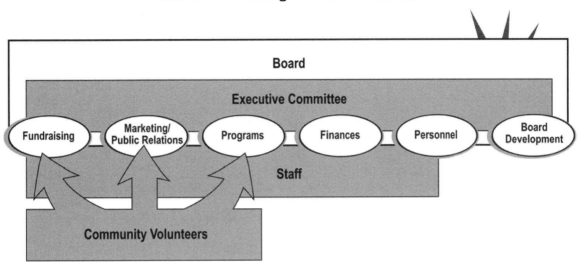

Community volunteers can be particularly useful on committees, including Fundraising, Marketing and Programs where their energy and knowledge of the community can complement the often limited energies of Board members – members who often are on several other Boards, as well. Also, staff members can provide tremendous value to Board committees because of their strong knowledge of the nonprofit, including its programs and operations. However, the Board Development Committee should be a primary responsibility of the Board members because they should see themselves as primarily responsible for the quality of their own Board operations.

Should Your Staff Members Attend Your Board Meetings?

It is often a major benefit to have staff attending at least portions of a Board meeting. Remember that the CEO is a staff member, as well, and his or her presence in Board meetings is often critical to the success of the Board and the CEO role. Attendance of other staff members can be a major benefit as well. For example, presentations by staff members to the Board are often very enlightening for Board members. They learn more about staff roles and the benefits staff provide for clients. Staff attendance to Board meetings should not be discouraged, just coordinated carefully.

There are times (for example, in Executive or in camera Sessions) when Board members should hold meetings that are private amongst themselves. This may be to consider the CEO's performance or deliberate about how to handle a pending lawsuit.

PART III:

HOW TO LEAD AND

MANAGE YOURSELF

How to Lead Others By First Leading Yourself

Skills to lead one are often the most neglected skills, yet they are the most important in being an effective leader of others. Therefore, this guide provides substantial information about leading oneself.

Understand the Typical Experiences of First-Time Nonprofit Leaders

They Rarely Have Adequate Training

Often, the first leadership position for an employee is that of supervisor. They are promoted to supervision because of their strong technical expertise – expertise in building a program or providing a service. Suddenly, the new supervisor is now charged with a whole new range of responsibilities, many of which have little to do with technical expertise.

People are not predictable. They have moods, illnesses, career expectations, crises in their family lives, etc. The supervisor's original field of expertise, especially if somewhat technical, can be useless when it comes to supervising people.

Sometimes Intimidated by Wide Range of Policies and Procedures

The new supervisor is suddenly faced with a wide range of rules and regulations – each of which the supervisor is responsible to enforce. The supervisor is often responsible for signing time cards, authorizing overtime, granting compensation time, dealing with performance problems, developing job descriptions, following hiring procedures, dealing with grievances, conforming to a complicated pay system, and the list goes on. It can be quite difficult to conform to today's wide range of employee laws, rules and regulations – and at the same time, produce a program or service.

New Supervisors Rarely Have Enough Time

No matter how many courses or degrees a new supervisor has completed, they are often surprised that management activities are so hectic and demanding. No matter how thorough the planning, managers rarely get to spend much time on any one activity. The role of most managers, whether new supervisors or executives, is interspersed with frequent interruptions. Any surprises in the work or lives of employees and volunteers are a sudden demand on supervisors.

New supervisors often expect to have complete knowledge of everything that goes on in their group. They do not want to encounter any surprises. So they spend more time reading, thinking, planning, communicating with employees – new supervisors often spend 60 hours a week on the job. Still, they do not feel they have enough time to do the job right.

New Supervisors Often Feel Very Alone

Each manager has a unique role in the organization. Each organization is unique. Usually there are no standard procedures for dealing with all of the numerous challenges that suddenly face management. Ultimately, it is up to each manager to get through the day. Faced with a great deal of pressure, little time and continuing demands from other people, the new supervisor can feel quite alone.

The supervisor is responsible to be an advocate for the organization and an advocate for the employee or volunteer. For example, if the organization implements an unpopular new policy, the supervisor is often responsible to communicate and justify that new policy to the employee or volunteer. In this case, management expects the supervisor to present and support the new policy, and the employee or volunteer vents his or her frustration to the supervisor. However, if the supervisor wants to promote the employee or present some other reward, he or she is now representing the employee's case to the rest of management. The supervisor is often alone, stuck in the middle.

The new supervisor wants to impress others as having deserved his/her promotion, as being in control of the situation. It is difficult to seek help from others in the organization. Even when there is someone to talk to, it is difficult to fully explain the situation – the new supervisor sometimes does not know how things got so hectic and confusing.

New Supervisors Often Feel Overwhelmed, Stressed Out

The new supervisor is responsible, often for the first time, for the activities of another employee or volunteer. The supervisor must ensure the employee or volunteer knows his or her job, has the resources to do the job and does the job as effectively as possible.

Until new supervisors develop a "feeling for the territory," they often deal with the stresses of supervision by working harder, rather than smarter. They miss the comfort and predictability of the previous jobs.

The stress and loneliness in the role of new supervisor can bring out the worst in people. If they deal with stress by retreating, they will retreat to their office and close the door. If they deal with stress as frustration, they will become angry and unreasonable with others. If they are used to getting strong praise and high grades, they will work harder and harder until their jobs become their lives.

Support and Development Are Critical for New Supervisors

Courses in supervision, delegation, time management, stress management, etc., are not enough. New supervisors need ongoing coaching and support. They need someone whom they can confide in. Ideally, they have a mentor in the organization who remembers what it is like to be a first-time supervisor, someone who makes himself or herself available.

If the experience of first-time supervision is successful, then the supervisor goes on to become a progressive, supportive leader and manager of other supervisors.

Understand Your Biases and How They Affect Others

Your biases play a major role in how you perceive others. Your perceptions are your reality, whether they are the reality for someone else or not. Differences in perception between you and others can make the difference between successful leadership and a complete disaster. So know your own biases! For example:

- Do you believe that leaders should "take charge" and lead from the front of the organization? If so, you might encounter frustration and resistance when working with others who believe that leaders should lead from the middle.

- Do you believe that, if an organization struggles for a year or so, it should just be shut down? If so, you might find it difficult to lead in a small nonprofit that is working hard to meet an unmet need in the community, but just cannot get enough resources.

- Do you believe that others should just "shut up and listen to you?" If so, they will probably only do what you say – and no more – until their frustration is overwhelming and they leave.

- Do you believe that nonprofits should operate like for-profit businesses? If so, you will be frustrated when others place more priority on mission, rather than on the "bottom line."

- Do you believe that meetings should start and end on time? If so, you will certainly be frustrated with people from cultures that place far less emphasis on time.

- Do you believe that most problems would be solved if people just did "what they were supposed to do"? What if people really do not know what they are supposed to do?

How to Articulate Your Professional Mission and Values

Your professional mission and values serve as your "compass" in life and work. They guide how you make decisions and solve problems, especially during complex and challenging activities. For many of us, our mission and values are implicit – we have not taken the time to clarify them explicitly or to write them down. Without explicitly proclaiming the mission and values from which we want to operate as leaders, we are prone to getting ourselves into situations – and operating in those situations – in a manner that does not match our nature and needs. Your professional mission and values can be communicated to others to help them to understand and trust you, which is critical in effective leadership. Therefore, it is important for leaders to carefully consider articulating their own mission and values, ideally into mission statements and values statements.

Developing Your Professional Mission Statement

There are various perspectives on mission statements. Some people believe the statements should describe an overall purpose. Some people believe the mission should also include a description of a vision, or future state. Some people believe the mission should also include a description of overall values. Mission statements can be just a few sentences long.

There are also various perspectives on how to develop a mission statement. The process of producing your own professional mission statement is as important as the mission statement itself. Therefore, it is important for you to carefully think about your own mission before you reference any mission statements produced by others.

When you write your professional mission statement, it should:

1. Succinctly describe the purpose of your career and leadership activities.

2. Mention the particular results (new knowledge, skills and/or conditions) that you work to help your people and you to achieve.

3. Mention any particular strengths and expertise that you have and will use.

4. Be clearly understandable by your people and you.

Developing Your Professional Values Statement

Your professional values statement describes the most important priorities in the nature of how you want to lead others and yourself. Some people might prefer to do a principles statement. Principles are descriptions of values in action and often begin with the phrase, "I will ..." or "I believe ..." Similar to the mission statement, the process of producing the values statement is as important as the values statement itself. The following guidelines will be helpful to you as you develop your own professional values statement.

1. **When identifying values, think about behaviors produced by those values.**
    Many of us struggle to directly identify desired values. We can get bogged down in words that seem too general, idealized – even romanticized – to be useful. Often, it helps first to identify desired behaviors and then the values that produce those behaviors.

2. **Consider relevant employment laws, for example, to protect minorities and disabled.**
    Identify behaviors or values that will help you avoid breaking these laws and follow the necessary regulations, for example, not to discriminate against others.

3. **Consider your own lens, biases, style, response to feedback and conflict.**
    You might identify behaviors and values that will help you to counter any potential misperceptions or obstacles that you might develop because of your own particular nature and needs.

4. **Consider any current, major issues in your work.**
    Identify the behaviors needed to resolve these issues and to identify which values would generate those preferred behaviors, for example, team building and more productivity.

5. **Consider any ethical values that might be prized by your people.**
    For example, consider expectations of clients, suppliers, funders and members of the local community, for example, strong reliability, honesty and integrity.

6. **From the above steps, select the top five to ten values.**
    You cannot be all things to all people, including to yourself. Even if you do include all the values on your statement, it is still important for you to carefully think about which values are most important to you.

7. **Associate with each value, two example behaviors which reflect each value.**
    Examples of behaviors for each value make the values much more explicit and understood to you and to others, for example, the behaviors of sharing communications and helping fellow staff members can be associated with the value of developing teamwork.

8. **Update the statement at least once a year.**
    The most important aspect of the statement is developing it, not the statement itself. Continued dialogue and reflection around your values cultivates awareness and sensitivity to act in accordance to your values. Therefore, revisit your statement at least once – preferably two or three times – a year.

How to Manage Your Motivation

One of the sure things that can be said about people who work in nonprofits is that they have a passion for the mission. Nonprofit leaders in the organization usually lead the pack in that regard. It is ironic, then that nonprofit leaders burn out and seem to do so at such a high rate. Perhaps, like many of us, they suffer from the illusion that the harder they work, the better things will get for everybody. Someone once called this the "Second Coming Syndrome." Someone else once compared continual, excessive hard work to falling off of a cliff: you always know your direction, there is lots going by and it is exhilarating – except for the last couple of inches.

Nonprofit leaders are like everyone else. They must manage for balance in their lives and their work. Besides, if the leaders do not seem motivated, then other staff will probably not be motivated either. Therefore, leaders in the organization must give attention to managing their own personal motivation – and it can be managed.

Guidelines

1. **Learn to delegate.**
   This is one of the most critical skills for a staff leader. Delegation involves assigning tasks to your employees along with the necessary authority and resources that they can learn to carry out the tasks in their own way. Assign the "what" and guide them to figure out the "how."

2. **Even if you do not like goals, set some goals, however small.**
   Without goals, you probably will not know if you are really accomplishing anything. Working hard is not necessarily an end in itself – especially if you expect your employees and volunteers to do the same thing. Set some small goals. It will be good practice for you if you have not done that before. (If you do not like goals, then you are in for a major challenge in leading a nonprofit because, without goals, it is very difficult to give direction and measure success.)

3. **Celebrate accomplishments.**
   Many hard-working people seem to believe that celebrating accomplishments is a form of complacency, that the job should be celebration in itself. Those beliefs can hold true maybe for the first couple years of the nonprofit leader's job. Then the grind gets old. It is critical for employees and volunteers to recognize that they are accomplishing something – it is usually not enough to be continually "working for the cause." Take time out to recognize what did get done and celebrate the accomplishments.

4. **Ask for help.**
   It can be quite difficult for nonprofit leaders to ask for help. Often, they are very passionate, hard-working people who want to be able to carry their own load. Thus, they are often reluctant to ask for help from others in the organization. This is a mistake, particularly for the Chief Executive Officer. The quality of the relationship between the Board Chair and Chief Executive Officer is one of the most important determinants of the success of a nonprofit. This relationship can be built around mutual support, especially if the Chief Executive Officer knows how to ask for – and value – the help from the Board.

5. **Find out what motivates you – it is not the same for everyone.**
    One of the most important learnings for new supervisors is that very different things can motivate different people. Consider the following reference.

    Consider "How to Support Your Employees and Volunteers' Self-Motivation" on page 227.

6. **Get some direct contact with your clients.**
    Few things are as motivational as hearing from a client how he/she benefited from the services of the nonprofit. Unfortunately, it is too easy for leaders to inadvertently become detached from providing direct service and to get lost in the management activities of the nonprofit. At least once a month, have a client come to a staff-wide meeting and share his/her experiences with the nonprofit.

7. **Post the mission of the nonprofit on the walls of all the rooms in your facilities.**
    It is amazing how many nonprofits give careful thought to the wording of their mission statements, and then file them away in file cabinets. Post your mission statement in all the rooms in your facility. Notice it each day. The mission statement depicts the reason that the nonprofit even exists.

8. **Follow simple guidelines of time and stress management.**
    With a few simple steps, you can make a lot of difference in managing your stress, often by first addressing how you spend your own time.

    Consider "How to Manage Your Time and Stress – Avoiding Burnout" on page 88.

9. **Watch your diet. Get enough sleep.**
    Do not resort to lots of caffeine and sugar to give you a boost. Research shows that the boost is usually followed by a major let down in energy. It is better to get up for a short walk, get some protein and do some stretches. Also, it is interesting how bleak the world looks to people who do not eat right or do not get enough sleep. A little bit of the right kinds of food and more sleep can make the world seem a lot better.

10. **Get some variety in your job.**
    Do not get lost in the "circle of paperwork." Often, the only way that you will get variety in your work is to schedule it. Schedule time to provide direct services to clients. Schedule time to help clean out the storage closet.

11. **Have personal goals.**
    Even if you have a few goals, at least those goals are in regard to your own development. Examples of goals might be to become acquainted with at least three other Chief Executive Officers or program managers of nonprofits that offer services similar to yours, or read a book a week, or even to start a hobby.

12. **Get some professional development.**
    Go to a course. Join a professional networking organization. Read professional journals that relate to your services. Join a Speakers Bureau to share your knowledge.

13. **Be sure that your job makes sense to you. Have an overall strategic plan.**
    One of the best outcomes from a strategic plan is that it helps to make sense of all of the work going on around people. People get some perspective and, thus, some meaning from their jobs.

Consider "How to Set Clear Purpose and Direction for the Nonprofit" on page 117.

14. **Write status reports.**
    Status reports can be weekly reports that document what you have accomplished over the past week, any highlights and trends and issues that currently exist, and what you plan to do next week. One of the most important outcomes from this activity is actually standing back and thinking about your job, and noticing that you are actually getting a lot done.

15. **Understand Founder's Syndrome.**
    This Syndrome can occur with almost anyone in the organization, not just the Founder. It is not unusual that the people who work the hardest in an organization (and are most prone to burnout) are also the people around whom all else seems to revolve. It is hard not to be the "hero" of the workplace, the person who gets everything done. Too often, this hero becomes the unintended villain when the organization succumbs to Founder's Syndrome.

Consider "Founder's Syndrome – How to Detect It, How to Avoid It" on page 283.

16. **Know when to leave.**
    It may be that you and your job just have to part, that you are simply no longer motivated in your work. It is a wise leader who can recognize this and arrange for a healthy transition to a new leader.

How to Appreciate – Critical Ability for Nonprofit Leaders

Why Is the Ability to Appreciate Accomplishments So Important?

Particularly with personnel in small- to medium-size nonprofits, it is rare that there is not a large amount of work to do. In addition, their mission is usually about meeting some large, unmet need in their communities. It is rare, too, that the nonprofits somehow completely meet those needs. For many personnel in nonprofits, it can seem like nothing ever gets done.

Because time is such a precious commodity in these nonprofits, it is common that their people cannot provide sustained effort to priorities and projects. Many times, they get put on "hold" for a few weeks as people attend to other sudden demands for their time, for example, developing a major grant proposal for funds that they suddenly found out about, the Chief Executive Officer's leaving for vacation, preparing for their annual meeting, or finishing a large program evaluation. For your employees, volunteers and you, it can seem that activities have stalled out completely.

For many of us, it can seem like we are stuck in a merry-go-round that never goes anywhere and we cannot seem to get off. By ignoring our accomplishments, we are ignoring vast portions of our lives and our work – our perspective can become skewed and incomplete. That perspective can be a major obstacle to the success of leaders in nonprofit organizations.

How Can You Maintain Appreciation for Appreciation?

As a leader, you can make a big difference in your effectiveness and that of your peoples' accomplishments if all of you have the ability to recognize and appreciate your accomplishments regularly. Consider the following guidelines.

1. **Convey the importance of appreciation when you start working with others.**
   Explain how important it is to recognize accomplishments as well as the tasks yet to be done. Mention it is really important in small- to medium-sized nonprofits.

2. **Ask staff members for ideas about how to regularly recognize completion of tasks.**
   Different cultures have different practices. Some might prefer a simple "Thank you," while others might prefer a ritual of some sort. Therefore, it is important early in your leadership role to get ideas from your people.

3. **When planning, build in acknowledgement of completion in plans.**
   Planning always results in a list of things to do. Too often, the design of the plans does not include means to recognize accomplishments. Planning is one of the best opportunities to regularly build in means to recognize accomplishments.

4. **Design project tasks so it is clear whether they were finished or not.**
   This is often one of the biggest challenges in developing a sense of appreciation. Ideally, goals, objectives and other tasks are designed to be SMART, an acronym for specific, measurable, achievable, relevant and timely.

5. **Regularly acknowledge the completion of the tasks or progress on tasks.**
   Always seek to find opportunities to appreciate the work of your people. That practice can be a powerful means to model behaviors that they learn from in their lives and work.

How to Keep It Real – Managing for Realistic Expectations

Many times, personnel in nonprofits are passionate and sometimes idealistic about what they want to accomplish. While those traits can be useful when working to make a major difference in communities and the world, they often pose major obstacles when trying to accomplish significant change in an organization. Also, it is not uncommon that when people have been struggling with a major issue, they urgently search for quick fixes to address those issues. That search can cause a great deal of despair and cynicism. Consequently, one of the most important requirements for successful leadership is for your people and you to share the same relevant and realistic expectations. Consider the following approaches:

1. **Use authentic behavior to verify whether plans are relevant and realistic.**
    It is important for your people and you to speak up if you have any confusion and concerns whatsoever about suggestions, recommendations, plans or actions. This is true particularly if plans and expectations seem unrealistic.

2. **Regularly ask your people for their perceptions of how the nonprofit is doing.**
    It is important that both your people and you frequently discuss the quality and progress of activities. One of the outcomes from those discussions is verification of your mutual expectations, as they may shift over time.

3. **Avoid quick fixes.**
    The typical nonprofit is short on time, money and people. There can be tremendous pressure to get a lot done and to do it quickly. However, it takes time to cultivate long-lasting change. You are far better off to take your time and do it right, than to have your people and you lose credibility in your leadership.

4. **Acknowledge both the ups and the downs that often occur in nonprofits.**
    Inexperienced leaders sometimes count on optimism and good wishes to motivate people for change. That approach may work for the short-term, but rarely for the long-term. So, trust and respect your people enough to tell them the whole story.

5. **Use written action plans, specifying who is doing what and by when.**
    At the end of each one-on-one and group meeting, always review who is going to do what and by when. Document plans and share them with others involved in the effort.

6. **Conduct coaching sessions around your employee's current issues and goals.**
    Coaching sessions can be useful for relevant and realistic action planning to specify who is going to do what and by when, and in particular, whether those plans are realistic. The sessions also collect key learning about plans and actions.

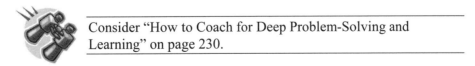

Consider "How to Coach for Deep Problem-Solving and Learning" on page 230.

How to Manage Your Time and Stress – Avoiding Burnout

The two topics of time management and stress management are often addressed together because they are so closely intertwined.

Myths About Stress and Time Management

1. **All stress is bad.**
   No, some stress is good and some is bad. Good stress can include excitement or thrills. The goal is to recognize your personal signs of bad stress and deal with them.

2. **Planning my time just takes more time.**
   Planning helps you work smarter, rather than harder. The attitude that stopping to plan is a problem is itself a symptom of stress and time management problems.

3. **I get more done in more time when I use caffeine, sugar, alcohol or nicotine.**
   Wrong! Research shows that the body always has to "come down." When it does, you will not be effective in your work, which offsets whatever gains you achieved from the boost from these stimulants.

4. **A time problem means there is not enough time to do what I need to do.**
   No, a time management problem is not using your time to your fullest advantage to get done what you want done. You need to know what you really want to do.

5. **The busier I am, the better I am using my time.**
   You may only be doing what seems urgent, and not what is important. Doing what is important often addresses the many matters that later seem to be urgent.

6. **I feel very hurried and busy, so I must have a time management problem.**
   Not necessarily. You should verify that you have a time management problem. This requires knowing what you really want to get done and if it is getting done or not.

7. **I feel OK, so I must not be stressed.**
   In reality, many adults do not even know when they are really stressed out until their bodies tell them so. They miss the early warning signs from their bodies.

Major Causes of Stress

1. **Not knowing what you want or if you are getting it – poor planning.**
   If you ask adults where they are needed, they can give you many answers. If you ask them what they want, they often struggle to answer.

2. **The *feeling* that there is too much to do.**
   One can have this feeling even if there is hardly anything to do at all. Knowing what you want to do often helps address the vague feelings that there is too much to do.

3. **Not enjoying your work.**
   This can be caused by lots of things, for example, not knowing what you want or not eating well.

4.   **Conflicting demands in your work.**
     Unless you have some sense of your priorities, it is likely that you will feel conflicting demands in your work.

5.   **Having insufficient resources to do your work.**
     As a leader, one of your most important resources is usually your time. You will benefit a great deal from finding your own style of time management.

6.   **Not feeling appreciated.**
     This can be a major problem for leaders. You can ask your people to tell you how you are doing. You have to accept and remember their compliments.

Biggest Time Wasters

1.   **Interruptions**
     There will always be interruptions. The interruptions are not the problem. The problem is how they are handled.

2.   **Hopelessness**
     People "give in," "numb out" and "march through the day." This is probably the worst time and stress management problem. Other guidelines in this section can help you to avoid this time waster.

3.   **Poor delegation skills**
     This involves not asking for help and/or sharing work with others. You can ask your people for help, consider working with colleagues or cut back your workload.

Common Symptoms of Poor Stress and Time Management

1.   **Irritability**
     Your family, friends, peers and employees usually notice this before you do. If they have noticed your symptoms, you will have to find a better means to manage your time and stress.

2.   **Fatigue**
     How many adults even notice this? We often work with a vague sense of tiredness. Your body sends the first message of problems, so learn to sense your own fatigue.

3.   **Difficulty concentrating**
     You can often get through the day without even concentrating. Thus, this symptom often goes unnoticed.

4.   **Forgetfulness**
     If you cannot remember what you did all day, what you ate today or whom you talked to, then you need to address your time and stress problem as soon as possible.

5.   **Loss of sleep**
     This affects everything else! Recognize what you can do to have a full night's sleep, for example, cut back on coffee or do not work late.

6.   **Physical disorders**
       Common symptoms are headaches, rashes, tics or cramps. At worst, consistent withdrawal
       and depression.

Wise Principles of Good Stress and Time Management

1.   **Learn your signs for being overstressed or having a time management problem.**
       Ask your friends about you. Perhaps they can tell you what they see when you are
       overstressed. Their feedback is often more accurate than your own perceptions.

2.   **Most people *feel* that they are stressed and/or have a time problem.**
       Verify that you really have a problem. What do you see, hear or feel that leads you to
       conclude that you have a time or stress problem?

3.   **Do not have the illusion that doing more will make you happier.**
       Is it the quantity of time that you want or the quality? If not quantity or quality, then what?

4.   **Stress and time problems usually require more than one technique to fix.**
       You do not need a lot of techniques, but usually more than one. Pick a few that are realistic
       and practical, get started, notice your successes and give yourself credit.

5.   **One of the major benefits of time planning is feeling that you are in control.**
       It might even help at this point to think about what you mean by "control." Does it mean
       that you control everything in your life or only what is most important in the long run?

6.   **Focus on results, not on "busyness."**
       This guideline is the main point about performance – a person can seem very busy, but that
       does not mean that he/she is actually accomplishing what is most important.

7.   **The trying counts – at least as much as finishing the perfect technique.**
       As people get older and wiser, they let go of frustrations around not achieving enough
       quantity of things. Instead, they focus on the quality of the process.

Simple Techniques to Manage Stress

There are many things people can do to cut down on bad stress. Most people probably even know
what they could do. It is not the lack of knowing what to do to cut down stress – it is doing what you
know you have to do. The following techniques are geared to help you do what you know you have
to do.

1.   **Talk to someone.**
       You do not have to fix the problem. Similar to addressing resistance and conflicts, it often
       makes a big difference just to recognize and name the problem.

2.   **Notice if any of the muscles in your body are tense.**
       Just noticing that will often relax the muscles. Pay attention to your neck, shoulders, arms
       and legs. Tightness? Soreness?

3.   **Ask your employees and volunteers if you are doing OK.**
       This simple question can make a lot of difference. Also, it further helps to build trust and
       openness between you and your employees.

4.   **Ask for help.**
      Ask peers. Hire some help. Get a mentor. Get a coach. Join a support or networking group.

5.   **If you take on a technique to manage stress, tell someone else.**
      They can help you be accountable to them and yourself. Otherwise, your attempts to use techniques can get lost in the other time and stress problems that you have.

6.   **Cut down on caffeine and sweets.**
      It is difficult to cut down on something without replacing it with something else instead. Do isometric exercises. Chew sugarless gum.

7.   **Use basic techniques of planning, problem solving and decision-making.**
      Concise guidelines are in this Field Guide. It might help to focus on the 20/80 rule. Remember, it is often the trying that counts.

8.   **Monitor the number of hours that you work in a week.**
      Tell your family, friends and peers how many hours that you are working per week now and how many hours that you intend to work.

9.   **Write status reports.**
      Reports can be drudgery to finish, but they are usually helpful to remind you of what you have done. You should be writing reports anyway.

10.   **"Wash the dishes."**
      Do something simple that you can feel good about. When following that guideline, as with others, starts with gumption: making that initial effort to move yourself.

Simple Techniques to Manage Time

The goal of time management should not be to find more time. The goal is to spend time on what you really need and want to be spending time on.

1.   **Start with the simple techniques of stress management above.**
      Many times, techniques of stress management are useful in managing time, as well.

2.   **Practice.**
      Practice asking yourself throughout the day: "Is this what I want or need to be doing right now?" If yes, keep doing it. If not, get help from family and friends.

3.   **Analyze your time.**
      Logging your time for a week in 15-minute intervals is not that hard and does not take up that much time. Do it for a week and review your results. This is both realistic and an objective way to analyze your time.

4.   **Create a "to do" list for the next day at the end of each day.**
      Mark items as "A" and "B" in priority. Set aside two hours right away each day to do the important "A" items and then do the "B" items in the afternoon. Let your voicemail or someone else take your calls during your "A" time. Limit email time until those top priorities are finished.

5.   **At the end of your day, spend five minutes cleaning up your space.**
     Use this time, too, to organize your space, including your desktop. That will give you a
     clean and fresh start for the next day.

6.   **Learn the difference between "Where am I needed?" and "What do I want?"**
     The former question is about your employee's time. The latter question is about yours.

7.   **Learn difference between "Do I need to do this now?" and "Do I need to do it at all?"**
     Finding the answers might require some careful reflection about what has been important in
     the past and what is important to you now.

8.   **Use a "Do Not Disturb" sign!**
     During the prime part of the day, when you are attending to your important items (your "A"
     list), hang this sign on the doorknob outside your door.

9.   **Sort your mail into categories: "read now," "handle now," "trash" and "read later."**
     You will quickly get a knack for sorting through mail. You will also notice that much of
     what you think you need to read was not really all that important anyway.

10. **Read your mail at the same time each day.**
     That way, you will likely get to your mail on a regular basis and will not become distracted
     into any certain piece of mail that ends up taking too much of your time.

11. **Have a place for everything and put everything in its place.**
     That way, you will know where to find it when you need it. Perhaps the most important
     outcome is that you have a *feeling* of being in control.

12. **Schedule 10 minutes to do nothing.**
     That time can be used to just sit and clear your mind. You will end up thinking more clearly,
     resulting in more time that is productive in your day. The best outcome of this practice is
     that it reminds you that you are not a slave to a clock – and that if you take 10 minutes out of
     your day, your work will not fall apart.

Understand How You Solve Problems and Make Decisions

Different people have quite different preferences and approaches for solving problems and making decisions. Those differences can often cause conflict between people unless they each understand their own particular preferences.

The following preferences represent probably the most common. It is important for you to note that any preference is not necessarily better than others. Certain preferences might work better in certain situations. The important point for you to realize is the diverse ways that people – including you – address problems and decisions. Consider that diversity when leading others.

Rational Versus Organic Approach to Problem Solving

Rational

A person with this preference often prefers using a comprehensive and logical approach similar to the following procedure. The rational approach, described below, is often used when addressing large, complex matters, for example, when conducting strategic planning.

1. Define the problem.

2. Examine all potential causes for the problem.

3. Identify all alternatives to resolve the problem.

4. Carefully select an alternative.

5. Develop an orderly implementation plan to implement that best alternative.

6. Carefully monitor implementation of the plan.

7. Verify if the problem has been resolved or not.

A major advantage of this approach is that it gives a strong sense of order in an otherwise chaotic situation and provides a common frame of reference from which people can communicate in the situation. A major disadvantage of this approach is that it can take a long time to finish. Some people might argue, too, that the world is much too chaotic for the rational approach to be useful.

Organic

Some people assert that the dynamics of organizations and people are not nearly so mechanistic as to be improved by solving one problem after another. Often, the quality of an organization or life comes from how one handles being "on the road" itself, rather than the "arriving at the destination." The quality comes from the ongoing process of trying, rather than from having fixed a lot of problems. For many people it is an approach to leading organizations. The following quote explains the organic (or holistic) approach to problem solving.

"All the greatest and most important problems in life are fundamentally insoluble ... They can never be solved, but only outgrown. This "outgrowing" proves on further investigation to require a new level of consciousness. Some higher or wider interest appeared on the horizon and through this broadening of outlook, the insoluble lost its urgency. It was not solved logically in its own terms, but faded when confronted with a new and stronger life urge."

From Jung, Carl, *Psychological Types (*Pantheon Books, 1923)

A major advantage of the organic approach is that it is highly adaptable to understanding and explaining the chaotic changes that occur in organizations and everyday life. It also suits the nature of people who shun linear and mechanistic approaches to projects. The major disadvantage is that the approach often provides little clear and consistent frame of reference around which people can communicate, feel comfortable and measure progress toward solutions to problems.

Intuitive Versus Sensing Approaches to Gathering Information

There are a variety of assessment instruments that are often referenced when helping people understand their own unique styles when solving problems and making decisions, for example, the Myers-Briggs Type Indicator® instrument. One of the dimensions of the Myers-Briggs is "Intuitive versus Sensing," which considers how a person gathers information. (Myers-Briggs is a registered trademark of Consulting Psychologists Press, Inc.).

Intuitive

Highly intuitive people often gather information instinctively. They thrive on ideas and possibilities. They might seem oblivious to what is going on around them, yet they often effectively solve problems and make decisions based on surprisingly valid information. Many times, they might not even know how they did it. Some experts on leadership and management assert that highly experienced people often have developed intuition that enables them to make quick, effective decisions. A major advantage of this approach is that it can save a great deal of time. A major challenge can be how to explain their choices to others.

Sensing

These people thrive on facts and information. They are detail-oriented and accuracy is extremely important to them. They are aware of their physical surroundings, of who is saying what. They solve problems and make decisions by considering the "data" around them. One of the major advantages of sensing people is that their actions are often based on valid information. Thus, they are able to explain their reasoning and their actions to others. A major challenge is the time and care required for them to solve problems and make decisions.

Thinking Versus Feeling Approaches to Process Information

Another major dimension of the Myers-Briggs Indicator® instrument is "Thinking versus Feelings," which considers how a person makes decisions about information.

Thinking

A thinking person often uses a highly objective, sometimes rational approach to organizing, analyzing and making decisions about information. At their extreme, he/she might shun consideration of emotions. The thinking person probably prefers the rational approach to problem solving as described above in this subsection. The advantage of this approach is that it often generates valid problem solving and decision-making. A major challenge can be that it might require an extensive amount of time to come to action.

Feeling

The feeling approach is used most often by individuals who are quite sensitive to their values in processing information. When people focus on their values, emotions often come into play. A major advantage of this approach is that it can help to ensure that people are happy and fulfilled in the situation – that their values have been considered during the process and are reflected in the outcome. A major challenge is that there are a variety of short-term factors other than the current major problem or decision that can influence a person's emotions, for example, his/her not having had enough sleep or having eaten right.

Understand How You Respond to Feedback and Conflict

How Do You Respond to Feedback?

One of the best ways to influence your employees and volunteers is to model the behavior that you want from them. Usually, you want them to be open to receiving feedback, whether the feedback is about the organization and its problems or even about the role that your people play in the problems. Thus, to model that kind of behavior, you want to be open to feedback yourself. Often, that is easier said than done.

In this context, feedback is information about your actions or performance and is information that you act on. This is in contrast to information that is about others or is either too vague or indirect to be useful to you.

Feedback from others might make you feel uncomfortable. However, you can manage your reactions in response to their feedback. Even if you feel threatened, frustrated or angry about the feedback, you can remind yourself that the feedback is not necessarily directed at you personally. Often, the feedback has more to do with another's fear about something than about you as a person.

You can also remind yourself that feedback from others is a valuable gift to you. For example, it is not uncommon that leaders get so highly involved in the organization's problems that they lose the professional objectivity required to be effective. Feedback from others can be valuable forms of learning in these situations.

How Do You Respond to Conflict?

Experienced leaders realize that conflict is a natural outcome from interactions among different people and from changes in an organization. Conflict can have a variety of causes, for example, differences in perceptions among people, feelings of fear or disrespect, power conflicts, poor communication techniques or just plain fatigue during organizational change.

Conflict is not inherently bad. Problems come from how the conflict is addressed. Effective conflict management includes focusing on the issue at the heart of the conflict, rather than on the personalities of the people involved. It includes using effective means of communication, such as effective listening, supportive questioning and noticing non-verbal (non-spoken) communications.

You want your employees and volunteers to advantageously recognize and manage their conflicts, rather than denying that those conflicts exist or engaging in ongoing destructive arguments with others. You can model successful conflict management by effectively responding to conflict within yourself.

It is not uncommon for people to have strong emotions, especially about major changes in the organization. It will be important for you to carefully respond to those emotions, including recognizing them and allowing people the freedom to express them. How you respond to conflict yourself is often how you respond to the strong emotions of others.

What Is Your Emotional Intelligence?

There are different definitions for emotional intelligence (EI), but it is probably fair to generalize that it is the ability to recognize our emotions and then manage our responses to those emotions in a manner that enhances our health and relationships with others. There are some basic guidelines that might be useful in enhancing your own EI. Consider the following basic guidelines:

1. Notice how you are feeling and be able to name the emotion, for example, mad, glad, sad or bad. Be careful not to get confused between your thoughts and feelings. Notice the difference between and then use "I feel …" and "I think …" statements.

2. Notice how you judge those emotions, for example, you might believe that "it is scary and bad to feel angry."

3. Notice what situations typically evoke those emotions in you.

4. Notice the difference between your emotions and your outward responses to those emotions – what others would see you do and say. Ask yourself how you choose to feel about something and whether your behavior is aligned with that choice.

5. Realize that it is OK to have strong emotional reactions. It is what you do with those emotions that can be a problem for you and others.

6. Notice how long you retain those emotions. What changes them?

7. Notice what makes you happy and plan for those situations on a regular basis.

8. Notice how you make conclusions about other peoples' feelings. What are they doing or saying?

Understand How You View Organizations

One of the most frequent reasons that experts and leaders argue about the best methods for organizational change is because they often have different perspectives, or lens, through which they view organizations. The impact of these differences is often underestimated. For example, you can have two different people study an organization and then provide very different descriptions of the same organization. Therefore, it is critical that people understand their own perspective and be sensitive to the perspectives of others.

 One of the most useful resources to explain these perspectives is *Reframing Organizations* (Bolman and Deal, Jossey-Bass, 1991). The authors depict four quite different and major organizational perspectives among researchers, writers, educators, consultants and members of organizations.

Table III:1 – Various "Lens" Through Which We View Organizations

Lens	Examples of What Is Noticed or Talked About from That Lens
Structural	Goals, objectives, roles, responsibilities, performance, policies and procedures, efficiency, hierarchy and coordination and control
Human Resource	Participation, feelings, fulfillment, communication, needs of people, relationships, motivation, enrichment and commitment
Political	Power, conflict, competition, authority, experts, coalitions, allocation of resources, bargaining and decision making
Symbolic	Rituals, culture, values, stories, different perspectives, language, expressions, myths, commitment and metaphors

Note that these are horizontal lens regarding what different people notice across the activities in organizations. There are also many vertical lens through which we view intra-personal dynamics, for example, the many perspectives put forth in the increasing amount of books on personal development.

It is important for you to realize that no lens, or perspective, is better than the others. Experienced leaders have learned that the more perspectives that they can get from their employees and volunteers about an issue in their organization, often the more accurate and useful are the plans to address that issue. Thus, the more lenses through which you can view organizations, the more useful you will be to your employees, volunteers and yourself.

How to Manage Your Own Professional Development

Professional development is learning how to be more effective in your current and planned roles in your like, work and career. Nonprofit leaders, in particular those leading small to medium-sized nonprofits, often tend to forget professional development – usually because there are not sufficient funds to pay for development. There are many free or low-cost sources of professional development. The key is to use them.

Free, or Low-Cost, Sources of Professional Development

1. **Join a professional organization.**
    There are a variety of organizations for nonprofit organizations, for example:

    a. National Council of Nonprofit Associations (NCNA) has chapters in many states (go to http://www.ncna.org/ on the Web) in the USA

    b. United Way forums for Chief Executive Officers (look in your Yellow Pages for your local United Way's telephone phone number)

    c. If the nonprofit is an association in the USA, then consider joining the local chapter of the American Society of Association Executives (go to http://www.asaenet.org)

2. **Join an online discussion group.**
    There are several groups listed in Appendix B.

3. **Read professional journals that relate to your services.**
    For example:

    a. *Nonprofit Times* (go to http://www.nptimes.com)

    b. *Chronicle of Philanthropy* (go to http://philanthropy.com)

4. **Attend workshops and seminars.**
    Many cities have local management support organizations or centers of nonprofit management. Contact local universities and colleges for courses on nonprofit management.

5. **Form a local book study.**
    Pick a book about nonprofit management (you are holding one). Call several of your peers. Invite them to get a copy of this guide, get together once a week or month and discuss certain topics from the guide.

6. **Regularly reflect on your activities in your job.**
    Your job can be a wonderful source of learning! Schedule even just 15 minutes a week to look back on your week. Ask yourself:

    a. What did I do?

    b. What did I learn from that? (Think of enhanced knowledge, skills or values.)

    c. How can I take that learning forward into my life and work?

7. **Keep in mind that you do not have to know it all in order to be effective at your job.**
Adults tend to learn best when they actually *apply* new information and materials to current, real-life challenges. Therefore, you will learn what you need when you need it.

8. **Consider forming your own peer group of leaders.**
In these groups, members help each other to reach goals by exchanging ongoing feedback and support.

Summary Principles for Staying Sane When Leading in Nonprofits

Everyone in management has gone through the transition from individual contributor to manager. Each person finds his/her own way to "survive." The following guidelines will help you to keep your perspective and your health.

1. **Monitor your work hours.**
The first visible, undeniable sign that things are out of hand is that you are working far too many hours. Note how many hours you are working per week. Set a limit and stick to that limit. Ask your peers, boss or Board for help.

2. **Recognize your own signs of stress.**
Different people show their stress in different ways. Some people have "blow ups." Some people get very forgetful. Some people lose concentration. For many people, they excel at their jobs, but their home life falls apart. Know your signs of stress. Tell someone else what they are. Ask them to check in with you every two weeks to see how you are doing. Every two weeks, write down how you are doing – if only for a minute. Stick in it a file marked "%*#)%&!!#$."

3. **Get a mentor or a coach.**
Ideally, your supervisor is a very good mentor and coach. Many other people have "been there, done that" and can also serve as great mentors to you.

4. **Learn to delegate.**
Delegating is giving others the responsibility and authority to carry out tasks. You maintain the accountability to get them done, but you let others decide how they will carry out the tasks themselves. Delegation is a skill to learn. Start learning it.

5. **Communicate as much as you can.**
Consider the following guidelines:

   a. Have at least one person in your life with whom you are completely honest.

   b. Hold regular meetings with employees – all of them in one meeting at least once a month, and meet at least once every two weeks with each of your direct reports. A common problem among new managers and supervisors (or among experienced, but ineffective ones) is not meeting unless there is something to say. There is always something to communicate, even if to say that things are going well and then share the health of your pets.

99

c. Err on the side of too much communication, rather than not enough. New managers and supervisors often assume that their employees know as much as they do. One of the first signs of an organization in trouble is that communications break down.

6. **Distinguish between what is important and what is urgent.**
One of the major lessons that experienced leaders have learned is to respond to what is important, rather than what is urgent. Phone calls, sick employees, lost paperwork, disagreements between employees all seem to suddenly crop up and demand immediate attention. It can seem like your day is responding to one crisis after another. As you gain experience, you quit responding to the crisis. You get an answering machine or someone else to answer the phone. You plan for employees being gone for the day – and you accept that people get sick. You develop a filing system to keep track of your paperwork. You learn basic skills in conflict management. Most important, you recognize that management is a process – you never really "finish" your to-do list – your list is there to help you keep track of details. Over time, you learn to relax.

7. **Recognize accomplishments.**
Our society promotes problem solvers. We solve one problem and quickly move on to the next. The culture of many organizations rewards problem solvers. Once a problem is solved, we quickly move on to the next one to solve. Pretty soon we feel empty. We feel as if we are not making a difference. Our subordinates do, too. So in all your plans, include time to acknowledge accomplishments – if only by having a good laugh by the coffee machine. Do take time to note that something useful was done.

How To Lead Others By First Understanding Them

It is critical that the managers, leaders and supervisors have very good skills in interpersonal communications. Many books have been written about good listening skills, verbal and nonverbal. One need not be an expert at the materials in these books in order to have good interpersonal communications skills.

How to Make Sure Your Employees Really Hear You

Usually, your most frequent form of communication is spoken words. As with non-verbal communication, spoken communication is highly dependent on the particular culture in which you are working. For example, culture can affect how people speak about conflict, use humor, are honest and direct with each other, use silence and use certain wording.

 Consider "How to Lead in Multicultural Organizations" on page 106.

Consider the following general guidelines, which might be useful in a wide variety of cultures.

1. **Know the main point that you want to convey.**
    Sometimes, people begin speaking with the hope that if they talk long enough, they are bound to say what they want to say. Before you speak, take the time to think about the main points that you want to convey.

2. **Convey one point at a time.**
    That approach ensures that the listener is more likely to continue to understand you, rather than being overwhelmed with too many ideas delivered at too fast a rate. You might even find that you understand your own thoughts more completely.

3. **Speak too slowly, rather than too quickly.**
    A good way to practice this guideline is to speak along with a news anchor when you are watching television. You will likely find that they speak much more slowly than you realize. They are professionals who have learned an effective rate of speaking.

4. **Vary your voice.**
    Always avoid monotone. A monotone voice might convey to the listener that you are bored or controlled. It is likely to lull you and/or the listener into a stupor. Varying your voice takes practice, but it is well worth the effort.

5. **State your conclusion before describing how you came to that conclusion.**
    Some speakers convey their recommendations or advice by conveying the necessary information to lead the listener to the same conclusions as the speaker's. Instead, it is often more reliable to first state your point and then explain it.

6. **People speak more frequently and completely when they are comfortable.**
    Therefore, get comfortable with the person to whom you are speaking. Skills in authentic expression can be useful in these situations. For example, if you are uncomfortable or confused, simply say so.

7. **Ask the listener to repeat the main points of what you just said to them.**
    This guideline ensures that the listener is indeed hearing what you wanted to convey. Be tactful when asking the listener to repeat what you said. For example, say "I want to be sure that I made sense to you just now, so I would appreciate if you could tell me what you heard me say."

8. **Ask others to provide feedback about your spoken communication.**
    One of the most powerful ways to learn about yourself is to ask others for feedback. Therefore, ask others about how you might improve your speaking skills.

See "How to Share Useful – and Respectful – Feedback" on page 236.

How to Recognize and Understand Non-Verbal Communications

Interpreting Other's Body Language

Resistance, confusion, distaste, passivity, etc., all show up in the body language of others, regardless of what they are saying verbally. Experienced leaders have learned often to trust what they see more than what they hear. Body language is always present. Too many speakers and listeners are unaware of body language.

The nature of a person's body language is highly dependent on the person's nature. For example, some people are intent on sitting or standing upright with their hands at their sides in a stance of attention and respect. Other people might slouch in their chair or extend their legs, in part, to convey that they feel comfortable around others in the room.

It is difficult to make overall conclusions about body language because it is culturally dependent. However, people trust non-verbal communication more than they do verbal (spoken) communication, so learn to notice non-verbal communication, and be aware of your own.

In general, notice:

1. **Style of voice, for example, loud, soft, frequent, irregular.**

2. **Movement of the body, for example, gestures, face, eyes.**

3. **Distance, space and time between speaker and listener.**

Specifically, notice:

1. **Eye contact**
    In the United States, this often conveys sincerity. In other cultures, though, it might convey aggressiveness or hostility.

2.   **Frequent movements of the body**
      Frequent movements might convey nervousness, poor listening.

3.   **Openness of the body**
      Arms crossed may mean defensiveness, which impedes communication.

Interpreting Your Own Body Language

Your body language is often the true "compass" about your impression of something. For you to remain authentic, you need to be in touch with your own non-verbal communication. Different people have different physical reactions in different situations. Consider the following:

1.   **Are you moving your arms and legs a lot?**
      If so, maybe you are afraid, frustrated or confused about something.

2.   **Is your mouth dry?**
      Then maybe you are afraid of something.

3.   **Is your body position closed?**
      Are your legs and arms crossed? Perhaps you feel attacked somehow?

4.   **Is your brow furled?**
      Perhaps you are confused – or you are really interested in what the other has to say.

5.   **Are you looking away from the others a lot?**
      Then there is likely something that is bothering you. Or, perhaps your style is to look away so you can think more clearly. If that is the case, realize that others might be seeing you as having poor eye contact.

6.   **Is your heart racing?**
      Perhaps you are afraid of others, or you are excited about a project you are undertaking.

How to Really Listen to Others

Listening is a critical skill for all adults to have. It is one of the most important skills for you to use as you learn about others. Also, it is one of the most important activities for you to use to establish a strong rapport with employees and volunteers.

There are many books about effective listening skills. The following common guidelines can help you to accomplish effective listening in the vast majority of situations.

1.   **Be sure you can hear the speaker.**
      It is surprising how often people do not really listen to other people. It is just as surprising how often people do not realize that they cannot even hear other people. So always make this your first guideline in any situation for effective listening.

2.   **Overall, attempt to listen 75% of time – speak 25% of time.**
      This is one of the most powerful guidelines. Use of the guideline depends on your situation. For example, if you are making a presentation, you will speak more. Otherwise, ensure that the other person speaks more than you do – and listen to them.

3. **Adopt a culturally compatible physical posture to show you are interested.**
This can be powerful means to show others that you are interested in hearing them. For example, you might lean forward and maintain eye contact. Whatever physical gestures you make, be sure they are compatible to the culture of the speaker.

Consider "How to Lead in Multicultural Organizations" on page 106.

4. **Do not think about what to say while you are also trying to listen to the speaker.**
Your brain goes four times faster than a speaker's voice. Thus, your brain can easily leave the speaker behind. Instead, trust that you will know how to respond to the speaker when the speaker is done.

5. **Notice the other's speaking style.**
Different people have different speaking styles. Do they speak loud or soft? Slow or fast? Are there disconnects between what they say versus what their body language conveys? Some people convey the central idea first and then support it with additional information. Other people provide information to lead the listener to the same conclusion as the speaker.

6. **Listen for the central ideas, not for all the facts.**
Experienced leaders develop a sense for noticing the most important information conveyed by their people. They hear the main themes and ideas from their employees. If you notice the major ideas, then often the facts "come along" with those ideas.

7. **Let the speaker finish each major point that he/she wants to make.**
Do not interrupt – offer your response when the speaker is done. If you do have to interrupt, do so to ensure you are hearing the other person. Interrupt tactfully. For example, put up your hand and say, "Might I interrupt to ask you to clarify something?"

8. **Reflect back and ask if you are hearing accurately.**
This is also one of the most powerful guidelines. Start by asking if you can reflect back, or summarize, to the other person after he/she has spoken. Then progress to where you can ask the person to summarize back to you what you have just said to him/her.

9. **Regularly share indications that you are listening to them.**
Those indications can be, for example, nodding your head, saying "Yes" to short points that you agree with.

10. **Learn the art of supportive questioning.**
Coaching involves the use of powerful questions to understand your other's perceptions, assumptions and conclusions. The coach must practice effective questioning skills to really understand others.

Consider "How to Coach for Deep Problem-Solving and Learning" on page 230.

11. **Ask others to provide you feedback about your communication skills.**
    Often, people do not know what they do not know about themselves. One example is the leader who prizes him/herself on strong listening skills, yet regularly interrupts others when they are speaking. Another is the leader who speaks only in conclusions, but does not share how he/she came to those conclusions. Thus, others do not understand the leader's rationale.

How to Put Yourself "in Their Shoes" – Your Skills in Empathy

What Is Empathy? Why Is It So Important?

Empathy is the ability to accurately put yourself "in someone else's shoes" – to understand the other's situation, perceptions and feelings from their point of view – and to be able to communicate that understanding back to the other person. Empathy is a critical skill for you to have as a leader. It contributes to accurate understanding of your employees and volunteers, their perceptions and concerns. It also enhances your communication skills because you can sense what others want to know and if they are getting it from you or not. Ideally, your employees and volunteers can learn skills in empathy from you, thereby helping them to become more effective leaders, managers and supervisors themselves.

Empathy is sometimes confused with sympathy. Sympathy involves actually being affected by the other person's perceptions, opinions and feelings. For example, if an employee is frustrated and sad, the sympathetic leader would experience the same emotions, resulting in the leader many times struggling with the same issues as the employee. Thus, sympathy can actually get in the way of effective leading.

Guidelines to Develop Empathy

1. **Experience the major differences among people.**
   One of the best examples of strong skills in empathy is people who have traveled or worked in multicultural environments. They have learned that the way they see and experience things is often different from others. People with little or no skills in empathy might have an intellectual awareness of these differences. However, until they actually experience these differences, their skills in empathy will probably remain quite limited.

2. **Learn to identify your own feelings – develop some emotional intelligence.**
   Many of us are so "processed" and "sophisticated" about feelings that we cannot readily identify them in ourselves, much less in others. For example, we might perceive thoughts to be the same as feelings. So when someone asks you how you feel about a project, you might respond, "I think we have a lot to do." Or, we might not distinguish between related emotions, for example, between frustration and irritability or happiness and excitement.

 Consider "What is Your Emotional Intelligence?" on page 96.

3. **Regularly ask others for their perspectives and/or feelings regarding a situation.**
   Silently compare their responses to what you might have thought they would be. This approach not only helps you to sharpen your own empathic skills, but also helps you to learn more about your employees and volunteers.

How to Lead in Multicultural Organizations

Cultural Diversity Has a Huge Affect on Perceptions of Leadership

In today's highly diverse organizations, the ability to work in diverse cultures is extremely important. An organization's culture is driven by the values throughout that organization. Employees need to feel that their values are recognized, understood and respected. They need to feel that their ideas and concerns are being heard. Those conditions create strong motivation and momentum for strong performance in their jobs. Also, to help your employees to make meaningful decisions – and to understand decisions that they may have made already – it is extremely important that you have some understanding of the culture and values of the organization.

It can be a major challenge to work in multicultural environments where others have values, beliefs and certain conventions that are distinctly different from yours. Differences between cultures can lead to increased resistance to leadership because others might not understand and trust you. Those differences can hamper the effectiveness of leadership, if not stop it altogether.

For example, Western cultures tend to be highly rational and value things that are very useful in meeting a current need. They value rugged individualism and competition. Some cultures might value patience, a sense of community and getting along with others, and still others might value direct authority and privacy. Some cultures may be overly deferential to the leader. Some cultures are deeply guarded about private matters.

You and your employees and volunteers might not even realize that you all have very different values. There are no universal laws to ensure conformity in each culture. Because of complexities in continually learning the cultures of your organization, it is critical for you to continually be open to differences and ask for help from your employees.

Although leading in multicultural organizations comes with its own unique challenges, it comes with many benefits, as well. There are few other such powerful experiences in which you can learn so much about people and organizations and also about yourself. The following guidelines are intended to focus on the most practical suggestions for working in multicultural environments.

Basic Guidelines to Culturally-Specific Leadership

The following guidelines might be useful, especially if you are new to the organization.

1. **Be aware of your personal biases, style, preferences, lens and focus.**
    This is critically important for successful leadership in any type of culture. You make a major difference in your organization, whether you know it or not, just by exposing it to your own nature and style of working. Thus, you need to understand nature.

2. **Realize that each part of an organization probably has a unique culture.**
    For example, the secretarial staff might interact with each other in a manner quite different from that of the program staff. In larger organizations, there are often several differences, for example, between senior management, program staff and support staff.

3. **Promptly convey to employees that you want to be sensitive to their culture.**
    You should start in your first interaction with them. State that you recognize that different people might work differently depending on their own personalities and the culture of the overall organization. Ask them how you can understand the nature of their organization.

4. **Consider getting a mentor, or representative, from the organization.**
    Attempt to get someone from the organization to help you understand their culture and how to work in a manner compatible with the culture of the organization. This request is not a sign of weakness or lack of expertise, rather it is an authentic request that better serves you and your employees.

Become Knowledgeable About Key Cultural Aspects

Consider asking others to help you understand how each of the following aspects might be unique in the culture of the organization. Key cultural aspects that might affect your leadership include:

1. **Assertiveness**
    Are members of your organization comfortable being honest and direct with each other? If not, how can you still be as authentic as possible and help them to be as authentic as possible, as well?

2. **Body language**
    Are there any specific cues that you can notice to help you to sense how others are experiencing you?

3. **Communication styles and direction**
    Is communication fairly direct and specific or more indirect and general? Does information flow mostly "upward" to executives or is it widely disseminated?

4. **Conflict**
    Is conflict considered bad and avoided? Or is conflict accepted as normal and directly addressed when it appears?

5. **Eye contact**
    Are members of the organization comfortable with sustained eye contact during communication or not?

6. **Gestures**
    Are there any specific gestures that can cause members of the organization discomfort or confusion?

7. **Humor**
    Is use of humor in the organization rather widespread? Is there anything about the use of humor about which you should be aware?

8. **Information collection**
    Should you be aware of any potential problems or use any certain precautions when conducting interviews or using assessments?

9. **Physical space**
    For example, are members of your organization quite conscious of having a minimum amount of space around them when they work or speak with others?

10. **Power**
    Are members attuned to certain people of power when solving problems and making decisions? Is power based on authority and/or respect?

11. **Silence**

Are members uncomfortable with silence during communication? Or is it a common aspect of communicating in their workplace?

12. **Time**

Is time a precious commodity that seems to underlie many activities, or can activities take as long as they need to take to be done effectively?

13. **Wording**

Are there certain words or phrasings that cause discomfort when people from different cultures interact?

Hints for Talking with Others About Management Activities

It is not uncommon for people of any culture to experience confusion or engage in protracted arguments about activities only to realize later on that they have been in agreement all along – they had been using different definitions for the same terms. Therefore, it is important to ensure that all of you are "speaking the same language" about activities. The following guidelines are most important when ensuring people continue to understand each other when talking about management activities.

Recognize Difference Between Terms That Refer to Results Versus Activities to Produce Those Results

It is common for people from different cultures to become confused because different people are talking about results and others about the activities to produce the results. For example, some people refer to the "plan" to be the document, and others refer to the "plan" to be the activity of developing the plan. It is usually most clear to use the term "plan" to refer to the document itself, and use the term "planning" for the activities that produces the plan.

Here is another example. Inexperienced leaders sometimes assert that, because employees do not have a tangible plan/document on the shelf and do not explicitly reference the document on a regular basis, the employees are not doing planning. That assertion can alienate the leaders from employees who believe that they have been doing planning all along (but probably implicitly) and also have a good plan – they just have not been calling their process "planning" and have not produced a written plan document. Therefore, it is important for you to recognize if your employees have their own form of a certain activity and how that form is carried out in the organization.

Be Able to Separate a Term from the Meaning of That Term

If your conversations with others about management seem to get stuck or mired in confusion, it often helps to separate terms from the intent of those terms. For example:

- Rather than talking about "vision" or "goals," talk about "what" the nonprofit wants to accomplish overall.

- Rather than talking about "strategies," talk about "how" to accomplish "what" you want to accomplish overall.

- Rather than talking about "action plans," talk about "who is going to do what, and by when."

Hints for Talking with Others About Leadership Activities

The topic of leadership has become so prominent and passionate with so many people that it sometimes causes great confusion. Here are a few tips to helping people to "stay on the same page" when talking about leadership.

1. **Be clear about whether you are talking about leadership roles or traits.**
    When people talk about leadership, they might be talking about traits of leaders, such as being charismatic, influential and ethical. However, when others talk about leadership, they might be talking about roles of leadership, such as the Board Chair or the Chief Executive Officer. Both discussions are about leadership, but both are about quite different aspects.

2. **Be clear about the domain of leadership about which you are talking.**
    For example, when talking about leading yourself, you might be talking about leadership skills, such as being assertive or having good time and stress management skills. When talking about leading other individuals, you might be talking about skills, such as coaching, delegating or mentoring. When talking about leading groups, you might be talking about skills, such as facilitation or meeting management. When talking about leading organizations, you might be talking about skills, such as strategic planning or business planning. In each of these four cases, the term "leadership" refers to different sets of skills.

How to Deliver Effective Presentations

Nonprofit leaders make presentations to a wide variety of audiences, for example: Board members, staff, funders, community leaders and groups of clients. Usually there is a lot that can be quickly gained or quickly lost from a presentation. A little bit of guidance goes a long way toward making a highly effective presentation.

Note that meeting management skills are often helpful in designing an effective presentation. Also note that the following guidelines are intended for general presentations, not for training sessions where your presentation is to help learners to gain specific knowledge, skills or attitudes in order to improve their performance on a task or job.

 Consider "How to Design Highly Effective Meetings" on page 188.

Basic Guidelines for Designing Your Presentation

1. **List and prioritize the top three goals that you want to accomplish with your audience.**
    It is not enough just to talk at them. You may think you know what you want to accomplish in your presentation, but if you are not clear with yourself and others, it is very easy – too easy – for your audience to completely miss the point of your presentation. For example, your goals may be for them appreciate the accomplishments of your organization, to understand your need for funding, learn how to use your services, etc. Again, the goals should be in terms of what you want to accomplish with the audience, not with the nonprofit.

2. **Be really clear about who your audience is and what they should learn in the meeting.**
    Members of your audience will want to know right away why they were the ones chosen to be in your presentation. Be sure that your presentation makes this clear to them right away. This will help you clarify your invitation list and design your invitation to them.

3.   **List the major points of information that you want to convey to your audience.**
When you are done making that list, ask yourself, "If everyone in the audience understands all of those points, then will I have achieved the goal that I set for this meeting?"

4.   **Be clear about the tone that you want to set for your presentation.**
For example, are you conveying hopefulness, celebration, warning, teamwork, etc.? Consciously identifying the tone to yourself can help you cultivate that mood to your audience.

5.   **Design a brief opening (about 5% of your total time presentation time) that:**

    a.   Presents your goals for the presentation.

    b.   Clarifies the benefits of the presentation to the audience.

    c.   Explains the overall layout of your presentation.

6.   **Prepare the body of your presentation (about 75% of your presentation time).**

7.   **Allocate 10% of the time to summarize the key points from your presentation.**

8.   **Allocate 10% of the time to answer any questions from the audience.**

Basic Guidelines About Presentation Materials

You might be handing out supplemental materials, for example, articles, reports, etc. along with making your presentation. You might also be handing out copies of your presentation, either as a report or as copies of the slides that you will be referencing during your presentation. You might be using transparency slides or showing slides from a personal computer onto a project screen.

1.   If you plan to project your slides from a computer onto a projection screen, then be sure to check out the computer system before people come into the meeting room, if at all possible.

2.   Use a consistent layout, or organization of colors and images, on your materials.

3.   If you present from slides, then allocate 3-5 minutes for each slide of your presentation. Include 5-8 lines of bulleted phrases on each slide.

4.   If you provide supplemental information during your presentation, then your audience will very likely read that information during your presentation, rather than listening to you. Therefore, consider distributing this information after you have completed your presentation. Or, hand it out at the beginning of your presentation and ask them not to read it until you have completed your presentation.

5.   If you hand out copies of your slides, be sure that the text on the handouts is large enough that your audience can read the handouts on the table in front of them without having to hold them up to their face. Be sure to leave space on the handouts for the audience to make notes on them.

Basic Guidelines About Your Delivery

1. If you are speaking to a small group (for example, 2-15 people), then try to accomplish eye contact with each person for a few seconds throughout your delivery.

2. Look up from your materials, or notes, every 5-10 seconds, and look into the audience.

3. Speak a little bit louder and a little bit slower than you normally would with a friend. A good way to practice this is to speak along with a news anchor when watching television.

4. Vary the volume and rate of your speech. A monotone voice is absolutely toxic to keeping the attention of an audience.

5. Stand with your feet at shoulder-length apart.

6. Keep your hands relatively still.

Communications Tools to Use With Employees and Volunteers

Effective communications is the "life's blood" of an organization. Organizations that are highly successful have strong systems of communications. One of the first signs that an organization is struggling is that communications have broken down. The following guidelines are basic in nature, but comprise the critical fundamentals for ensuring strong ongoing, internal communications.

1. **Each employee writes a one-page weekly status report to his/her supervisor.**
    These reports may seem a tedious task, but they are precious in ensuring that the employee and supervisor have mutual understanding of what is going on. The reports also come in very handy for planning purposes. They make otherwise harried employees stand back and reflect on what they are doing. In the dated report, include description of:

    a. What tasks were done last week.

    b. What tasks are planned next week.

    c. Any current highlights, trends or issues regarding your activities.

2. **Chief Executive Officer conducts staff-wide meetings (meeting with all employees).**
    Employees greatly appreciate that the CEO finds time to talk to them, and the opportunity to meet their CEO in person.

    a. For clarity, focus and morale, be sure to use agendas and ensure follow-up minutes.

    b. Mention any significant events for staff, for example, birthdays.

    c. Review the overall condition of the organization.

    d. Consider conducting "in service" training about the organization where employees take turns describing their roles to the rest of the staff.

    e. Consider bringing in a client to tell his/her story of how the organization helped them.

3. **Each supervisor conducts meetings with all employees together.**
    Have these meetings even if there is not a specific problem to solve – just make them shorter. Holding meetings only when there are problems to solve cultivates a crisis-oriented environment where managers believe their only job is to solve problems.

    a. Prepare for these meetings by reviewing the employee's weekly status report.

    b. For clarity, focus and morale, be sure to use agendas, take minutes and ensure follow-up minutes.

    c. Facilitate the meetings to support exchange of ideas and questions.

    d. Use these meetings for each person to briefly give an overview of what they are doing that week. If the meeting includes 10 people or less, then have each person give a one-minute description of what they did last week and plan to do next week.

    e. Have each person bring his/her calendar to ensure the scheduling of future meetings accommodates everyone's calendar.

3. **Each supervisor conducts one-on-one, monthly meetings with each employee.**
    This ultimately produces more efficient time management and supervision.

    a. Review overall status of work activities.

    b. Hear status from both the supervisor and the employee.

    c. Exchange feedback and answer any questions about current products and services.

    d. Discuss career planning, training plans, performance review plans, etc.

4. **Volunteer coordinators meet regularly with major volunteers.**
    If the nonprofit has people who volunteer on a regular basis, for example, 5-10 hours a week, then the Volunteer Coordinator should meet with those volunteers at least monthly. These volunteers often have as much knowledge, expertise and opinions to offer as employees, and should be treated as such. (If a nonprofit has enough volunteers to warrant consistent attention to their recruitment, selection, training, scheduling and record keeping, then the nonprofit should consider establishing at least a part-time Volunteer Coordinator role.)

5. **Use memos.**
    It is much more effective if important day-to-day information is written to people rather than said to people. Use of memos, or even e-mail messages, is ideal in these situations. In your memos or e-mail messages, include:

    a. "Subject" line, with a phrase describing the topic of the memo.

    b. "To" and "From" lines.

    c. "Date."

    d. "Summary" describing the highlights in a paragraph near the top of the memo.

e. "Action" specifying what you want the recipients to do with the information in the memo, for example: to respond, to take note, to starting doing something, to stop doing something, etc.

f. "Signature" line, that includes the signature of who wrote the memo.

6. **Every employee gets an Employee Manual.**
The Employee Manual includes all of the up-to-date personnel policies of the nonprofit organization.

 Consider "How to Use An Employee Manual" on page 202.

PART IV:

HOW TO LEAD

– AND CHANGE –

NONPROFITS

How to Set Clear Purpose and Direction for the Nonprofit

Leading is setting direction and then motivating oneself, others, groups or an organization to follow that direction. There are many ways to lead, ranging from highly participatory to highly directive. The direction for an organization is usually established during strategic planning. Most organizations do some form of strategic planning – some without knowing it because planning can be done in a very explicit, comprehensive and systematic manner or in a rather implicit, partial and spotted manner. The former is usually the more effective approach to planning.

This section provides guidelines sufficient for you to develop a basic strategic plan from which you can begin or continue to effectively lead the organization. It will be helpful to recruit the involvement of a Planning Committee, comprised of key Board and staff members, to follow the guidelines in this section about strategic planning.

It is not within the scope of this Field Guide to provide comprehensive guidelines and procedures to carry out a complete, in-depth strategic planning process. You can get step-by-step guidelines for developing an in-depth strategic plan from the guidebook, *Field Guide to Nonprofit Strategic Planning and Facilitation*, from Authenticity Consulting, LLC. Additional resources are suggested at the end of this topic.

All Else Flows From Your Strategic Planning

Strategic planning, when well done, identifies or clarifies:

1. Major trends, rules and regulations, and expectations of stakeholders that influence the nonprofit's purpose, priorities and operations.

2. Specific needs among specific groups of clients, the results (outcomes) that would meet those needs, the programs and services that would achieve those outcomes, and the specific groups of clients to be served by the program and services.

3. The organization's purpose (mission), overall goal (its vision), nature of how it wants to operate (its values), and the priorities and accomplishments (goals) to work toward the mission and vision.

4. How the organization and its resources should best be structured and organized to best operate according to the mission, vision, values and goals.

5. Milestones, or objectives, that together accomplish each of the goals.

6. Resources (people, money, facilities, etc.) needed to achieve those goals and objectives.

7. How the strategic plan (which documents the mission, vision, values, goals and objectives) will be developed and how its implementation will be monitored.

The most important part of strategic planning is not the strategic plan document itself, but rather the planning process, which, in reality, is always an ongoing process. Good organizational leadership is essentially an ongoing process of good strategic planning and implementation.

Particularly for small nonprofits, the process of strategic planning should be carried out in a highly practical fashion. It is important during planning to do the 20% of effort that generates 80% of a good plan. The remaining 20% of a good plan often comes from actually implementing the plan itself. While matters about the mission, vision and values are certainly very important, do not get distracted into spending most of your planning time and energy on those matters. Strategic planning should always include solid action planning which specifies who will do what and by when in order to achieve the goals and associated objectives.

Strategic Planning – How, Who and When

How Should Strategic Planning Be Done?

There are many perspectives on the strategic planning process, including on the various terms and steps in the process. Some experts assert that organizations should start by examining their mission, vision and values statements. Others assert that organizations should start by analyzing what is going on in their external and internal environments, and then using the results of that analysis to update the mission, vision and values statements. Most experts assert that planners should identify major goals, set strategies to achieve the goals, and perform action planning that identifies who will be doing what and by when in order to achieve the goals. Action planning is followed by first identifying what resources are needed to implement the strategies and then specifying those resources, for example, in an annual operating budget.

Who Should Develop the Plan?

Board members and leaders among staff must be highly involved in clarifying the mission statement. They also should be involved in writing the vision and values statements, if the organization decides to develop vision and values statements. They also should be highly involved in identifying strategic goals. Staff members are often involved with the Board in identifying strategic goals and associated objectives to achieve each of the goals. Staff members are also highly involved in action planning. However, some nonprofits prefer that Board and staff members work together in all aspects of strategic planning, especially if the nonprofits are new, small or have members who prefer highly egalitarian and team-oriented approaches to activities.

If you have not done strategic planning before, consider recruiting an experienced facilitator. A nonprofit should obtain an outside facilitator (that is, someone to facilitate who is not a member of the nonprofit) if any of the following are true:

- The nonprofit has not conducted strategic planning before.

- For a variety of reasons, previous strategic planning was not deemed to be successful.

- There appears to be a wide range of ideas and/or concerns among organization members about strategic planning and current organizational issues to be addressed in the plan.

- There is no one in the nonprofit who feels that he/she has sufficient facilitation skills.

- No one in the nonprofit feels committed to facilitating strategic planning for the nonprofit.

- Leaders believe that an inside facilitator will either inhibit participation from others or will not have the opportunity to fully participate in planning themselves.

- Leaders want an objective voice, that is, someone who is not likely to have strong predispositions about the nonprofit's strategic issues and ideas.

When Should Strategic Planning Be Done?

Strategic planning should be done:

- When an organization is just getting started.

- In preparation for a new major venture, for example, developing a new program.

- At least once a year in order to be ready for the coming fiscal year.

It also should be done if:

- There are many new Board members who need to agree on the direction of the nonprofit.

- There are many recurring problems in the nonprofit.

- The nonprofit wants more robust fundraising and funders require a strategic plan.

Sample Planning Process for Short-Term Strategic Plan

The length of time for strategic planning depends on whether the organization has done planning before, how many strategic issues and goals the organization faces, whether the culture of the organization prefers short or long meetings, and how much time the organization is willing to commit to strategic planning. However, for small nonprofits in particular, the planning process might be too long if it drags out over several months. Therefore, it is often much better for small nonprofits to spend several weeks to do a top-level, short-term strategic plan than to spend several months or longer doing a more detailed, long-term strategic plan.

Here is an example of a basic strategic planning format, which results in a short-term, strategic plan that can be embellished later by staff adding more detailed action plans, if necessary. The plan is focused on the coming six-month period. Some strategic planning experts might complain that the following procedure does not produce a highly "strategic" plan, that is, the procedure does not include getting input from all major stakeholders, analysis of external factors, etc. However, the following recommended procedure is likely to "jump start" a highly practical plan from which you can later develop a longer term plan.

1. **Have a meeting to announce planning process to Board members and key staff.**
    a. The Board Chair and Chief Executive announce to Board and staff that a strategic planning process will soon be underway. The announcement includes explanation of the purpose and benefits of strategic planning, and the role of Board and staff in the process. The Chair and/or Chief Executive explain who will be involved in the planning process. Time is allowed for Board and staff to ask questions in their respective meetings.

b. All Board and certain staff members are asked to think about current challenges that the organization faces and/or goals that they recommend for the organization to achieve over the coming six months. Staff are encouraged to talk to other staff to get ideas, as well.

c. The next upcoming planning sessions are scheduled.

2. **In a half-day Board retreat, identify major challenges over the next six months.**
    Include Board members and key staff. Activities include:

    a. Introductions by the Board Chair and/or Chief Executive along with their explanations of the organization's benefits from strategic planning and the organization's commitment to the planning process. Explanations should indicate that the planning process will focus particularly on the next six months.

    b. The facilitator provides an overview of the process. The facilitator might be an external facilitator, that is, someone from outside the organization, or an internal facilitator who has previous experience in strategic planning.

    c. Brief review of the mission (and the vision and values, if applicable) with the bulk of time spent on identifying current, major challenges to address over the next six months. Challenges are clarified and prioritized. Participants may suggest goals to meet the challenges, as well.

    d. Finalize which challenges will be targeted over the next six months.

    e. Finalize which goals will be achieved in order to address each of the challenges.

    f. Before the next meeting, a subcommittee is asked to draft the strategic plan document that describes the major challenges and the goals to address each challenge.

3. **Finalize action plans for each goal and then draft the strategic plan document.**
    The next planning meeting is attended primarily by staff. Some Board members might attend as well, especially Board leadership and any Board members assigned to Board committees whose activities are closely involved in achieving the goals.

    a. An action plan is developed for each of the goals, including what objectives are needed to achieve each goal, along with who will be doing what and by when in order to achieve each objective.

    b. A subcommittee is asked to update the drafted plan to include the action plans, and to provide the plan to Board members before the next Board meeting.

4. **In the next Board meeting, Board members authorize the strategic plan document.**
    Board members:

    a. Discuss the drafted plan document.

    b. Suggest any changes. If changes are in order, they should be coordinated promptly with staff.

    c. Approve the final draft of the document by signing the document.

In the above example of a planning process, various subcommittees might be charged to gather additional information and distribute it between meetings.

No matter how serious planners are about their strategic planning, they usually have strong concerns about finding the time to attend frequent planning meetings. This concern can be addressed by ensuring that meetings are well managed, and by having several shorter meetings rather than one or two longer meetings.

How to Develop Your Basic Strategic Plan

 For a complete set of worksheets that you can use to fill in the draft of your strategic plan, go to http://www.managementhelp.org/np_progs/sp_mod/sp_frame.htm .

Draft Your Initial Mission Statement

Your description of your mission statement should briefly describe the purpose of your organization, whom it serves and how it serves them. The mission is the compass for the decisions by the Board and other leaders in the nonprofit. Your mission statement is particularly important to program planning because it guides the overall relationship between the activities of your overall organization and your program. There should be strong alignment between the mission of your organization and the goals of your program. Therefore, you should give careful thought to the development of your mission statement.

Example:

> "To support individual and community development in Minneapolis by ensuring all adults between the ages of 18 and 65 achieve gainful employment in the community."

Draft Your Initial Vision Statement

Your description should depict the overall benefits that your community and clients will achieve from participating in your programs. It should help guide Board members' decisions.

Example:

> "Every adult in Minneapolis is fulfilled by employment that contributes to his or her individual and community development."

Draft Your Initial Values Statement

The values statement should describe the overall priorities, or principles, that guide how you want the nonprofit or program to operate.

Example:

"We believe that:

- Employment provides opportunity for adults to develop the community and themselves;

- Every person deserves an opportunity for gainful employment;

- Gainful employment of all citizens is a responsibility of all citizens."

Analyze Outside Environment of Nonprofit Now

Take a wide look around at the world outside the nonprofit and how it might affect the nonprofit and its clients. This external analysis looks at societal, technological, political and economic trends affecting the organization. This may include trends in donations, recent or pending legislation, federal funds, demographic trends, or degree of access to trained labor and competition. In your external analysis, do not forget to consider stakeholders' impressions of the organization including funders, clients and community leaders. If you have limited resources for this external analysis, then be sure to at least consider the needs of current and potential clients, what funders are funding efforts to meet those needs, and what collaborators might you work with.

From this information, try to identify 4-5 opportunities facing the nonprofit now, for example, more clients for programs, more access to clients, useful technologies for more efficiency, strong relationships with stakeholders that might produce more collaboration or funding, and increasing societal priorities to address the needs met by your programs.

From this information, try to identify 4-5 threats facing the nonprofit now, for example, decreasing number of clients, less access to clients, little innovation in the technologies used by your programs, poor public relations with stakeholders, and changes in laws that might decrease attention to your programs.

Note that opportunities and threats can seem very similar. What might seem like an opportunity to one person might seem like a threat to another because not enough of the opportunity seems present to that other person. Many times, opportunities and threats can seem like two opposite ways of looking at the same situation. For example, the threat of decreasing funds can be an opportunity to increase efficiencies in operations to reduce expenses. The perspective is up to the planners.

For another comprehensive list of considerations about the external environment, go to http://www.managementhelp.org/plan_dec/str_plan/drvnforc.htm .

Analyze Inside Environment of Nonprofit Now

Now consider the quality of operations inside your organization, for example, of the Board, programs, staff, marketing, finances, fundraising, facilities and evaluations. Think about the nonprofit's strengths and weaknesses.

From this information, try to identify 4-5 strengths of the organization, for example, strong expertise among staff, effective Board, strong public image, strong outcomes produced by programs and strong motivation of Board and staff members.

From this information, try to identify 4-5 weaknesses of the organization, for example, high turnover of Board and staff members, continual financial crises, complaints from clients and poor facilities.

Consider "Useful, Free Nonprofit Organizational Assessments" on page 267.

Identify Your Most Important 5-7 Issues to Address For Now

Think about your external and internal analyses. Which issues (usually threats and/or weaknesses) seem most important to address for now? Usually, it is best to describe in terms of a question. How can we establish a new Chief Executive Officer position? How do we strengthen and develop our Board so it can be more effective in helping to set direction and raise funds? How do we establish overall direction for our nonprofit? How do we enhance our management skills? How can we get more money in the future, especially when donations seem to be decreasing? How can we serve more homeless clients in our area, especially when current, and likely new, laws are disenfranchising our clients from our services? How do we respond to increased competition?

Identify Your Goals to Address Each Issue Now

Consider what must be done (what goals must be achieved) to address each of the issues that you identified from considering the threats and weaknesses. Consider what strengths you can use and what opportunities you might take advantage of in order to achieve the goals. (Planners refer to this step as a SWOT analysis. SWOT is an acronym for strengths, weaknesses, opportunities and threats. Think about the SWOT information that you can identify so far from doing the external analysis.)

The following sites might have examples of SWOT analyses:
1. http://www.consultancymarketing.co.uk/swot.htm .
2. http://www.historyoftheuniverse.com/human.html#swot .
3. http://erc.msh.org/quality/example/swot.cfm .
4. http://foba.lakeheadu.ca/zahaf/2014/SWOT.pdf .

Example:

> Issue #1: How do we establish a full-time CEO position?
>
> 1) Goal 1.1: Obtain funds to pay CEO for at least one year.
>
> 2) Goal 1.2: Establish and operate Board Search Committee.
>
> 3) Goal 1.3: Search Committee recommends CEO candidate.
>
> 4) Goal 1.4: Board selects new CEO.

Develop Action Plans for Each Goal

For example, for Goal 1.1 above:

Objectives for Goal 1.1	Date of Completion	Responsibility	Status and Date
1.1.1. Recruit fundraiser/trainer.	1/1/09	Program Director	
1.1.2. Schedule Board and CEO training about fundraising.	1/1/09	Program Director	
1.1.3. Conduct training.	1/21/09	Program Director	
1.1.4. Draft short-term fundraising plan.	2/1/09	Program Director	
1.1.5. Board approve plan.	2/8/09	Program Director	
1.1.6. Implement plan.	2/8/09	Program Director	
1.1.7. Pay CEO salary.	6/1/09	Program Director	

How Do You Ensure Implementation of Your Plan?

The following guidelines will help ensure that the strategic plan is implemented.

1. **In planning, involve the people who will be responsible for implementing the plan.**
   Use a cross-functional team (representatives from each of the organization's major programs or services) in planning in order to ensure that the plan is realistic and collaborative.

2. **Ensure the plan has realistic vision, goals and objectives.**
   During planning, continue to ask planners, "Is this realistic? Can we really do this?" When implementing the plan, adjust deadlines as needed in order to keep the plan relevant.

3. **The Board Chair and Chief Executive should show very visible support.**
   For example, they should clearly convey the purpose of the planning to Board and staff members, and should stress that they will monitor implementation of the plan.

4. **Organize the overall strategic plan into smaller action plans.**
    Be sure that the plan specifies who is going to do what and by when in order to achieve the goals and associated objectives in the plan.

5. **Build in regular reviews of the status of the implementation of the plan.**
    Board and staff meetings are very good opportunities to quickly review status. During reviews, monitor achievement of goals and objectives according to their deadlines.

6. **Translate plan's goals and objectives into job descriptions and performance goals.**
    Unless the plan is integrated into the day-to-day activities in the nonprofit, the plan is very likely to sit on a shelf, collecting dust.

7. **Be sure one internal person has ultimate responsibility to ensure implementation.**
    Even though one person is responsible to coordinate the plan's activities (often the Chief Executive Officer), Board members are still responsible to monitor the implementation.

8. **Ensure Board members regularly review status reports on the plan's implementation.**
    This is one of the members' most important jobs – to be sure that the nonprofit is meeting the needs of the community by implementing a community-driven strategic plan.

For more information on strategic planning, go to
http://www.managementhelp.org/strt_org/strt_np/strt_np.htm .

Consider the *Field Guide to Nonprofit Strategic Planning and Facilitation* from Authenticity Consulting, LLC, available by clicking on the link "Publications" at http://www.authenticityconsulting.com/ .

How Your Board and Staff Together Can Lead the Nonprofit

Ultimately, Board members have the responsibility and accountability for the direction, purpose and priorities of the nonprofit. However, research suggests that the most successful and well-respected nonprofits are led by a strategic partnership of the Board and Chief Executive. Thus, the guidelines in this section are best addressed by this working partnership.

Consider "How Your Board and CEO Can Work in Strategic Partnership" on page 48. Also, consider "How Much Should Your Board Be Involved in Management" on page 73.

How to Make Sure Your Stakeholders Are Always Heard

Nonprofits are public trusts. They exist to serve the needs of the community. They are obligated to the community – a community that often permits nonprofits to be exempt from requirements made to other forms of business. In return, the public expects to be heard. They count on the nonprofit's leaders to ensure that the voice of the community is heard. Therefore, leaders must focus strong attention to listening to their stakeholders. This activity is sometimes called "inbound marketing." This activity is critical to the primary job of nonprofit Board members and leaders among staff to verify that their nonprofit is indeed effectively and efficiently meeting a specific need in the community.

Far too often organizations focus on aggressive advertising, promotions and media campaigns that go *at* their stakeholders: funders, clients and other groups in the community. Too many organizations do not really *listen to* their stakeholders.

Guidelines for Effective Leadership of Inbound Marketing

If your Board uses Committees, then a Marketing Committee would be helpful in this area, although a Program Committee could also oversee inbound marketing, which involves market research.

1. **Understand laws and regulations that apply to the nonprofit.**
   This includes filings with appropriate government agencies, benefits and limitations of corporate status, conformance to corporate Articles, By-Laws, etc.

2. **Know who the major groups of stakeholders are for the nonprofit.**
   Consider Board members, staff, clients, funders and community members.

3. **Establish policies to regularly collect information from stakeholders.**
   Collect information about unmet needs in the community, impressions of the nonprofit, and other nonprofits working to meet needs similar to those met by the nonprofit.

4. **Ensure strategic planning includes feedback from stakeholders.**
   Collect input from Board members, staff, clients, funders, the community, etc. Ask, "What does each stakeholder consider to be 'success' for the nonprofit?"

5. **Ensure the mission is centered on meeting verified needs in the community.**
    Mission statements should describe at least the community need that is being met among which groups of clients by using which methods. Verify that those needs even exist.

6. **Design and conduct Annual Meetings.**
    In the meeting, take time to ask others about what they need from the nonprofit and what would meet that need.

7. **Ensure means to effectively verify results achieved among clients.**
    Conduct practical outcomes-based evaluations that collect information from program clients about whether their desired results are being met or not.

8. **Ensure Board members represent, or understand, your important constituents.**
    Constituents often include clients, funders, collaborators, community leaders, suppliers, government agencies, etc. Also consider groups of clients, regions and community values.

How to Ensure That Relevant and Realistic Strategic Planning Takes Place

Strategic planning establishes purpose and overall direction for the nonprofit, including where it should to be at some point in the future and how it is going to get there. In a previous section, this guidebook explained that "all else flows from strategic planning" in a nonprofit. The process has been emphasized so much that all variety of proponents and opponents has voiced their opinions about the process. Some nonprofit leaders recoil at hearing the phrase "strategic planning" because it represents to them a long, tedious process, which, far too often, results in a report that sits collecting dusts on the shelf. That need not be the case. Leaders can help ensure that the process is carried out in a highly flexible, relevant and realistic fashion.

When deciding how to go forward, the nonprofit might decide to use a process called "strategic planning" or something else. Whatever process the nonprofit chooses to use, leaders have the responsibility to ensure that the process establishes clear direction and alignment for all of the important parts of the nonprofit. Also, leaders must ensure that, regardless of which planning process is used, the nonprofit is focused on meeting a strong, verified need in the community and is progressing toward meeting that need.

Guidelines for Effective Leadership of Strategic Planning

If your Board uses Committees, then an ad hoc Strategic Planning Committee would be helpful in this area.

1. **Actively participate in strategic planning, whether formal or informal.**
    A major responsibility of Board members is to ensure that the nonprofit has a clear purpose and direction, and has guidelines to work toward both of these. Developing and implementing a strategic plan usually fills that responsibility.

2. **Ensure strategic planning includes feedback from stakeholders.**
    Far too often, strategic planning tends to include only the opinions of those internal to the organization. Consequently, a "beautiful ladder can be built entirely to the wrong roof" – the plan includes wonderfully worded mission and vision statements, but little else that directly

applies to needs in the community. Therefore, in planning, include the perspectives of Board members, staff, clients, funders and the community.

3. **Craft your mission statement to describe who you serve, for what results and how.**
    The mission statement is the key communication to constituents. Mission statements can be in a wide variety of formats. However, the statements should reflect what you are doing for your constituents, not just for your organization.

4. **During planning, always ask, "Is this realistic?"**
    Many nonprofit plans sit on shelves, collecting dust because the vision and goals were completely unrealistic. It is better to have a plan with a few realistic goals than to have a plan with many inspirational goals, most of which are far too ambitious to achieve.

5. **Be sure that the goals from the strategic plan are integrated throughout the nonprofit.**
    The plan specifies what most important priorities for the nonprofit to address. The nonprofit cannot do that if its various functions are not all aligned with addressing those priorities. Functions include Board operations, programs, marketing, staffing, finances and fundraising.

6. **Regularly monitor status reports regarding implementation of the plan.**
    Top-level information about mission, vision and values and lofty goals have no foundation if there is no specification of who needs to do what and by when in order to work towards those top-level priorities.

 Consider the free, online self-directed, learning module about strategic planning at http://www.managementhelp.org/np_progs/sp_mod/str_plan.htm .

 See the topic, "Strategic Planning," in the Free Management Library[SM] at http://www.managementhelp.org/plan_dec/str_plan/str_plan.htm .

 Also consider the publication, *Field Guide to Nonprofit Strategic Planning and Facilitation,* from Authenticity Consulting, LLC. Go to the "Publications" link at http://www.authenticityconsulting.com .

How to Make Sure Your Board's Operations Are Always High-Quality

Guidelines for Effective Leadership of Board Development

Like the physician who has an unhealthy lifestyle, but takes very good care of his/her patients, the Board rarely gives attention as to how it is doing overall. Board development helps ensure that the Board is working smarter rather than harder. The following guidelines are directly in regard to ensuring that activities within the Board are always high quality. Note that it often is the Chief Executive who supports the Board to be doing its job.

If your Board uses Committees, then a Board Development Committee would be helpful in this area.

1. **Clarify what skills are needed among Board members to effectively govern.**
   The approach that you use to recruit Board members depends on whether you are staffing the Board to get expertise to achieve strategic goals and/or representing the voices of diverse stakeholders. If you are staffing primarily according to passion for mission, then be sure that the members do more than have passionate meetings.

2. **Orient Board members about the unique aspects of the nonprofit.**
   Ensure members know about the nonprofit's history, programs, successes and other Board members. Be sure to review Board policies, specifically By-Laws, Board calendar, comparison of Board and staff roles, Board attendance, conflict-of-interest, Board self-evaluation, CEO's job description, committees and ethics policy.

3. **Train members to be effective Board members.**
   Train Board members about the roles and responsibilities of a governing Board of Directors. Review the fiduciary duties and associated responsibilities, job descriptions and the major types of decisions made by Board members.

4. **Effectively organize Board expertise and resources to achieve goals.**
   You might use committees or task forces to organize members around important strategic priorities. The extent of involvement of Board members depends on the factors listed above

5. **Use a Board calendar of important events to ensure all those events are conducted.**
   To ensure that all important Board activities are conducted, reference an annual calendar of about when the Board does a self-evaluation, evaluates the CEO, does strategic planning, produces a budget, approves updated policies and procedures, etc.

6. **Evaluate the Board to ensure maximize performance.**
   Board self-evaluation might need just 30 minutes a year from each member in order to complete a questionnaire about the quality of operations of the Board. Results of that self-evaluation usually are extremely useful to the Board.

Consider the free, online, self-directed, learning module about Boards at http://www.managementhelp.org/np_progs/brd_mod/boards.htm .

See the topic, "Boards of Directors," in the Free Management Library[SM] at http://www.managementhelp.org/boards/boards.htm .

Consider the guidebook, *Field Guide to Developing, Operating and Restoring Your Board,* from Authenticity Consulting, LLC. Go to the "Publications" link at http://www.authenticityconsulting.com .

How to Verify Your Programs Always Meet Needs of Your Community

Programs are the primary strategies by which a nonprofit meets a specific need in the community. Therefore, the nonprofit's leaders must have strong knowledge of programs, especially as to whether they are indeed meeting the specific community needs that the nonprofit was formed to meet.

Guidelines for Effective Leadership of Programs and Services

If your Board uses Committees, then a Programs Committee would be helpful in this area.

1. **Know what the nonprofit's program are – many leaders often do not.**
    It is amazing how long Board members can serve a nonprofit, but when asked what the programs are, members are not able to identify them. Ask the Chief Executive to describe specifically what the programs are for the nonprofit.

2. **Understand each program, including the need it is to meet in the community and how.**
    This requires that client groups provide continual feedback to the nonprofit about the clients' needs. It also requires that the nonprofit identify certain outcomes (impacts or benefits) among clients that the program will work to achieve among client groups.

3. **Ensure programs are consistent with the mission and goals of the nonprofit.**
    Do not stray into providing programs that seem useful, but that might already be offered by other nonprofits, or that might be so outside the nonprofit's focus that the programs would cost far too much in time and distraction to do.

4. **Ensure programs are sufficiently resourced.**
    Major resources include people, expertise, funding and facilities. Resources also can include time and attention from the nonprofit's leaders and external stakeholders constituents.

5. **Ensure programs continue to meet the needs of clients – conduct evaluations.**
    This requires ongoing outcomes evaluations that focus on:

    a. Identifying indicators, or measures, that suggest what impacts or benefits (outcomes) the programs are helping clients to achieve.

    b. Collection of ongoing feedback from clients and program staff regarding the achievement of those measures for clients.

    c. Conclusions about the ultimate effectiveness of programs in achieving the desired outcomes for client groups.

6. **Ensure the various programs are highly integrated in purpose and operations.**
    It is not uncommon that various programs almost seem to stand apart from each other, as if the nonprofit is really running various separate other organizations. A tight integration of programs means savings and efficiency from sharing resources.

Consider the free, online, self-directed, learning module about marketing
at http://www.managementhelp.org/np_progs/mkt_mod/market.htm .

Consider the guidebook, *Field Guide to Nonprofit Program Design,
Marketing and Evaluation,* from Authenticity Consulting, LLC. Go to
the "Publications" link at http://www.authenticityconsulting.com .

How to Ensure Fair Management of Your Employees and Volunteers

The human resources (employees and volunteers) are the nonprofit's most important asset. It is
critical that all paid staff (including the Chief Executive) and volunteers be recruited, trained and
supervised according to up-to-date personnel policies and procedures that are approved by the Board.

Guidelines for Effective Leadership of Human Resources

If your Board uses Committees, then a Personnel Committee would be helpful in this area.

1. **Ensure the nonprofit has up-to-date written personnel policies and procedures.**
    Employee laws today are so numerous and complex that nonprofits have to have written
    policies and procedures in order to ensure compliance to laws, rules and regulations. An
    expert on employment laws should review policies on a regular basis. All staff (paid and
    volunteer) should have copies of the policies and procedures in the form of an employee
    handbook. The Chief Executive and other management staff, in particular, should be trained
    to ensure compliance. The Board should formally approve the personnel policies.

2. **Ensure employee and volunteers are retained according to expertise, not personalities.**
    Employees and volunteers should not be hired or recruited primarily because they know
    someone in the nonprofit or because they are likeable. Focus on the requirements of the job
    and ensure that a job description accurately describes those requirements. Then reference
    the job description to fill the position.

3. **Ensure all employees and volunteers are fully resourced to do their jobs.**
    It is very important to give them a brief orientation of the nonprofit program's, other
    employees and volunteers, and resources available to help them (for example, job training,
    computers, procedures, internal experts, etc.). Sometimes they might seem like they are
    poor performers when instead they just need better training and resources.

4. **Ensure all staff and volunteers receive regular written evaluations.**
    Too often, nonprofit leaders assume that people are doing fine because they keep showing up
    for work each day. High-performing people usually want to know how they are doing and
    how they can improve. The best way to convey that information is to provide written
    evaluations. Those evaluations also serve as a valid benchmark, or indicator, if leaders need
    to take some form of performance-related action later on.

5.   **Ensure all employees receive fair and equitable benefits and compensation.**
     There are many online salary surveys that suggest pay ranges for various positions. Even if
     a nonprofit cannot pay compensation that is well within these ranges, the Board still should
     approve a formal policy to determine, not only how much employees should be paid, but
     also to ensure that they are treated fairly when compensation is determined.

> Consider the free, online, self-directed, learning module about staffing at
> http://www.managementhelp.org/np_progs/sup_mod/staff.htm .

How to Ensure Strong Leadership in Fundraising

A recent trend among funders is to expect Board members to take a very active role in leading
fundraising, including making their own monetary contributions to the organization. Board and key
staff members can approach funders, not only to solicit funds, but also to develop relationships with
funders. Funders expect nonprofits to present a clear case for the need for funds and clear methods
for continuing to verify that funds are spent in an effective fashion. If a fundraiser is hired, Board
members should follow ethical practices in hiring and supervising those consultants. Therefore,
nonprofit leaders must conduct fundraising activities in a highly focused, plan-based fashion that
directly follows from the nonprofit's mission and goals.

Guidelines for Effective Leadership of Fundraising

If your Board uses Committees, then a Fundraising Committee would be helpful in this area.

1.   **Work smarter, rather than harder – do not do the same techniques even harder.**
     Nonprofits often do the same few techniques to raise money, for example, an annual
     fundraiser that requires an extensive amount of time from Board and staff members, but that
     generates very little in revenue. Or, they burst out a large number of grant proposals, all
     with the same wording. They would benefit much more from planning their fundraising as
     described below.

2.   **Do prospect research to identify all sources of funding and likely amounts from each.**
     Prospect research can identify the percentage of funding that a nonprofit with similar
     nonprofits in your locale might get from individuals, foundations, corporations and
     government, for example, 30% from individuals, 30% from foundations, 20% from
     corporations and 20% from government. That sets a benchmark, or measure, from which you
     can target your expected levels of funding from fundraising efforts to those sources. Prospect
     research also reminds your organization to go well beyond doing the same approaches to
     fundraising (for example, doing annual events).

3.   **Ensure development and approval of a comprehensive Fundraising Plan!**
     This should be the primary job of a Fundraising Committee. The Plan should specify:

     a.   The overall fundraising target or amount to be raised and by when.

     b.   Percentage to be raised from among the different types of sources, including individuals,
          foundations, corporations and/or government (that requires prospect research).

c.   Specific sources in each type, for example, names of specific individuals or specific foundations.

d.   How each of those sources will be approached and by whom.

e.   How status of fundraising will be tracked.

4.   **Ensure that all Board members remain actively involved in fundraising activities.**
A Board Fundraising Committee or task force should ensure that the Fundraising Plan is developed and implemented – but all Board members should take part in implementing the Plan. Board members should get a short training from staff about programs, including who is served and what successes have occurred so far, along with providing members a set of talking points so members feel comfortable approaching funders.

5.   **Ensure that funds are spent according to the requirements and specifications of donors.**
Board members must ensure that the funds continue to be spent in the manner that was described in the grant proposals that produced those funds. Otherwise, there can be lawsuits for misappropriation of funds and the nonprofit will lose all credibility with funders.

6.   **If fundraisers are hired, be clear about expectations to them and hire them ethically.**
For example, many experts assert that it is unethical to hire a fundraiser and expect him/her to pay his/her fee or salary with the monies that are raised. Instead, fundraisers should be paid an amount regardless of the amounts raised. Also, distinguish between the type of fundraiser who can help you with your planning and those who primarily write many grants.

See "How to Hire and Work With Consultants" on page 173.

7.   **Carefully monitor implementation of the Fundraising Plan.**
Is the Plan being implemented? Are you getting the results that you desired? If not, what should be done? Put more priority on implementation? Get more resources? Extend deadlines in the Plan?

8.   **Ensure that all donated funds are reported as required by law and funders.**
Sometimes nonprofits forget about funders once the nonprofits receive the checks. That is a mistake. Usually, foundation, corporate and government funding is accompanied by stringent reporting requirements that the nonprofit report how the funds were spent, including in which programs and what the results were from the expenditures.

Consider the free, online, self-directed, learning module about fundraising at http://www.managementhelp.org/np_progs/fnd_mod/fnd_raise.htm .

See the topic, "Nonprofit Fundraising and Grantwriting," in the Free Management Library[SM] at http://www.managementhelp.org/fndrsng/np_raise/np_raise.htm .

Can a Nonprofit Make a Profit From Programs and Services?

Yes. There is an age-old misconception that "nonprofit" means that the organization cannot make any excess monies – even that nonprofits should only raise monies primarily from fundraising. There is an increasing trend for nonprofits to engage in "earned-income" ventures where they generate significant funds from fees for services or products. They, in turn, use this increased revenue to offset the amounts that they must raise via fundraising. Many foundations and major funders even prefer that nonprofits undertake this "commercial" activity because it results in more financial self-reliance and sustainability on the part of the nonprofit.

Nonprofits that engage in activities where a substantial portion of their revenue is from sales of goods and services that are not directly in regard to their tax-exempt purposes (as described on their Form 1023 in the USA) have to pay taxes on that portion of revenue, the "unrelated business income." In the USA, that income must be reported on the Form 990-T to the Internal Revenue Service (IRS). If a "substantial" portion (as yet undefined by the IRS) of revenue is from unrelated business income, then the tax-exempt nonprofit could lose its tax-exempt status. If it plans to generate sizeable portions of its revenue from unrelated business income, then it might consider forming a for-profit subsidiary. In that situation, the nonprofit should seek counsel from a tax expert who is well versed in tax-exempt law.

You can benefit from the free advice shared by thousands of people on the free forum about earned income at http://www.npenterprise.net .

Nonprofit earned-income ventures are similar to those in for-profits in that they require careful business planning, including market research about the potential products and markets, perhaps feasibility or market testing, product development planning, identifying needed staffing, structuring the approach to managing the venture, and computing final costs to develop and sell the product.

This might seem like a lot of effort, but many nonprofits are probably already doing some form of business planning in order to successfully deliver programs to clients – these nonprofits probably are just not referring to their activities as business planning.

There is more information about earned-income ventures at http://www.managementhelp.org/soc_entr/soc_entr.htm#anchor80808 .

How to Effectively Promote the Nonprofit to Others

Those who are new to the nonprofit world might think that nonprofits should not have to "sell" their services. After a few months in a nonprofit, many people realize that "selling" is needed in the nonprofit world at least as much in the for-profit world. However, nonprofit personnel may not be nearly as effective at understanding how to sell.

First, it helps to understand what we are talking about. Advertising and promotions are aimed at continuing to bring a service to the attention of potential and current clients. Successful advertising and promotions depend very much on knowing what groups of clients your program aims to serve, what features and benefits of the program you want to convey to the clients, and what methods of communication will be most effective in reaching those clients. Sales is a "partnership" between the program and the client, geared to explore the client's needs and assess if there is a suitable match or not. If there is a match, the salesperson helps the client to take advantage of the program's services. Public relations might be viewed as advertising and promotions, not of a specific program, but of the entire nonprofit organization.

One of the Board's major responsibilities is to represent the nonprofit to the community. Ideally, the Board is comprised of representatives from the nonprofit's major stakeholders. Thus, Board members are poised to be very effective in advertising, promotions, sales and public relations for the nonprofit. (This activity is sometimes called "outbound marketing.")

Guidelines for Effective Leadership of Outbound Marketing

If your Board uses Committees, then a Marketing Committee would be helpful in this area.

1.   **Be sure that all the nonprofit's leaders understand the nonprofit's programs.**
As mentioned above, the leaders often do not know what the nonprofit's programs are. They should know each program, who it serves, the results that the program aims to achieve, the methods used by the program, and the types of results that have been achieved so far.

2.   **Define an overall desired image for the nonprofit – how should people view it?**
For example, should the nonprofit be known primarily for its strong programs, or its diverse values, or its strong relationships in the community? Should the nonprofit adopt a slogan, or a concise phrase, that helps to convey that image? Should the nonprofit standardize on a graphic, or logo, to convey its unique identity?

3.   **Develop an overall Promotions (or Marketing) Plan – ideally for each program.**
In the Plan, for each different, specific group of clients, specify:

   a.   The specific benefits that each different group will achieve from the different programs.

   b.   The different messages that will be conveyed to each different group. (When selecting the messages, consider the different needs and wants for each of the different groups.)

   c.   How each group prefers to get its messages, for example, some prefer television, some prefer the radio, some prefer newspapers, etc.

   d.   Who will convey the messages by using the preferred communications approaches with each group.

   e.   When those messages will be conveyed.

   f.   How implementation of the Promotions Plan will be tracked.

4.   **Develop a Public Relations Plan about the entire organization.**
Whereas a Marketing Plan ideally is about marketing each program, that is, a Plan for each program, a Public Relations plan is about marketing the entire organization. Develop a Plan that specifies:

   a.   The unique identity, or branding, of the nonprofit, along with any slogan, mission, etc.

   b.   The major stakeholders of the nonprofit, for example, clients, funders, collaborators and community leaders.

c. What the nonprofit wants each group of stakeholders to believe or feel about the nonprofit.

d. The communication channels that might be preferred by each group of stakeholders.

e. The messages to convey to each group via its preferred channel(s).

f. Who will convey the messages and by when.

5. **Ensure leaders work from a public relations or media kit, talking points, etc.**
Each Board and staff member is a representative of the nonprofit in the community. They deserve a short training about how to effectively describe each program and the entire organization to the community.

6. **Carefully monitor implementation of the Promotions and Public Relations Plans.**
Are the Plans being implemented? Are you getting the results that you desired? If not, what should be done? Put more priority on implementation? Get more resources? Extend deadlines in the Plans?

Consider the free, online, self-directed, learning module about marketing at http://www.managementhelp.org/np_progs/mkt_mod/market.htm .

Consider the guidebook, *Field Guide to Nonprofit Program Design, Marketing and Evaluation,* from Authenticity Consulting, LLC. Go to the "Publications" link at http://www.authenticityconsulting.com .

How to Ensure Sound Management of Finances and Taxes

The reality of how well, or how poor, a nonprofit is doing is reflected in the nonprofit's finances (if the financial numbers are anywhere accurate). When funders consider whether to provide funds to nonprofits, they usually consider how well the finances are tracked and managed. Overseeing financial management also means overseeing management of assets, such as facilities, major equipment, etc. Even though a nonprofit might be exempt from paying certain federal, state/provincial and local taxes, there still might be certain payroll deductions that need to be withheld from staff paychecks, if staff are employed.

Guidelines for Effective Leadership of Financial Management

If your Board uses Committees, then a Finance Committee would be helpful in this area.

1. **Develop up-to-date fiscal policies and procedures and have them Board-approved.**
These policies specify how finances and monies will be collected, managed, reported and dispersed in a highly accurate and controlled fashion that conforms to laws and regulations and minimizes the likelihood of loss, fraud or malfeasance. New organizations might obtain sample policies and modify them according to the organization's nature and needs.

Sample financial policies are available at http://www.mncn.org
/doc/Sample%20Financial%20Procedures%20Manual.PDF .

2. **Approve an annual operating budget.**
    Usually, the budget is developed and approved near the end of the strategic planning
    activities when planners have identified what resources will need to be obtained and
    supported in order to achieve the goals in the strategic plan.

3. **Establish internal controls for the handling of cash and the approval of expenditures.**
    Fiscal policies and procedures usually specify how cash should be managed, for example,
    that the person who tracks incoming invoices is not the same person who writes checks to
    pay the invoices, thereby minimizing any likelihood that one person could steal funds
    without getting caught.

4. **Ensure all federal and state/provincial payroll taxes are paid.**
    Tax-exempt nonprofits can avoid paying certain taxes. However, payroll taxes must be paid
    from wages and salaries paid to members. In the USA, taxes are for Social Security and
    Medicare. Be sure these taxes are being paid.

5. **Report and review the trends, issues and highlights regarding the finances.**
    Instead of leaders reviewing columns of numbers, have the Board Treasurer and/or Chief
    Executive provide a summary report, in addition to the numbers. The report explains:

    a. Highlights to notice about the numbers, for example, an account that is significantly
        overspent or underspent.

    b. Trends to notice about the numbers, for example, significant tendencies in certain
        accounts that might result in overspend or underspend, which might result in an issue
        later on.

    c. Issues, for example, an account that is so overspent or underspent that Board members
        need to take action on that item now.

6. **Review financial reports, especially cash flow and budget-versus-actual reports.**
    For new or small organizations, a cash-flow statement is extremely important to review
    because it shows whether the nonprofit has the funds to pay its near-term bills or not. The
    Statement of Financial Activities (an income statement) should be reviewed at least quarterly
    and more often if the nonprofit is struggling financially. A Statement of Financial Condition
    (balance sheet) should be reviewed at least quarterly, as well.

7. **Ensure a Form 990 is filed on an annual basis in the USA.**
    Tax-exempt nonprofits normally do not have to file if its gross receipts are under $25,000.

To learn about reporting requirements, go to
http://www.irs.gov/charities/article/0,,id=96103,00.html .

8. **Ensure the nonprofit has adequate insurance coverage.**
    For example, the nonprofit might need general liability insurance to cover situations where someone is hurt on the premises, workers compensation if an employee is hurt on the job, property insurance if a major asset is damaged or destroyed or lost, or Directors and Officers (D&O) Insurance for Board members if someone sues the Board for its actions or lack of actions.

9. **Consider financial audits and/or reviews by external auditors.**
    There are different types of audits and reviews. Typically, an audit is verification by an outside expert of the nonprofit's financial management practices and its financial numbers in terms of accuracy and completeness. There are requirements for nonprofits to have an audit under different circumstances, depending on the state in the USA, if the nonprofit raises more than a certain amount of donations/funding or has grants over a certain threshold. Audits are good way to verify that the numbers on the financial reports are accurate – that is always a strong reassurance to Board members. A review is an analysis by an outside expert on some aspect of financial management, usually of the financial numbers, to report on the quality of that aspect.

10. **Be sure that Board members are trained to analyze and decide on finances.**
    Far too often, only one Board member – the Treasurer – really understands the finances. Some members even pride themselves that they refuse to try to understand finances – it is "just not their thing." Having that stance is irresponsible. Board members' responsibilities for the nonprofit cannot be delegated to anyone else, especially to only one Board member. There should be at least one other Board member who knows the details of the finances, and who probably is on the Finance Committee. All Board members should be trained about how to analyze financial reports, detect where attention is needed, and make necessary decisions to address any issues.

Consider the free, online, self-directed, learning module about finance at http://www.managementhelp.org/np_progs/fnc_mod/fnance.htm .

See the topic, "Nonprofit Fundraising and Grantwriting," in the Free Management Library^{SM} at http://www.managementhelp.org/finance/np_fnce/np_fnce.htm .

Sample financial policies are available at http://www.mncn.org/doc/Sample%20Financial%20Procedures%20Manual.PDF .

How to Advocate for Public Needs – and Lobby Legally

Lobbying consists of activities to directly influence a specific piece of legislation (the creating or modifying of a law), for example, by contacting legislators or hiring lobbyists. This is in comparison to advocacy, which is promoting a position about an issue, for example, sharing information with the public about the need for cessation of smoking.

Nonprofits exist to serve the general public, not only one specific group of people. In return, the general public grants nonprofits the special rights to avoid paying certain taxes and to collect donations that can be deducted from the donor's tax liabilities. Tax-exempt nonprofits that engage primarily in lobbying can be viewed as working to benefit only one specific group of people, and could lose their tax-exempt status, depending on the amount of lobbying they do and report.

Because of this concern, there is a common misconception that nonprofits should not be engaged in lobbying, lest their organizations lose their tax status. Actually, one of the responsibilities of the nonprofit's leaders is to represent the nonprofit to stakeholders, including to enhance conditions for clients of the nonprofit's programs. Board and staff members can, and are expected to, do lobbying. However, there are certain requirements that must be met in order to retain a favorable tax status.

In the USA, the amount of lobbying activities, including preparation, development of an agenda to push to legislators and/or lobbyists, and the dollars spent on these activities, must be "insubstantial" as mentioned in the 1976 Lobby Law. Although the Internal Revenue Service (IRS) does not quantifiably define "insubstantial," a general rule of thumb seems to be less than 10% of revenues. Organizations that choose to engage in an amount of lobbying activities over that amount, and wish to retain their tax status, can elect 501(h) status with the IRS by filing Form 5678. Organizations that want to spend an amount of 20% should consider re-filing the Form 1023 with the IRS to apply for 501(c)(4) status, rather than 501(c)(3) status.

Guidelines for Effective Leadership of Lobbying Activities

If your Board uses Committees, then a Public Policy Committee would be helpful in this area.

1.   **Learn the limitations placed on nonprofits that engage in lobbying.**
     As explained above, nonprofits can – and should – engage in lobbying.

For more information on lobbying, go to http://www.nonprofits.org/npofaq/11/08.html . Also see the Charity Lobbying in the Public Interest website at http://www.clip.org .

An excellent book on this topic is *The Nonprofit Board Member's Guide to Lobbying and Advocacy* by Marcia Avner (Amherst H. Wilder Foundation, 2004).

2.   **Carefully craft a Public Policy Plan with messages and methods to influence legislation.**
     Similar to the design of a Public Relations Plan as itemized in the above section about oversight of outbound marketing, you should clearly identify:

    a.   The specific social issues you want to address.

    b.   The specific results that you want in order to address regarding each issue.

    c.   Who you need to influence in order to get those results.

    d.   How you will influence each of those people.

It may even be worth hiring a professional in public relations or lobbying to help you because you probably will have a very small amount of time with a legislature. Professionals know how to craft and convey a message in a way that is most powerful in getting the attention and consideration of the decision makers.

3.   **Carefully monitor implementation of the Plan.**
Is the Plan being implemented? Are you getting the results that you desired? If not, what should be done? Put more priority on implementation? Get more resources? Extend deadlines in the Plan?

For more information about lobbying, go
http://www.managementhelp.org/tax/np_tax.htm#anchor230047 .

How to Track Performance of Nonprofit, Board and People

Performance is effectively achieving goals and objectives in a timely manner – goals that are directly aligned with the mission and strategic priorities of the organization. A primary responsibility of a nonprofit's leaders is to ensure that the nonprofit remains a high-performing nonprofit. Without specific goals to achieve – or at least monitoring for "best practices" – for the organization, programs and management, leaders have little or no reliable means by which to measure performance.

Guidelines for Effective Leadership of Performance Management

If your Board uses Committees, then an Executive Committee would be helpful in this area, especially if the Executive Committee is comprised of Chairs of each of the other committees.

1.   **Specify goals – what will be achieved, how much, who will achieve them and by when.**
Attention to specifying goals in plans often is as important – or more important – than extensive attention on the wording used in mission, vision and values statements. Specify goals in strategic plans and especially in plans for Board development, program growth, finances and fundraising. Do not worry about the specification of goals having to be perfect the first time, just do your best for now. The specifications can always be changed.

2.   **Monitor status toward achieving specific goals – and then adjust accordingly.**
On a regular basis, monitor whether the goals are being achieved or not. If goals are not being achieved, then increase priority on achieving the goals, allocate more resources to achieve them, or extend the deadlines to reach the goals.

3. **Monitor for "best practices" in different governance and management functions.**
   As mentioned in this guide, there can be wide disagreement about what constitutes "best practices." However, particularly for new or struggling nonprofits, they are much more likely to benefit from at least monitoring if the best practices are being followed than if those nonprofits ignore the best practices altogether.

   Consider "Useful, Free Nonprofit Organizational Assessments" on page 267.

4. **Invite each Board member to evaluate his/her performance on the Board.**
   This can include each member privately using a basic self-assessment tool that asks the member questions about the quality of his/her participation on the Board. Members could be invited to share the results of their self-evaluations in order to get help to improve their participation.

5. **Ensure all Board members formally evaluate the entire Board, at least annually.**
   This includes all members privately completing an assessment tool that asks questions about the quality of the overall Board operations. These Board evaluations often can be done very quickly and conveniently.

6. **Ensure annual, formal evaluation of the Chief Executive (if a CEO role is on the staff).**
   Board members should ensure the CEO has certain responsibilities to carry out, as specified in the CEO's job description. Also, the CEO should have certain annual goals to achieve (performance goals) and these goals should closely align with those in the strategic plan.

   Consider "How Your Board Can Evaluate Your CEO" on page 56.

7. **Ensure evaluation of staff, according to procedures in personnel policies.**
   All staff, including the CEO, deserve feedback about the quality of their performance. That feedback, including in the form of performance evaluations, should be done according to guidelines in up-to-date personnel policies.

8. **Most important, evaluate programs to verify they are meeting community needs.**
   This means ensuring that outcomes-based program evaluations occur to verify that each program is indeed meeting the needs that the nonprofit was formed to meet.

   Consider the free, online, self-directed, learning module about evaluation at http://www.managementhelp.org/np_progs/evl_mod/evl_mod.htm .

   Consider the guidebook, *Field Guide to Nonprofit Program Design, Marketing and Evaluation,* from Authenticity Consulting, LLC. Go to the "Publications" link at http://www.authenticityconsulting.com .

How to Identify and Avoid Risks to the Nonprofit

The nonprofit's leaders are responsible to ensure the reliable, ongoing and effective operations of their nonprofit. That includes ensuring that the most critical assets and functions are protected from sudden loss or significant damage. It also includes ensuring the means to quickly recover from those unfortunate situations. Most nonprofits have very limited resources, so damage or loss to any of them usually means a significant – even traumatic – loss to operations. Therefore, risk management is an extremely important topic for Board members to address.

Guidelines for Effective Leadership of Risk Management

If your Board uses Committees, then a Finance Committee or Audit Committee would be helpful in this area.

Avoiding Sudden Loss or Damage

1. **Compensate the CEO commensurate to his/her capabilities and responsibilities.**
    One of the most frequently cited reasons that CEOs of nonprofits leave their jobs is because of significantly low pay. Very often, they could make 30% to 50% more in the for-profit sector or in working independently, for example, as a consultant. Board members must recognize this and not rely on CEOs working for low pay because "we're a nonprofit."

2. **Undertake ongoing CEO succession planning.**
    If the CEO suddenly left that position because of illness, death, firing or other reasons, it would be traumatic for the nonprofit. Board members are responsible to minimize that affect on the nonprofit, as much as possible.

 Consider "How Your Board Can Ensure Smooth Succession to New CEO When Needed" on page 56.

3. **Ensure up-to-date job descriptions for all Board roles and critical staff roles.**
    In case any of their positions needs to be filled soon, at least there will be general descriptions so that others can more quickly understand the positions in order to help fill them as soon as possible.

4. **Ensure protected and stable facilities.**
    Computers and peripherals should have consistent levels of electrical protection, so that electrical surges do not damage them. Facilities should have adequate fire protection, including water sprinklers that would not damage critical electrical components. All important information and materials should be locked, including password protection on computer files.

Avoiding Damaging Acts

1. **Have up-to-date, Board-approved personnel policies for paid and volunteer staff.**
    Personnel policies specify how personnel should be hired, supervised and fired in accordance with employment laws that ensure fair, equitable and legally compliant treatment of others. Personnel, particularly those who supervise others, should be trained on the policies.

2. **Conduct background checks on potential new hires.**
Background checks can detect if a person has committed crimes, major or minor in nature, that might suggest tendencies for how the person will act in the workplace. These checks also ensure the public that the nonprofit's Board and staff members are suitable for working with the public.

3. **Conduct Board orientations once a year for members.**
Board orientations make members aware of the unique aspects of the Board and nonprofit, including the Board's policies, for example, about ethics, conflict-of-interest, whistleblowers and document retention/destruction.

4. **Establish a Whistleblower Policy.**
The policy should specify how Board members, staff and others can safely report an alleged or actual organizational behavior or practice event is illegal, unethical or inappropriate, without retaliation to the whistleblower.

5. **Establish a Board Ethics Policy.**
The policy should specify the types of behaviors to conduct and/or to avoid in order to ensure that Board members conduct themselves in a manner that treats others fairly, equitably and that is legally compliant.

6. **Ensure accurate and Board-approved meeting minutes.**
The minutes formally document Board members' deliberations, decisions and actions and, thus, serve as an accurate record to explain or justify to others the intentions, participation and actions of Board members.

7. **Establish up-to-date, Board-approved fiscal policies and procedures.**
These procedures ensure that the activities in financial management are conducted in a highly thorough, accurate and useful manner that also minimizes the likelihood of malfeasance, including theft, fraud or misappropriation of funds.

8. **Annually conduct a financial audit and/or review.**
The audit or review verifies the usefulness and accuracy of some or all aspects of financial management and, thus, greatly increases the likelihood that financial numbers and reports are indeed accurate.

Recovering from Loss

1. **All major functions should have written plans that specify current goals and priorities.**
Organizations can more quickly recover if plans are documented so that personnel can quickly reference them to continue addressing important priorities. These should include the strategic plan, program plans, staffing plans, marketing plan and fundraising plan.

2. **Establish written procedures for routine tasks in the workplace.**
These procedures can be referenced by personnel to quickly restore and resume the practices, thereby reducing adverse impact on operations as a result of a major interruption in operations. Procedures might in regarding, for example, to ordering supplies, operating facilities, bringing clients into a program, delivering services and evaluating services.

3. **Keep contact lists of personnel and major stakeholders.**
Document their names, the role that the personnel have with the nonprofit, and contact information so they can be contacted, especially to help restore operations.

4.   **Have suitable insurance coverage.**
     Consider general liability insurance in case someone sues because of workplace injury.
     Consider property insurance in case property is damaged or lost. Consider professional
     liability insurance in case someone sues as a result of what he/she perceives as malpractice
     in programs. Consider Directors and Officers Insurance to pay any lawsuits lost by Board
     members when someone sued the Board, alleging damage because of members' actions or
     inactions. Consider workers' compensation insurance in case someone is injured on the job.

5.   **Establish a Document Retention/Destruction Policy.**
     The policy should specify which documents are retained for how long before they can be
     destroyed. It also should specify how the nonprofit will completely cooperate if any
     documents are required by agencies investigating the nonprofit or its affiliates.

Sample policies are in the Board topic in the Free Management
Library at
http://www.managementhelp.org/boards/boards.htm#anchor1322914 .

There is more information and materials on risk management at
Nonprofit Risk Management Center at http://www.nonprofitrisk.org .

How to Ensure Sustainability of Nonprofit, Programs, People and Money

Sustainability often is misunderstood. It is more than generating enough money to keep paying the
bills. True long-term, organizational sustainability for an organization involves four dimensions,
including strategic, programs, personnel and finances. If sufficient attention is given to the first three
dimensions of sustainability, then financial sustainability is much more likely to occur – and much
easier to accomplish. The following guidelines help leaders ensure sustainability in each dimension.

Guidelines for Effective Leadership of Practices for Sustainability

If your Board uses Committees, then an Executive Committee would be helpful in this area,
especially if it is comprised of Chairs of other committees, because that form of Executive
Committee is more likely to have representatives from each of the four dimensions of sustainability
as listed below.

Strategic Dimension of Sustainability

1.   **Ensure realistic vision and strategic goals for the organization.**
     If these are not realistic, then the organization will be trying to do too much. As a result, it
     will very likely run out of resources, including money and people.

2.   **Ensure realistic strategies to achieve the vision and goals.**
     Even if the vision and goals are realistic, if the efforts to achieve them are unrealistic, then
     the organization will have the same problems as mentioned above.

3. **Modify the vision, goals and strategies to remain realistic when implementing plans.**
    One of the most important parts of a plans is often forgotten – procedures for how to change the plans. Consider extending deadlines to achieve goals or dropping them altogether if that is what it takes to ensure long-term sustainability.

Program Dimension of Sustainability

1. **Verify what clients truly need, versus what they only want – or programs will fail.**
    Clients will come to programs based on what they want, and they will stay based on what they need. If programs are meeting the true needs of clients, then programs will fail. Consider basic market research to verify what the clients really need.

2. **Evaluate effectiveness and outcomes of programs to verify they are meeting needs.**
    Effectiveness is in regard to the quality of program's processes in delivering services. Outcomes are in regard to the actual changes in clients as a result of participating in programs. Consider doing process and outcomes evaluations for each program.

3. **Change program methods, if needed, to improve quality in order to meet client needs.**
    Programs should undergo continuous improvement in order to remain effective. Listen to the opinions of the clients about the program. Consider results of program evaluations. Then make changes to the programs accordingly.

Personnel Dimension of Sustainability

1. **Ensure staff has sufficient expertise, training and resources to provide programs.**
    Even if the vision, goals and strategies are realistic and the programs are designed well, staff members have to continue to operate high-quality programs. Often, that is a matter of staff members having strong expertise, getting training and having sufficient resources.

2. **Ensure staff members are using all of their resources to provide programs.**
    This is a matter of effective supervision. Ensure there is effective delegation to staff members (setting goals, sharing feedback, adjusting performance) and evaluation of staff such that members are always doing their best.

3. **Ensuring redundancy and succession planning for staff in case people leave.**
    In a typical nonprofit, programs and other operations would be damaged significantly if involved staff members suddenly were no longer available. Ensure that key staff members have suitable "backup" personnel who also can do much of their jobs, and that guidelines and procedures exist for jobs, as much as possible.

Financial Dimension of Sustainability

1. **Identify how much funding (fees and/or fundraising) is needed to offset expenses.**
    Develop an annual budget and identify any deficits to know how much funding is needed, so that fundraising targets and/or fees can be adjusted accordingly to rid those deficits.

2. **Do adequate prospect research to identify *all* likely sources in fundraising.**
    Do not do the same fundraising activities, but even harder. For example, fundraising events often require a substantial amount of time and often do not generate much in funds. Research all sources among individuals, foundations, corporation and government.

3. **Allocate sufficient funding to administration and programs.**
    Know how much money each program needs. To do that, develop program-based, or functional, budgets. Those budgets identify the expected revenues and expenses associated with each program, along with a percentage allocation of overhead (expenses common to all budget, for example, the salary of the Chief Executive, facilities, costs, etc.) to each.

4. **Track expenditures and revenues to promptly address financial priorities and issues.**
    Nonprofits, especially if they have ever experienced financial hardships, often do a good job of tracking expenditures. Two reports are useful in particular, a budget-versus-actual report and cash-flow reports.

5. **Ensure adequate reserves and contingencies of funding if revenues are very low.**
    Establish a policy to set aside some percentage of your revenue, for example, 10% to be available in case of emergency. When budgeting, plan a couple of scenarios, one where all expected revenue arrives and another where, for example, only 70% of revenue arrives. Then, if there is a shortage of revenue, the nonprofit can reference the latter scenario to more quickly respond.

How to Ensure Transparency and Accountability in Governance and Operations

Nonprofits are entrusted by their communities to successfully meet a variety of public and social needs in the community. In return, the public can grant the nonprofits tax-exempt and/or charitable status. The communities expect the nonprofits to continually prove that the work they are doing is really meeting the needs of the community – the communities want to know what the nonprofits are really doing. The nonprofits need to be transparent and accountable to the public.

Board transparency means Board members always providing full disclosure and explanation of the nonprofit's governance, finances and effects on communities, and also willingly supporting stakeholders' efforts to understand that information. Board accountability means members continually making the nonprofits and themselves responsible to meet the expectations of stakeholders, and verifying with those stakeholders that their expectations are indeed being met.

The Sarbanes-Oxley Act of 2002 in the USA (commonly referred to as SOX) instituted certain requirements to make publicly traded companies more legally and ethically compliant, especially in financial practices, by increasing transparency and accountability of governance. For example, some requirements include establishing a skilled and independent Board Audit Committee (a Board committee comprised of independent Board members); the CEO and financial officers certifying accuracy of financial statements; and instituting policies for avoiding conflict of interest, having whistleblower protection and for retention/destruction of documents. Although the requirements apply primarily to publicly traded companies, the policies on conflict-of-interest, whistleblower and document retention/destruction can apply to nonprofit corporations, as well.

There is more information about *Sarbanes-Oxley* at
http://www.abanet.org/abastore/books/inside_practice/july_2005/oxley.htm

Guidelines for Effective Leadership to Ensure Transparency and Accountability

If your Board uses Committees, then a Finance Committee or Audit Committee would be helpful in this area.

1. **Recruit independent Board members.**
    These are members who are not staff members, have no other business affiliation with the nonprofit, and are not very close and personal friends of any executives in the nonprofit. Independent Board members are much more likely to challenge opinions and decisions offered by the CEO and other Board members.

2. **Establish a Board Conflict-of-Interest Policy.**
    The policy should explain conflict of interest, give examples, and specify what Board members can do to report and avoid apparent or real conflict-of-interest situations.

3. **Establish a Whistleblower Policy.**
    The policy should specify how Board members, staff and others (the Whistleblower) can readily report apparent or actual events of illegal, unethical or inappropriate behaviors and practices, without retribution to the Whistleblower.

4. **Establish a Document Retention/Destruction Policy.**
    The policy should specify which documents (hardcopy and computer-based) are retained and for how long, how documents are protected, and how documents are made readily available in the event of potential or actual criminal proceedings that might involve those documents.

5. **Establish a Board ethics policy.**
    The policy should suggest behaviors for Board members to follow and/or avoid in order to ensure legally compliant, fair and equitable dealings when acting as members of the nonprofit's Board.

 Sample policies are in the Board topic in the Free Management Library at http://www.managementhelp.org/boards/boards.htm#anchor1322914 .

6. **Utilize financial audits and/or reviews.**
    The reporting of accurate financial information to the public is a strong requirement for achieving transparency and accountability. One approach to verifying financial accuracy in is via reviews and/or audits. Not all nonprofits are required to undergo annual financial audits. (Nonprofits should identify requirements for audits by contacting the appropriate government agency, for example, the Attorney General's office in their state in the USA.) There are different types of financial analysis and services related to audits and reviews, ranging from a basic review of financial practices to the auditing for financial practices and their resulting financial data. A significant benefit of a review, especially an audit, is having an outsider's objective conclusions and recommendations regarding financial practices and/or information.

7. **Board review and approval of the annual filing to appropriate tax agency.**
    Certain charitable organizations in the USA must file an IRS Form 990 (or Form 990-EZ or Form 990-PF) to the Internal Revenue Service. Board members formally approve the Form, thereby, indicating that each member asserts that the information is accurate.

8. **Train Board and key staff members how to analyze and decide about finances.**
    Frequently, nonprofit Boards have one member – the Treasurer – who is comfortable dealing with "the numbers," each and every Board member is responsible to ensure that the numbers are accurate and that the nonprofit is making the best decisions about those numbers. Therefore, all Board members should receive relevant, up-to-date and accurate financial information, and all should be trained how to understand and respond to that information.

9. **Make publicly available, information about finances, governance and operations.**
    For example, on the nonprofit's website, provide: Articles of Incorporation, By-Laws, most recent strategic plan, annual report, list of Board members, Board policies, Form 990s, recent audited financial reports, and list of funders.

10. **Finally, be accountable to verify that programs are meeting community needs.**
    Accountability is about more than efforts to avoid losing lawsuits – it is about Board members doing their primary job to verify that their nonprofit is indeed meeting the need in the community that the nonprofit was formed to meet.

How to Lead Organizational Change and Capacity Building

There are increasing social problems to be solved by nonprofits, at a time when there is increasing competition for funding. The workforce is more diverse than it has ever been, so leadership and management styles must accommodate this diversity. Funders and the public are expecting more accountability in spending of funding and results of programs. Nonprofit organizations are undergoing significant changes like never before. As a result, one of the most important applications of leadership in nonprofits is leadership of change in the organization.

Why Change and Capacity Building Can Be Difficult to Accomplish

Change can be difficult for you to accomplish for a variety of reasons.

- **People are afraid of the unknown.**
  They communicate their fear through direct means, such as complaining about the plans for change. Or, they communicate their fear indirectly, for example, by not attending meetings to plan the change.

- **People think things are just fine.**
  This might occur if the leaders in the nonprofit have not adequately communicated the need for the change.

- **Many people are inherently cynical about change.**
  This cynicism often occurs if earlier attempts at change were unsuccessful, and not explained to employees and volunteers.

- **Many doubt there are effective means to accomplish successful change.**
  They may have read publications in which writers assert that most organizational change efforts fail.

- **There may be conflicting goals in the organizational change effort.**
  Conflicting goals might be, for example, to significantly increase resources to accomplish change, yet substantially cut costs to remain viable. That conflict can occur, especially if staff members were not involved in plans for the change.

- **Change often goes against values held dear by members in the organization.**
  The change may go against how members believe things should be done. For example, they might disagree that nonprofits should pursue "making a profit" when implementing plans for an earned-income venture.

- **The original reason for the change, changes.**
  This situation is not uncommon, particularly in nonprofits with clients whose needs are rapidly changing or in nonprofits with rapidly changing environments.

- **People get burnout during the change effort.**
  Organizational change usually takes longer to achieve than most people expect. Some experts assert that successful change can take from several months to several years.

- **Leaders of the change end up leaving the organization.**
  Especially in smaller nonprofits or nonprofits with very limited resources, leaders might not believe they are receiving sufficient value for what they are investing in the nonprofit. They might conclude that it is better to just leave. Or, the change may not be going as expected, and the leaders are asked to leave.

- **Participants do not understand the nature of planned change.**
  Frequently, participants expect the change to be according to a well-designed, well-organized effort that has few surprises. When surprises do occur, they lose faith in the change effort and seek to abandon it.

Requirements for Successful Organizational Change in Nonprofits

There is not one standard procedure for accomplishing successful, significant change in all types of organizations. However, there has been a substantial about of research lately about what seems to be in common among projects for change that are deemed to be successful by the leaders in the organizations. So rather than looking for a procedure, perhaps it is most reasonable to consider a set of guidelines based on that research. Cummings and Worley (1995) describe a comprehensive, five-phase, general process for managing change, including: 1) motivating change, 2) creating vision, 3) developing political support, 4) managing the transition and 5) sustaining momentum. As you read the following paragraphs, think about how the guidelines might apply in your organization.

Phase 1: Motivating Change

This phase includes creating a readiness for change in the organization and developing approaches to overcome resistance to change. General guidelines for managing this phase include enlightening members of the organization about the need for change, expressing the current status of the organization and where it needs to be in the future, and developing realistic approaches about how change might be accomplished. Next, organization leaders need to recognize that people in the organization are likely to resist making major changes for a variety of reasons, including fear of the unknown, inadequacy to deal with the change and whether the change will result in an adverse effect on their jobs. People need to feel that their concerns are being heard. Leaders must widely communicate the need for the change and how the change can be accomplished successfully. Leaders must listen to the employees and volunteers – people need to feel that the approach to change will include their strong input and ongoing involvement.

Phase 2: Creating Vision

Leaders in the organization must articulate a clear vision that describes what the change effort is striving to accomplish. Ideally, people in the organization have strong input to the creation of the vision and how it can be achieved. The vision should clearly depict how the achievement of the vision will improve the organization. It is critically important that people believe that the vision is relevant and realistic. Research indicates that cynicism is increasing in organizations in regard to change efforts. People do not want to hear the need for the latest "silver bullet" that will completely turn the organization around and make things better for everyone all the time. They want to feel respected enough by leaders to be involved and to work toward a vision that is realistic, yet promising in the long run.

Often the vision is described in terms of overall outcomes (or changes) to be achieved by all or parts of the organization, including associated goals and objectives to achieve the outcomes. Sometimes, an overall purpose, or mission, is associated with the effort to achieve the vision, as well.

Phase 3: Developing Political Support

This phase of change management is often overlooked, yet it is the phase that often stops successful change from occurring. Politics in organizations is about power. Power is important among members of the organization when striving for the resources and influence necessary to successfully carry out their jobs. Power is also important when striving to maintain jobs and job security. Power usually comes from credibility, whether from strong expertise or integrity. Power also comes from the authority of one's position in the organization.

Some people have a strong negative reaction when talking about power because power often is associated with negative applications, for example, manipulation, abuse or harassment. However, power, like conflict, exists in all human interactions and is not always bad. It is how power and conflict are used and managed that determine how power and conflict should be perceived.

Matters of power and politics are critically important to recognize and manage during organizational change activities. Change often means shifts in power across management levels, functions, programs and groups. To be successful, the change effort must recruit the support of all key power players, for example, senior management, subject matter experts and others who are recognized as having strong expertise and integrity.

A strong mechanism for ensuring alignment of power with the change effort is to develop a network of power-players who interact and count on each other to support and guide the change effort. Means to manage power can include ensuring that all power-players are involved in recognizing the need for change, developing the vision and methods to achieve the vision, and organization-wide communication about the status of change. Any recommendations or concerns expressed by those in power must be promptly recognized and worked through.

Phase 4: Managing Transition

This phase occurs when the organization works to make the actual transition from the current state to the future state. In consultations, this phase usually is called implementation of the action plans. The plans can include a wide variety of "interventions," or activities designed to make a change in the organization, for example, creating and/or modifying major structures and processes in the organization. These changes might require ongoing coaching, training and enforcement of new policies and procedures. In addition, means of effective change management must continue, including strong, clear, ongoing communication about the need for the change, status of the change, and solicitation of organization members' continuing input to the change effort.

Ideally, the various actions are integrated into one overall Change Management Plan (or an overall Strategic Plan) that includes specific objectives, or milestones, that must be accomplished by various deadlines, along with responsibilities for achieving each objective. Rarely are these plans implemented exactly as planned. Thus, as important as developing the plan, is making the many ongoing adjustments to the plan with key members of the organization, while keeping other members up-to-date about the changes and the reasons for them.

Phase 5: Sustaining Momentum

Often, the most difficult phase in managing change is this phase when leaders work to sustain the momentum of the implementation and adjustment of plans. Change efforts can encounter a wide variety of obstacles, for example, strong resistance from members of the organization, sudden departure of a key leader in the organization, or a dramatic cut in funding. Strong, visible, ongoing support from top leadership is critically important to show overall credibility and accountabilities in the change effort. Those participating in the change effort often require ongoing support, often in the form of provision of resources, along with training and coaching. The role of support cannot be minimized – despite its importance during organizational change, the role of support is often forgotten. Employee performance management systems play a critical role in this phase of organizational change, including in setting goals, sharing feedback about accomplishment of goals, rewarding behaviors that successfully achieve goals and accomplish change, and addressing performance issues.

Major Roles During Change and Capacity Building

The process of organizational change can include a variety of key roles. Various individuals or groups can fill these roles at various times during the change process. Sometimes, individuals or groups can fill more than one role.

Change Initiator

It is conventional wisdom among experts in organizational change that successful change is often provoked by a deep "hurt" or crisis in the organization, for example, dramatic cut in funding, loss of a key leader in the organization, warnings from a major funder, or even actions of a key competitor. It is not uncommon then that someone inside the organization reacts to that deep hurt and suggests the need for a major change effort. Often the person who initiates the change is not the person who becomes the primary change agent.

Change Agent

The change agent is the person responsible for organizing and coordinating the overall change effort. Different people can fill the change agent role at different times during the project. For example, an outside consultant might be the first change agent. After the project plan has been developed and begins implementation, the change agent might be an implementation team comprised of people from the organization. If the change effort stalls out, the change agent might be a top leader in the organization who intercedes to ensure the change process continues in a timely fashion.

Champion for Change

Change efforts often require a person or group who continues to build and sustain strong enthusiasm about the change. This includes reminding everyone of why the change is occurring in the first place, and the many benefits that have come and will come from the change process. The champion might be the same person as the change agent at various times in the project.

Sponsor of Change

Usually, there is a one key internal person or department that is officially the "sponsor," or official role responsible for coordinating the change process. In large organizations, that sponsor often is a department, such as Human Resources, Strategic Planning or Information Technology. In smaller organizations, the sponsor might be a team of senior leaders working to ensure that the change effort stays on schedule and is sustained by ongoing provision of resources and training.

Leadership, Supervision and Delegation

In this Field Guide, leadership is defined as setting direction and influencing people to follow that direction. A person can lead themselves, other individuals, other groups or an entire organization. Supervision is guiding the development and productivity of people in the organization. Effective supervisors are able to achieve goals by guiding the work of other people – by delegating.

Note that supervisors exist throughout a nonprofit organization, depending on the particular structure of the Board and staff. For example, the Board of Directors supervises the Chief Executive Officer (CEO), the CEO supervises program directors or executive assistants, and program directors supervise other program staff.

The topic of leadership has become one of the most prominent topics in all of management literature today. It is almost impossible to find a general management book that does not include frequent mention of the topic of leadership. There are a variety of reasons for this, one of the most important being that successful organizational change requires strong, ongoing and visible leadership in support of that change. Leaders must model the type of behaviors that they want to see in their organization. Other reasons include:

- Leaders who work with others in the organization to clarify those desired results define the vision and goals, or desired results, for change.

- Leaders in the organization must "walk their talk" – they must behave according to the same values and behaviors that are to be accomplished by the change effort.

- Leaders must ensure the ongoing accountabilities, resources and support to ensure that actions are taken to accomplish the overall change effort.

There simply is no substitute for the role that leadership and supervision play in accomplishing successful organizational change. Thus, it is extremely important that leaders and supervisors in the organization have a strong understanding of basic principles of successful change in organizations.

How to Regularly Measure Overall Health of the Nonprofit

One of the biggest questions that lurk – consciously or unconsciously – at the back of leaders' minds is "How's our nonprofit really doing? Are we verifying that we're effectively and efficiently meeting specific needs in the community?" Despite the importance of this question, nonprofit leaders rarely pursue means to measure the overall health of their nonprofit, even though there are a variety of free, easy-to-use tools available. The tools are usually comprehensive questionnaires that ask about the occurrence of certain "best practices" in the organization or the tools suggest standards of excellence for the nonprofits to pursue in their operations. The tools might ask questions or suggest standards for operations, including: Boards, strategic planning, programs, staffing, finances, fundraising, facilities and evaluations.

Use of the tools, especially questionnaires, can take as little as 30 minutes from each Board member and senior staff member, and the analyses and reporting of results can take 2-3 hours – this is time very well spent for the health of the organization.

Guidelines for Measuring Health of the Nonprofit

If your Board uses Committees, then a Planning Committee would be helpful, for example, if the assessment is being done as part of the strategic planning process.

1. **Annually, do the quick assessment near the beginning or middle of the fiscal year.**
   This timing is intended to produce results of the assessment that can be considered during strategic planning (strategic planning often is best to do in the middle of the fiscal year in time to produce an approved budget for the next fiscal year).

2. **Or do the assessment whenever the nonprofit seems to have many chronic struggles.**
   For example, an assessment is useful if the nonprofit continues to have financial shortfalls, high turnover, or frequent conflicts among Board and staff members. The assessment is a great way to identify the "root causes" of issues, rather than focusing only on symptoms.

3. **Be careful not to consider the tools as if they portray the "perfect" nonprofit.**
   The practical purpose of these tools is to identify the most important functions or practices that need to be improved in the nonprofit for now, not to identify each and every little issue. Answers to the questions should be informed by your own understanding of the nonprofit.

4. **Appoint a small group of Board and staff members to oversee assessment activity.**
   The group would identify which tool to use, notify others about the purpose of the tool and how to use it, and coordinate the analysis and reporting of results. They might be a project team that works closely with an outside consultant to administer the assessment.

5. **If it is the nonprofit's first time to do an organizational assessment, consider help.**
   You might hire a consultant to work with the group, including to recommend a tool, guide the planning and communication about use of the tool, analyze and report the results, and generate recommendations to address any issues found in the results.

6. **Include recommendations from the assessment in the strategic and Board plans.**
   Be sure that the recommendations somehow are captured in other plans, which greatly increases the likelihood that the recommendations will be followed. The best plans (strategic plans, Board development plans, marketing plans, program plans, etc.), include specification of who will do what and by when and also a means to track implementation.

Consider "Useful, Free Nonprofit Organizational Assessments" on page 267.

How to Focus on Real Causes of Problems, Not Just Symptoms

Leaders are charged to make very important decisions about their nonprofits. In their roles, they often hear about major, ongoing problems. Often, they do not fully understand the situations and so they end up making the wrong decisions. Staff members also do not understand how to identify the true causes of problems. So everyone ends up focusing on the symptoms of the problems, rather than solving the problems. Here are some common examples:

- The nonprofit keeps running out of money. Board and staff members continue to believe that the solution to their problems is to keep doing more fundraising – but the cash crises continue to occur. So the Chief Executive blames the Board for not doing enough fundraising.

- Programs have very poor attendance. Board members continue to tell the Chief Executive that he/she must do a better job of getting the word out – but increased advertising is not making any difference. So the Board blames the Chief Executive.

- Leaders continue to notice increasing conflicts and high turnover among Board and staff members. Board members tell the Chief Executive to get some leadership training. The Chief Executive does and later tells the Board that the problem is also caused by poor strategic planning. Board members disagree and lose confidence in their Chief Executive.

In these examples, the Board and Chief Executive are dealing with the symptoms of the problem, rather than the real causes. Wise leaders can see beyond the symptoms to get at the real solutions. Table IV:1 and the rest of this section describe one way to understand the inner workings of nonprofits and how to be more successful at resolving problems for the long-term. Notice how the functions in a nonprofit seem to occur in a cycle, from top to bottom and back to the top again. As you read the rest of this section, notice how problems often show up as symptoms in functions near the bottom of the table, but are resolved by addressing functions at the top.

155

Table IV:1 – Cycle of Important Functions in Nonprofits

Inputs: Unmet community needs, input from stakeholders, funding, laws and regulations, etc.		
System Loop	**Major Functions**	**Comments**
Planning	Strategic planning for organization – establish: (mission? vision? values? goals?)	• All activities are integrated with each other.
	Planning for each program – determine: (clients? outcomes? services? marketing? costs?)	
	Resource planning – need what: (people? fundraising/revenue? technologies? other?)	• Driving force behind all activities is leadership among Board and staff.
Developing	Revenue / fundraising development (for major activities)	
	Board, staff and volunteer development (recruiting, training, organizing)	
	Development of other resources (facilities, supplies, policies, procedures, etc.)	• Leadership sets direction, guides resources toward the direction, and makes adjustments to keep resources on track.
Operating	Supervision and teamwork	
	Program operations	
	Advertising and promotions	
	Facilities management	• Strategic goals set direction for organization and suggest performance goals for Board and staff.
	Financial management	
	Administration	
Evaluating	Board	
	Individuals	
	Programs	• Communicating about these goals is key to achieving them.
	Processes	
	Organization	
Outputs: Community needs that were verified to have been met by the nonprofit, for example, by conducting program outcome evaluations		

156

Table IV:1 includes the roles and integration of standard management functions, including the planning, implementation and evaluation of programs, staffing, marketing, finances, fundraising and facilities. The relationships between these functions and common symptoms are described here.

Planning

1. **Poor strategic planning causes symptoms throughout the organization.**
   During strategic planning, members of the Board and staff determine the overall purpose (mission) and direction (vision and goals) for the nonprofit, as well as the methods (values, strategies and programs) for the nonprofit to work toward the purpose and direction. The strategic planning process provides direction and efficiency to all other major functions in the organization. Thus, if strategic planning is not done well, symptoms of the problem can show up in Board operations, programs, staffing, fundraising and finances. To address these symptoms, strategic planning must be improved.

2. **Poor program planning causes symptoms, especially in finances and fundraising.**
   During program planning, the marketing research (or "inbound marketing") activities are conducted to identify: specific community needs for the nonprofit to meet, what outcomes are needed to meet those needs, what specific groups of clients to serve, and how to serve them to achieve those outcomes. Thus, if program planning is not done well, programs will not be targeted where they are needed or will not be meeting the needs of clients. This will result in poor participation of programs and in decreased revenues and ineffective fundraising. Many problems commonly associated with financial shortfalls and fundraising are really the result of poor program planning. Until program planning is improved, attempts to improve fundraising and financial management are likely to be ineffective.

3. **Poor resource planning causes symptoms, especially in staffing and funding.**
   During resource planning, planners identify what resources (the best Board and staff members, money, trainings, facilities, etc.) are needed to most effectively work toward the mission and provide the best programs. Thus, if resource planning is not done well, the Board and staff members might not be the best for the nonprofit, and funding might be inadequate. Facilities might be insufficient, as well. This can cause related symptoms, such as conflicts and burnout among Board and staff members. Many problems commonly associated with Boards, staffing and funding are really the result of poor resource planning, which, in turn, needs good strategic and program planning.

Developing

4. **Successful fundraising needs good strategic, program and resource planning.**
   Fundraising is often a key component of resource development, which might also include earned-income, in-kind donations, or human resource development. Strategic and program planning clarifies what programs are needed and identifies budgets for the coming years. Program planning specifies how much money the programs might earn (expected revenues), how much money they might cost (expected expenses) and if there are any deficits (expenses exceeding revenue) for the programs. The deficits often are addressed by fundraising. If the planning for fundraising is not based on good strategic and program planning, then the fundraising target (the amount to raise by fundraising) will always be vague and changing, resulting in much frustration among those doing the fundraising. In addition, funders will quickly recognize that the nonprofit has not been doing the right kind of planning, so they will not be likely to invest in the nonprofit. Problems associated with fundraising often are symptoms of problems in strategic and program planning.

5. **Board, staff and volunteer development need good strategic and program planning.**
    Members of the Board and staff are developed first by identifying what expertise is needed to achieve the goals in the strategic and program plans. Then the best members are recruited, trained and organized in a manner that best achieves the goals in the strategic and program plans. If those plans are not done well, then ongoing confusion, conflicts and inefficiencies can occur, resulting on high turnover and poor performance of the Board and staff. Program and administrative operations can suffer. Problems with Board and staff members can be symptoms of poor overall planning and resource development, including recruitment, selection, organization and development of members.

6. **Successful operations require clarification of roles, and some policies and procedures.**
    There are a variety of types of resources (other than money and people) that needed to be obtained and developed, for example, facilities, equipment, roles, policies and procedures. Perhaps most important among these resources are roles, policies and procedures. They form the "glue" that aligns and integrates the resources of money and people. If they are not established, they can cause significant symptoms, such as increasing inefficiencies, conflicts and turnover. The best solution to these conflicts might be to clarify roles, policies and procedures, rather than chastising people to make them get along better with each other.

Operating

By now, you understand that problems that show up in the day-to-day activities (for example, in supervision, program operations, financial management, fundraising, advertising, etc.) are often symptoms of larger problems in planning and resource development. Thus, to address those symptoms for the long-term, Board and staff members must ensure that planning and resource development were done well. Without that understanding among Board and staff members, they will likely continue to focus primarily on the symptoms, making things much worse in the long term.

Below, are descriptions of other major functions in nonprofits and how they are integrated and related to each other.

7. **Supervision and teamwork**
    A supervisor is someone who oversees the progress and productivity of people who report directly to the supervisor. Thus, a Board supervises the Chief Executive Officer, and a CEO supervises, for example, the Program Director (if the nonprofit chooses to have a CEO or any paid staff at all). Teamwork is about how people work together to coordinate goals, roles, leadership and communication. The activities of supervision and teamwork are critical to the success of a nonprofit because those activities ensure that goals are established in accordance with strategic and program goals, progress toward the goals is monitored, and adjustments are made among individuals to more effectively achieve the goals. Many times, recurring problems in other types of operating activities are really symptoms of poor teamwork.

8. **Program operations**
    This includes the ongoing activities that provide services directly to the clients. The nature of these activities depends on the types of needs met by the program. For example, health services often require highly trained program staff and technologies. Food shelves require large facilities to store groceries. The success of programs depends a great deal on the effectiveness of strategic and program planning and of teamwork in the organization.

9. **Advertising and promotions**

These "outbound" marketing activities are geared to inform stakeholders (clients, funders, community leaders) about new and current programs, and also to keep those programs in the minds of stakeholders. Many times, problems in advertising and promotions are the result of poor program planning, such as unclear identification of what specific groups of clients should be served, the needs of each group, and how the programs meet each need.

10. **Facilities management**

This includes identifying what major facilities will be needed and managed, such as buildings, equipment and computer systems. The need for major facilities is identified during resource planning. Thus, problems caused by lack of facilities often are a result of poor resource planning. Ineffective use of facilities might be a symptom poor staff development.

11. **Financial management**

Activities of financial management include documenting financial transactions (bookkeeping), generating and analyzing financial statements, and making adjustments to budgets based on the various analyses. This is usually done to Board-approved fiscal policies and procedures. Many times, people report problems with finances when they really mean problems with inadequate funding. Those problems are often caused by ineffective program planning, resource development and/or fundraising activities. Problems that are truly about financial management often can be addressed by training personnel about bookkeeping, and about generating and analyzing financial statements.

12. **Administrative activities**

This includes the extensive range of detailed activities that must be coordinated and conducted on a daily basis to ensure the efficient operations of the nonprofit. Many people think of these activities as clerical, or "paperwork." Problems with administrative tasks often are the result of poor resource planning and staff development, or lack of appreciation for policies and procedures.

Evaluating

13. **Board self-evaluation**

Members of the Board of Directors should regularly evaluate the quality of their activities on a regular basis. Activities might include staffing the Board with new members, developing the members into well-trained and resourced members, discussing and debating topics to make wise decisions, and supervising the CEO. Probably the biggest problem with Board self-evaluation is that it does not occur frequently enough. As a result, Board members have no clear impression of how they are performing as members of a governing Board. Poor Board operations, when undetected, can adversely affect the entire organization.

14. **Staff and volunteer (individual) performance evaluation**

Most of us are familiar with employee performance appraisals, which evaluate the quality of an individual's performance in their position in the organization. Ideally, those appraisals reference the individual's written job description and performance goals to assess the quality of the individual's progress toward achieving the desired results described in those documents. Continued problems in individual performance often are the results of poor strategic planning, program planning, staff development and communications. If overall planning is not done effectively, individuals can experience continued frustration, stress and low morale, resulting in their poor overall performance. If goals that result from planning are not clearly communicated, the individual may not understand how to succeed or perform effectively. Experienced leaders have learned that continued problems in performance are not always the result of a poor work ethic – the recurring problems may be the result of larger, more systemic problems in the organizations.

15. **Program evaluation**
Program evaluations have become much more common, particularly because many donors demand them to ensure that their investments are making a difference in their communities. Program evaluations are typically focused on the quality of the program's process, goals or outcomes. An ineffective program evaluation process often is the result of poor program planning – programs should be designed so they can be evaluated. It can also be the result of improper training about evaluation. Sometimes, leaders do not realize that they have the responsibility to verify to the public that the nonprofit is indeed making a positive impact in the community. When program evaluations are not performed well, or at all, there is little feedback to the strategic and program planning activities. When strategic and program planning are done poorly, the entire organization is adversely effected.

16. **Evaluation of cross-functional processes**
Cross-functional processes are those that span several systems, such as programs, functions and projects. Common examples of major processes include information technology systems and quality management of services. Because these cross-functional processes span so many areas of the organization, problems in these processes can be the result of any type of ineffective planning, development and operating activities.

17. **Organizational evaluation**
Ongoing evaluations of the entire organization are a major responsibility of all leaders in the organization. Leaders sometimes do not recognize the ongoing activities of management to actually include organizational evaluations – but they do. The activities of organizational evaluation occur every day. However, those evaluations usually are not done systematically. As a result, useful evaluation information is not provided to the strategic and program planning processes. Consequently, both processes can be ineffective because they do not focus on improving the quality of operations in the workplace.

This section stressed the importance of having good strategic planning. Consider the book, *Field Guide to Nonprofit Strategic Planning and Facilitation*, from Authenticity Consulting, LLC. Go to the "Publications" link at http://www.authenticityconsulting.com .

This section also stressed the importance of having good program planning. Consider the book, *Field Guide to Nonprofit Program Design, Marketing and Evaluation*, from Authenticity Consulting, LLC. Go to the "Publications" link at http://www.authenticityconsulting.com .

How to Make Sure Your Board Participates in Change

Especially in projects for change in small- to medium-sized nonprofits, the Board can be the leverage point – the point in the project that can make the biggest difference – for success in the projects because the Board is the ultimate authority in the nonprofit. To ensure that Board members have strong participation in major projects for change, consider the following guidelines.

Benefits of Board Involvement in the Project

1. **The Board ensures the project is fully resourced and shows political support.**
    Board members have full authority for allocation of resources for the nonprofit. Consequently, Board members can ensure that the project has all necessary resources, including people, money and time. Their allocation shows strong political support for change, which can sustain ongoing motivation and momentum for change.

2. **The Board ensures that project plans are developed and implemented.**
    The Board supervises the Chief Executive Officer, having full authority over the CEO. Although staff members (including the CEO) usually develop and implement many of the action plans in the project for change, the Board can ensure that those plans are fully developed and completely implemented.

3. **Board members provide a wide range of useful expertise.**
    Board members often have a wide range of useful skills for governing the organization, such as planning, leadership, management, supervision and problem solving. They may also have technical knowledge of the organization or the industry. Those skills can be useful during a project for change.

4. **The Board provides time and energy to help implement plans for change.**
    Staff members often are already overloaded. Giving them yet more work to do (during your project) can completely overload them such that they collapse altogether, which could significantly damage the organization. Although the Board is responsible to govern the organization by establishing broad plans and policies, Board members still can help with implementation of various plans by helping to develop and oversee development of plans. Plans might be to address issues in strategic planning, programs, marketing, staffing, financial management or fundraising.

5. **The Board can provide objective assessments on project issues and results.**
    Board members usually are not involved a great deal in the day-to-day activities of a project. Consequently, they often retain an objective perspective on the activities and results of the project. Their perspective can be useful when addressing issues in the project and evaluating results of the project.

6. **Involvement of Board members is a powerful means to Board development.**
    One of the best ways to get good Board members is to give them something to do. One of the best ways to get rid of Board members is to give them something to do. Your project can be useful means to give Board members something to do – and, thus, to develop the Board.

Ensuring the Board Is Highly Involved in the Project

1.   **The Board should be involved in the first meetings about the project for change.**
In projects that are intended to accomplish significant change in a nonprofit, members of the Board certainly should be aware of – and have approved – the project. That often includes approving a budget to obtain and support resources used in the project.

2.   **Educate Board members about successful organizational change.**
Members of the Board are almost always volunteers to the nonprofit organization. Thus, they usually already have full-time jobs and are quite busy. Still, you should briefly educate them about what it takes to accomplish successful organizational change. You might provide them a short article, or brief presentation.

Consider "Requirements for Successful Organizational Change in Nonprofits" on page 150.

3.   **Involve at least one Board member in a Project Team.**
In projects for change, you should try to form a Project Team comprised of key personnel from the organization. The Team oversees development of a change management plan. Ensure that at least one Board member, ideally the Board Chair, is included on the Team.

4.   **Board members should be highly involved in activities that affect the Board.**
Board members should participate in various aspects of the project, depending on its scope. For example, if the project includes Board development and development of the CEO position, Board members should be highly involved in setting and achieving project goals.

5.   **Include Board development in the project if many issues exist in the organization.**
If the organization has many problems, then it is likely that the Board has major problems, as well. Otherwise, the Board would have been effectively governing and the many organizational issues would not have existed. Also, one of the most powerful approaches to addressing problems among staff and programs is to build up the Board to help you to address those problems. Therefore, the Change Management Plan should have a goal to develop the Board.

6.   **If there are CEO and/or staffing issues, form a Board Personnel Committee.**
A Board Personnel Committee is responsible to ensure that staffing (including the CEO) is carefully planned and fully utilized. That includes providing ongoing coaching to the CEO to ensure that his/her role is competently filled. A Board Personnel Committee can be of tremendous value to coach the CEO through the struggles of making major changes.

7.   **All Board members should be copied on project reports.**
All Board members have a responsibility to govern the organization. All Board members should always be able to access any information inside the nonprofit organization. Consequently, they should be copied on reports about the status of your project.

8.   **The Board should formally approve the Change Management Plan.**
Formal approval of the Plan by the Board helps to ensure that Board members have seen and will support the Plan. It also gives the Plan much more credibility to all members of the organization.

9.   **The Board Executive Committee should "police" implementation of action plans.**
Ensure that the Board Executive Committee regularly reviews the implementation status of
the Change Management Plan. If the nonprofit has many issues, if often helps if the
Executive Committee is comprised of Chairs of all Board committees. That design helps the
Executive Committee to always be aware of what the other committees are doing.

10.   **Board members should be highly involved in reviewing evaluation results.**
Finally, Board members should ensure that the project actually addresses the most prominent
issues in the organization. They should regularly review results of evaluations of project
activities as those activities occur. Also, they should review results of evaluations of the
quality of final results from the project.

How to Structure the Nonprofit and Its People

One of the most common ways that organizations make sure that the results of a change effort are maintained for the long term is by way of restructuring all or parts of the organization. There is an increasingly used phrase that "structures determine behaviors, which determine events." That phrase reminds us that, many times when we notice undesirable behaviors or events (for example, poor performance, conflicts or high turnover among staff members), the cause is not the people involved, rather the cause is the poorly designed structures in which staff members must work. In the context of organizations, structures are the organization's designs, plans, policies and procedures. There also is a common phrase, "form follows function," which means (again, in the context of organizations) that the structures should be designed to best maximize the effectiveness and efficiencies of the functions in the organization. Therefore, when undertaking organizational change to solve problems or to make things even better, organizational structures should get a lot of attention during projects for change.

How to Organize or Re-Organize People

Important Terms in Organizing People

- Span of control
  This is in regard to the number of employees and/or volunteers who work for you, or report to you. (These are your "direct reports.") You will want enough people in the nonprofit or your group to get the work done. However, you also have to be careful that you do not have so many people that you cannot keep track of (or be helpful to) them all. It is common that supervisors have, for example, anywhere from one or two to even 10 or 15 people. Having up to 15 people can be very difficult to supervise!

- Authority
  In your role as a leader, you have some formally granted influence to make decisions, pursue goals and to get the resources to pursue the goals. Authority in a managerial role may exist only to the extent that your people agree to grant you this authority or follow your orders. That is why it is so important to effectively work with your direct reports, so that they understand what you are doing and why.

- Responsibility
  Your responsibilities are your obligations when carrying out your assignments or conducting certain activities in your role. It is very important that a person who has responsibility for certain activity also be given the appropriate authority to get and use the resources needed to do that activity.

- Delegation
  Delegation includes giving someone the responsibility to achieve a desired result and the authority to have the resources to achieve those results. When delegation is done well, the person is assigned the results, but is given the freedom to choose how to achieve the results.

- **Accountability**
  This is having the responsibility for achieving desired results and for proving that those results were achieved. For example, a Chief Executive Officer can hold a program manager accountable for a program to achieve its intended outcomes for the program's clients.

- **Chain of command**
  Your chain of command includes all of the employees and/or volunteers who eventually report to you, including your direct reports and all others who report to them, etc.

- **Job (or position)**
  A job is a collection of tasks and responsibilities that an employee or volunteer is responsible to conduct. Jobs, or positions, have titles, such as Chief Executive Officer.

- **Task**
  A task is a unit of work, that is, a set of activities needed to produce some result, for example, vacuuming a carpet, writing a memo, sorting the mail, etc. Jobs often are comprised of numerous tasks.

- **Job description**
  A job description is a list of the general tasks, or functions, and responsibilities of a position. Typically, they also include to whom the position reports, qualifications needed by the person in the job in order to perform the job very well, and the salary range for the position. Job descriptions are usually developed by conducting a *job analysis*, which includes examining the tasks and sequences of tasks necessary to perform the job.

- **Role**
  A role is the set of responsibilities or expected results associated with a job. A job usually includes several roles.

Primary Considerations When Organizing People

In the past, organizations were designed primarily by working from such abstract concepts as differentiation and integration of activities. Applications of those concepts too often were vague, confusing and frustrating. Now we have access on the Web to a vast range of examples of organizational designs and job descriptions that we can reference. However, organizations should never just adopt the design or descriptions that they find elsewhere. They should always modify them to suit the nature and needs of their own organization. The following guidelines will be helpful.

1. **Realize that there is no one "perfect" way to organize people in your organization.**
    There are a variety of ways that you might organize the furniture in your house in order to optimize your comfort and activities around the house. There probably is no one perfect design that works for everyone all the time. Organizing people is similar. You do the best you can to organize it in the best design for now, and then keep changing it as you need to.

2. **Consider how people are organized in organizations with similar missions, size and age.**
    For example, if yours is a new social service organization, then consider similar organizations in your locale or elsewhere. New and small- to medium-sized nonprofits often have very similar designs, or ways of organizing people.

 Consider "Some Common Structures of Nonprofits" on page 17.

3. **Differentiate between programs.**
    It is very useful to develop program-based budgets that depict the expenses and revenues associated with each program. Also, funders tend to fund specific programs. Therefore, it is important to be able to recognize the difference between different programs. Any services that are intended to provide different results might be recognized as separate programs. For example, if you provide transportation to get people to your training programs, but lately you have also been transporting clients to do their shopping or to visit their relatives, then transportation and training might be two separate programs.

4. **When identifying jobs, review job descriptions in similar organizations.**
    Examples of job descriptions can give you a basic impression of how duties and responsibilities might be grouped together into one job. Now with the Web, people now can view examples of a wide range of job descriptions for many different roles in many different types of organizations. As mentioned above, you should never merely adopt another job description exactly as it is. You should always modify descriptions according to the nature and needs of your organization by following guidelines in this section.

Examples of many job descriptions are available on the Web at http://www.job-descriptions.org/ .

5. **Who should the person in each job, or position, report to?**
    Notice which positions must closely rely on each other in order to do all of their jobs. Those positions might best be organized under the same supervisor. Be careful, though, that the supervisor does not end up having more direct reports than he/she can keep track of. Discuss the situation with the supervisor and then closely watch if he/she is indeed able to keep track of all his/her direct reports. Also consider who else has the most capability to do the job, has the most control of the resources needed to do the job, or has the most experience in supervising people. The person who most closely meets these qualifications might be the best person to supervise the person in the job. The person might report to a group of people. However, it often is most effective if the person ultimately reports to one person, or one supervisor.

6. **How can communication and coordination best be coordinated between positions?**
    Again notice which positions must closely rely on each other in order to do all of their jobs. Make sure that these positions regularly share information, for example, in staff meetings or status reports.

7. **Communicate the new organization and closely monitor to see if changes are needed.**
    The best way to communicate the new organization is by using organization charts (see the section immediately below). Closely listen to the opinions and recommendations of your people to discern if any changes should be made to the new organization.

Consider "How to Develop New Staff Positions" on page 168.

How to Design Organization Charts

When you are done organizing people, one of the most straightforward means to describe the new organization to others is by providing them an organization chart. The organization chart is clear depiction of the positions in the organization and how they relate to each other.

 Consider "Some Common Structures of Nonprofits" on page 17.

Important considerations in the design of an organization chart are:

1. **Depict the chain of command from the top to the bottom of the chart.**
   The public owns the nonprofit. The Board of Directors is ultimately responsible to ensure that the nonprofit is governed in an effective way in order to serve the needs of the public. Therefore, depict the "Public" or "Community" in a box at the top of the page with "Board of Directors" in a box immediately underneath.

2. **Depict positions, rather than only names of people in the positions.**
   The chain of command is based on the relationships of the positions in the organization, not on the people in the positions. Therefore, always label the positions with their titles, for example, "Chief Executive Officer" or "Program Director." Optionally, you can include the names of the people in those positions under the titles.

3. **Depict the chain of command between the positions.**
   Draw solid, or continuous, lines between boxes (or positions) where the person in the upper box is the supervisor, or the person with direct authority, over the people in the boxes immediately underneath. If people in various positions have strong influence on each other's jobs (for example, by providing strong expertise or significant resources), but do not have direct authority over each other, then connect the boxes with dotted, or broken, lines to depict that influence, but lack of authority.

4. **Be sure to indicate authorization of the organization chart.**
   The chart should depict that it is official and formally used in the organization. A signature line at the bottom of the page will serve this function. The chart usually is signed by someone in a position depicted near the top of the page.

5. **Be sure to put a date on the chart.**
   The designs of organizations can change rapidly. It is healthy to change the design of an organization if its major priorities, plans and policies have changed. Therefore, be sure to put a date on each version of the chart, so you can refer to a specific version of the chart.

6. **Issue the new organization chart and the reason for it, and invite input from others.**
   Always describe the reasons for the current design. If you are re-organizing an established group, then mention that it is healthy for organizations to re-organize. Be clear that you are open to the opinions of others and how they can provide them to you. Finally, ask for the patience of those involved as the new organization design is further refined.

How to Identify When Need Staff Roles are Needed

Formal Method – Reference Strategic and Program Plans

This is much is easier if the organization has been conducting planning, especially strategic and program planning. When determining staffing needs, consider the following guidelines.

The strategic plan should specify strategic goals and the objectives to achieve each goal. The plan should include an action plan that specifies who will do what and by when in order to achieve the goals. The plan should include a listing of the resources needed to implement the action plan. These resources should include, for example, funding, facilities and expertise (people). When analyzing your staffing needs, reference the action planning and the associated list of what expertise is required from people.

Consider "How to Set Clear Purpose and Direction for the Nonprofit" on page 117.

Informal Method – Grow/Change Based on Current Feedback

Often, leaders realize the need for a new organizational position when employees or volunteers continue to report being short-handed and they mention that certain tasks are not being done. This issue can point to the need for new people. (This issue can also point to other causes, for example, inadequate supervision or training.)

How to Develop New Staff Positions

Activities to develop new positions should be in accordance with the most current, Board-approved personnel policies and procedures. Be sure to understand the role of those policies.

Consider "How to Develop and Update Your Personnel Policies" on page 199.

1.   **Draft a job description.**
     Management should draft a job description which specifies the general responsibilities of the new position along with some of the specific duties of the job, the title for the position, and also any special skills, training or credentials required to do the job.

     a.   Do not merely seek job descriptions from other organizations and adopt those as is. Your open position is unique and job descriptions are very important so you should develop your own – the process of completing the job description is usually quite enlightening.

     b.   Note which job activities are essential and which are non-essential.

     c.   Add whom the position reports to and whether the position is full-time or part-time.

d. Consider if the position requires any special physical skills. This may be important when considering accommodations to candidates with physical disabilities and effects. Various government agencies have employment laws in this regard, for example, the Americans with Disabilities Act in the USA.

e. If a paid employee must fill the position (see the next sections to consider if a volunteer or consultant is more appropriate), determine whether the position should be salaried or hourly. Usually, highly skilled and/or professional jobs are salaried, while entry-level positions are hourly.

f. Invite employees or volunteers to review and edit the drafted job description.

g. Consider including a six-month probationary period for the new position and if you do so, be sure to update your personnel policies to describe your organization's use of the probationary conditions. A probationary period allows you to fire an employee during the six months if you have concerns and greatly decreases the chances you will be sued for wrongful termination.

 Examples of many job descriptions are available on the Web at http://www.job-descriptions.org/ .

2. **Would a volunteer be most appropriate to fill the role?**
Consider filling the position with a volunteer if the job involves activities that are:

a. Fairly routine

b. Unskilled

c. Not necessarily time-critical (that is, must be done by a certain deadline)

Volunteers are also useful when there simply is no money to pay someone to do the job.

 Consider "Do Not Forget About Using Volunteers" on page 171.

3. **Would a consultant (independent contractor) be most appropriate?**
At this point, consider if a consultant might fill the new position. For example, it is common for small- to medium-sized nonprofits to hire accountants as consultants. Generally, if the activities associated with your new role require any of the following, then consider hiring a consultant:

a. Highly skilled personnel for a fixed and limited duration

b. Unskilled personnel for a fixed and limited duration, but it is not likely that you can find a volunteer to fill the role

c. A unique set of resources or tools that are not commonly available and would come with a professional (for example, a graphics designer)

Note that the consideration whether to hire an employee or an independent contractor is a very serious one. If the wrong choice is made, then you may be assessed strong fees and penalties.

See "How to Hire and Work With Consultants" on page 173.

4.   **Determine the approximate cost of the new role.**

   a.   Estimate the salary range for the new position. Set this range by talking to other organizations with similar product or services, or by scanning classified sections of newspapers with ads for similar roles. You can also reference various salary surveys.

Consider "Basics of Benefits and Compensation" on page 203.

Idealist.org has a list of nonprofit salary surveys at http://www.idealist.org/en/career/salarysurvey.html .

   b.   Finalize how much the position will cost the organization by adding "fringe" to the salary. Fringe includes costs of benefits planned for the new role, including health and dental and life insurance, and retirement benefits, along with Workers Compensation and any pension plans. Depending on the state in which you live, you may be required to pay certain employment taxes for part-time people, often if they are at or over half-time. For planning purposes, fringe might be estimated at 40% of the salary.

   c.   Additional costs of the position result from training, equipment, rental of space, postage, copying, etc. You should develop a compensation program, with policies that outline the procedure for determination of salary and benefits.

5.   **For major, new employee positions, get feedback and authorization from the Board.**
         In small nonprofits where addition of a staff member is very significant or if the new position is a management position, then the Chief Executive Officer may want to work with the Board Chair to prepare for communication of the new job to the Board. Propose the new position to the Board by attaching a proposal letter to the drafted job description along with description of how the position will be funded and sending it to all Board members for their review before the next Board meeting. At the next Board meeting, invite open discussion and questions about the new role. Seek the member's authorization for the new position.

6.   **Finalize the job description.**
         Update the job description with relevant feedback from the Board. It is important that the job description be as accurate as possible because it is the basis for determining compensation, conveying the role to the new employee and conducting regular performance appraisals. Be sure to note the version of the job description by including the date on the bottom. The job description should be reviewed and updated annually, usually by the employee and/or volunteer and the person's supervisor during the performance review cycle.

Do Not Forget About Using Volunteers

As mentioned previously in this guide, volunteers often are useful when a job or role involves activities that are fairly routine, unskilled and/or do not have urgent deadlines. Volunteers are also useful if there simply is no money to pay someone to do the job. New nonprofit organizations are often run entirely by volunteers. Members of the Board of Directors are volunteers.

It is common for nonprofits that utilize a large number of volunteers, for example, 20 or more, to appoint a Volunteer Coordinator. The position may be part-time or full-time, depending on the number of volunteers to lead and supervise.

Volunteer Management Programs

A common misconception is that the use of volunteers is quite different than the use of employees. Actually, the activities to ensure the effective use of volunteers very closely resembles the activities to ensure the effective use of employees, except that volunteers do not receive benefits and compensation. That is why it is important that your personnel policies be up-to-date regarding use of volunteers as well as employees. Many of the activities to supervise volunteers can be done by following the guidelines for supervising employees as listed elsewhere in this guide, for example, for defining roles, recruitment and selection, training, supervising, evaluating, rewarding and terminating volunteers.

Consider "How to Develop and Update Your Personnel Policies" on page 199.

1. **Draft job descriptions of the roles that volunteers are to play in your organization.**
    The job description for volunteer roles is often more detailed than descriptions for employees, and often resembles a list of recurring activities or tasks to be conducted by that role. The description might also include specific times for these tasks to be completed.

2. **Recruit and select volunteers based on the job description.**
    Volunteers should be carefully recruited and selected, just like employees. It is appropriate to do reference checks of the backgrounds of potential volunteers, particularly if they will be providing direct services to clients. Volunteers should sign a contract that specifies their services and when they will be provided.

3. **Train volunteers.**
    Volunteers should be trained how to do their tasks. In addition, they deserve orientation to the nonprofit, including its mission, programs, facilities, etc. Volunteers should also be briefed on relevant personnel policies.

4. **Schedule volunteers.**
    This can be a major challenge. Scheduling often is a time-consuming activity for Volunteer Coordinators.

5. **Supervise volunteers to ensure strong performance, or high-quality services.**
    Volunteers are often supervised by a Volunteer Coordinator role. The activities to supervise volunteers should be very similar to supervising employees, other than determining benefits and compensation.

6.   **Evaluate the work done by volunteers.**
      Volunteers usually appreciate hearing feedback about how they are doing. Therefore, schedule reviews with them, particularly to understand what might keep them coming back to volunteer.

7.   **Reward volunteers for their efforts.**
      There are a variety of ways to reward volunteers. (See the section, "Recognizing and Retaining Volunteers," below.)

8.   **Terminate volunteers.**
      If a volunteer is not working out, then he or she should be terminated. This process should be carefully carried out, similar to the process to fire an employee. It is wise to have a personnel policy in this regard.

9.   **Keep records of their attendance and services.**
      Volunteers often want record of their contributions to use as references for jobs or evidence of contributions for tax purposes.

Finding Volunteers

There are usually many sources of volunteers in a community, depending on the extent of skills, time and energy that you require from your volunteers. It is often much easier to recruit volunteers if the nonprofit has been conducting effective marketing about its programs and services. The following are some common sources of volunteers.

1.   Contact other nonprofit organizations that use volunteers.

2.   See if there is a volunteer center near you.

3.   Contact local universities, colleges, professional organizations or large corporations, particularly if you are seeking volunteers with specialized skills.

4.   Place ads in local neighborhood newspapers.

5.   Put flyers and posters around your neighborhood.

6.   Ask former clients.

7.   Ask friends of staff.

8.   Ask organizations for senior citizens.

9.   In the USA, explore if there is an Executive Service Corps (ESC) organization near you.

10.   Contact the local United Way to ask for sources of volunteers.

Recognizing and Retaining Volunteers

One of the best ways to retain volunteers is for them to feel that their contributions are being recognized.

1. Mention the volunteer's contributions to the organization during the annual meeting.

2. Include mention of the volunteer's accomplishments in the nonprofit's newsletter.

3. Include mention of the volunteer's accomplishments in an article in the local newspaper.

4. Present a certificate of gratitude. Make this presentation during an annual meeting.

5. Offer to write references for their job searches and personnel files.

6. Include their names on the nonprofit's Web site.

7. Let them see the result of their volunteer services on the actual clients of the nonprofit's programs.

8. Hold an event dedicated to recognizing volunteers, for example, a dinner.

9. Give volunteers discounts to programs and services.

10. Be sure that the volunteer gets a chance to express what they want to be doing and then try to match their preferences with tasks available in the nonprofit.

How to Hire and Work With Consultants

Good Reasons to Hire an External Consultant

- The organization has limited or no expertise in the area of need, for example, to develop a new program for clients.

- The time of need is short-term, for example, less than a year, so it may not be worth hiring a full-time, permanent staff member.

- The organization's previous attempts to meet its own needs were not successful, for example, to facilitate planning or to develop a new internal process.

- Organization members continue to disagree about how to meet the needs and, thus, bring in a consultant to provide expertise or facilitation skills to come to consensus among them.

- Leaders want an objective perspective from someone without strong biases about the organization's past and current issues.

- A consultant can do the work that no one else wants to do, for example, historical data entry. (Some would argue that this is not really a consulting project.)

- A funder or other key stakeholder demands that a consultant be brought in to help further develop the nonprofit organization.

Poor Reasons to Hire an External Consultant

The following reasons are likely open to disagreement – some people would argue that some or all of the following are good reasons to hire a consultant.

- The organization wants a consultant to lend credibility to a decision that has already been made, for example, the Board of Directors has decided to reorganize the nonprofit, but the Chief Executive Officer disagrees – so the Board members hire a consultant to lend expert credibility to their decision. Many consultants might consider this to be an unethical reason to hire a consultant.

- A supervisor does not want to directly address a problem of poor performance with one of the employees, so the supervisor hires a consultant to do the job that the employee should be doing. This is an irresponsible action on the part of the supervisor.

- The organization does not want to pay benefits (vacation pay, holiday pay, pension, etc.) or go through the administrative processes to withhold payroll taxes (social security taxes, federal taxes, etc.), so the organization hires a consultant. This reason for hiring a consultant is likely to be illegal, and could result in the organization paying fines and penalties to the appropriate government agency.

Major Types of Consultants to Nonprofits

1. **Technical consultants**
   They usually provide highly specialized content expertise regarding certain specific systems and processes in the organization, for example, computer systems, financial and accounting systems, market research, fundraising, lobbying and advocacy, or facilities management. Many nonprofits hire technical consultants. The types of services provided by these consultants are often referred to as technical assistance.

2. **Program consultants**
   They usually provide highly specialized "content" expertise that is unique to certain types of program services, for example, expertise about health care, education or childhood development. Their services might also be referred to as technical assistance, depending on how specific and focused their services are.

3. **Management consultants**
   They help leaders and managers be more productive at planning, organizing, leading and coordinating resources in the organization. Applications for their services might include leadership, management and supervisory development. The types of services provided by these consultants might be referred to as either technical assistance or organizational development activities (see the next paragraph).

4. **Organizational development consultants**
    This type of consultant helps organizations improve performance, often by focusing on changing a significant portion of the organization or the entire organization itself. These consultants often use a wide variety of approaches, tools and techniques to affect various systems and functions across the organization, for example, technical assistance, coaching, facilitation and training.

Generalists and Specialists

Some people refer to specialists and generalists as overall, major types of consultants. They might refer to technical consultants as specialists. Many people would consider organizational development consultants to be generalists.

Whether program consultants and management consultants are generalists or specialists depends on the nature of their services. The more specific the nature of their services, the more likely they would be referred to as specialists.

Functional or Focused Services

Recently, the terms "functional" and "focused" have been used to refer to servicing a specific system, function or process, for example, marketing systems, financial systems or information technology. Functional and focused activities are considered similar or the same as technical assistance.

Types of Consulting Can Overlap

The distinctions among the types of consultants can be blurry. For example, a management consultant, program consultant or technical consultant might operate as an organizational development consultant if he/she works in a manner that affects a significant portion or all of the organization.

Also, each type of consultant might be needed at various times in a project. For example, an organizational development consultant might work with a client to identify the most important problems in an organization. Later on, a management consultant might be needed to train and coach various leaders and managers during the change effort. You might also bring in various program and technical consultants to contribute their specific expertise to the change effort.

Where to Get Consultants

1. Contact professional associations, for example, networks of organization development practitioners, facilitators, trainers, fundraisers, accountants, lawyers and computer users.

2. Contact local large corporations; they often have community service programs and can provide a wide range of management and technical expertise.

3. Consult the local telephone company's Yellow Pages under the category "Consultant" and "Volunteering."

4. Call a local university or college and speak to someone in the college of Human Resources, Training and Development, or Business Administration.

5. Ask other organizations for ideas, particularly those that have similar services and head-count size, for contacts and references.

Nonprofits can often get consultants to provide services on a pro bono basis. It is worth asking the consultant, especially if the consultant is in strong agreement with the community's need for the nonprofit's services.

How You Can Make Consultancies Productive as Possible

1. Know what you want before you get a consultant. Imagine what you would have if the consultancy worked out perfect. Keep that vision when you start to look for a consultant.

2. Get Board agreement on the hiring of the consultant. Ideally, (if your Board uses committees) appoint a committee such as the Personnel Committee or Project Committee to oversee the consultant progress.

3. Do not become dependent on a consultant. Be sure that the project has a start and stop point.

4. If possible, do not limit the consultant to recommending action. Get the consultant involved in implementing recommendations.

5. Fix causes, not symptoms. Do assessments, look closely at what you see and hear, then figure out the cause. It is often not what you see or hear that is the root cause of problems, rather it is the nonprofit's structures, roles, plans, etc., that cause the problems.

 Consider "How to Regularly Measure Overall Health of the Nonprofit" on page 153 and "How to Focus on Real Causes of Problems, Not Just Symptoms" on page 155.

Getting and Hiring the Best Consultant

(This section includes advice graciously provided by Barbara Davis, Consultant, St. Paul, Minnesota.)

1. Give interested people the information they need to understand your needs by using a "request for proposal" (RFP) or "request for quote" (RFQ); direct conversation may work as well.

2. Get a written proposal from every interested party. Do not just talk to one consultant.

3. Get a bid on the fee and reimbursable expenses.

4. Look at more than one proposal and examine them all carefully.

5. Interview the best prospects and check their references. Consider their extent of expertise, listening skills, ability to adapt to the nature of your organization, ability to coach to ensure the organization can address the problem in the future, etc.

6. Do not pick someone based only on price.

7.   Be sure there is no conflict of interest with the consultant that you want to hire. The consultant should not be faced with conflicting roles if working for your organization. For example, the consultant should not also be on your Board of Directors or be a member of your staff.

8.   Write a good contract including:

    a.   Start and stop date of the agreement.

    b.   List of specific, tangible "deliverables" that will be produced by the consultant.

    c.   Checkpoints at which you can evaluate programs, for example, have a Phase I, Phase II, etc.

    d.   Project completion date, including date for deliverables.

    e.   Payment schedule (consider making partial payments based on provision of each deliverable or project phase).

    f.   Agreement on reimbursable expenses.

    g.   Specification of the roles and responsibilities of the consultant and of your organization.

    h.   Name of person in your agency who has the authority to agree to expenditures or approve work.

    i.   A clear understanding of who will do the actual consulting.

    j.   "Bail-out" clause, ideally that you can immediately bail out by providing notice in writing.

    k.   Confidentiality about sharing any information regarding your organization and its activities.

    l.   Ownership of any materials used and/or produced during the project.

    m.   Scope of the agreement: that it supercedes any other agreements that you have with the consultant regarding that project.

Additional Advice

Help Consultants Understand Your Organization

A few basic techniques can greatly help the consultant to understand your organization, particularly if brought in to work organization-wide on non-technical issues.

1. **Help the consultant to understand your services, markets and stakeholders.**
    Provide them with copies of your strategic plans, budgets, policies, most recent annual report, organization charts and advertising/promotions/sales literature. If there is a full range of these types of documents, your organization probably values careful documentation when making important decisions, and will likely prefer the same from the consulting project. If these documents appear to be very comprehensive and include a great deal of graphs, figures and numbers, then your organization probably highly values careful research, analysis and conclusions, and will prefer the same in the consultation project.

2. **Give the consultant a sense for the overall nature of your organization.**
    For example, are staff members highly independent and work alone or do they prefer to work in teams? Do you aim for consensus during decision-making, even if it takes a long time to get, or do you resort to using the authority of management? Are there strong traditions you require based on the diversity of your workforce? How does the staff feel about using consultants?

3. **Give them a sense for the overall priorities of your organization.**
    You might attempt to identify the general life stage of the nonprofit, such as start-up, developing/building, stabilizing, declining, etc. The stage will indicate your overall priorities as well, for example, getting any help you can get, grabbing more market share and/or more clients and/or more revenue, developing a wide range of careful documentation, divesting resources while ensuring client needs are met, etc.

Include Frequent Evaluations, Including Project Follow-Up

The extent of the consultant's and client's participation in evaluating the project is often an indicator of how much they really see themselves responsible for the overall, long-term quality of the consulting project.

1. **The consulting project should be evaluated regularly.**
    For example, include a brief evaluation at the end of each meeting (about the process used in that meeting), at mid-point in the planning effort and at its end. Specify in the contract that certain deliverables (tangible products, such as reports, presentations, project reviews, etc.) be delivered during the project. Ideally, the project is evaluated at three months and six months after completion. Be sure to focus on whether the consultant's recommendations were implemented or not and whether the project's goals were reached or not.

2. **Establish criteria early on from which the consulting effort will be evaluated.**
    Establish criteria by having you and the consultant specify what constitutes a successful consulting project and process. Get descriptions to be as detailed as possible so that it will be easier to evaluate the project's success in the future.

3. **Do not base evaluations mostly on feelings.**
    Avoid this mistake by specifying, as much as possible, behaviors that will reflect a successful consulting project.

Be Sure You Have "Independent Contractor" Relationship

A major, recent issue with some government agencies is the distinguishing between independent contractors and employees. Some organizations hire what they consider to be "independent contractors," but what the agencies conclude are really "employees." In these cases, the agencies demand that the organizations pay employees' taxes and also pay certain penalties. Consequently, a nonprofit must be very careful when entering into a relationship with a consultant in order to ensure that government agencies will not deem the relationship to be an "employee" relationship.

For example, in the USA, the Internal Revenue Service (IRS) is diligent about this matter and has issued guidelines about how to discern if a relationship is really more of an employee relationship than an independent contractor relationship. The IRS guidelines are similar to guidelines in Canada. Whether someone is deemed by the IRS to be an employee or an independent contractor depends primarily on the extent of control the nonprofit has over the person: the less control in the relationship, the less likely the IRS will deem the person to be an employee. Consider the following actions when attempting to define the relationship with an independent contractor:

1. Carefully specify your relationship with the person in a written contract.

2. The terms of the relationship (specific services, fees, project start and stop dates, etc.) should all be specified in the contract.

3. Attempt to arrange fees to be based on results or tasks, rather than on time.

4. In the contract, specify the relationship to be with an "independent contractor" who is responsible to pay his or her own taxes.

5. The person doing the work should have all or considerable discretion in how services are carried out, including the process and scheduling.

6. The person doing the work should be responsible to obtain and pay for his or her own training to carry out the services.

7. The person should not be required to carry out his or her services at the offices of the client.

8. The person should have or be making obvious efforts to advertise and retain business with other clients.

9. The person should have his or her own place of business.

The more a person appears as a manager in the organization (that is, makes operating decisions, supervises people, is responsible for resource allocations, etc.), the more likely that a government agency will deem the service provider an employee, and not an independent contractor.

Currently, the Internal Revenue Service in the USA uses a set of questions to help determine which status (employee or independent contractors) best fits the role. To see these questions, go to http://www.irs.gov/govt/fslg/article/0,,id=110344,00.html .

PART V:

HOW TO LEAD TEAMS

How to Organize Highly Effective Teams

Most successful projects, changes and learning occur in teams in the workplace. Therefore, it is very important for leaders to know how to design, develop and lead highly effective teams.

Types of Teams You Could Use

There are many types of teams you could use in the workplace. The type you choose depends very much on the nature of the results that the team is to accomplish.

1. Formal and informal teams

    These are usually small groups of employees or volunteers who come together to address some specific goal or need. Management appoints formal teams, that is, teams that are intentionally organized and resourced to address a specific and important goal or need. Informal teams are usually loosely organized groups of people who come together to address a non-critical, short-term purpose.

2. Committees

    Committees are organized to address, major ongoing functions or tasks in an organization, and the membership of the committees often is based on the official position of each of the members, for example, committees in Boards of Directors.

3. Problem-solving teams

    These teams are formed to address a particular, major problem currently faced by the organization. Often, their overall goal is to provide a written report that includes recommendations for solving the problem. Membership often is comprised of people who perceive and/or experience the problem, as well as those who can do something about it.

4. Self-directed and self-managed teams

    These types of teams are increasingly used where a) team members are working to address a complex challenge in a rapidly changing environment, and b) the strong ownership and participation of members are extremely important. These types provide great latitude in how members achieve the overall results to be achieved by the teams. The role of leader in a team might change during the team activities depending on where the team is in its stage of development (see below) and/or achieving is results.

Understand How Teams Grow (Life Stages of Teams)

When developing a team, it helps a great deal to have some basic sense of the stages that a typical team evolves through when evolving into a high-performing team. Awareness of each stage helps leaders to understand the reasons for members' behavior during that stage, and to guide members to behavior required to evolve the team into the next stage.

1. **Forming**

    Members first get together during this stage. Individually, they consider "What am I here for?", "Who else is here?", "Who am I comfortable with?", etc. During this stage, it is important for members to get involved with each other, including introducing themselves to each other. The team leader may require clear and strong leadership during this stage in order to facilitate the clarity and comfort required for members to evolve to the next stage.

2.   **Storming**
      During this stage, members are beginning to voice their individual differences, join with others who share the same beliefs, and try jockey for position in the group. Therefore, it is important for members to continue to be highly involved with each other, including to voice any concerns in order to feel represented and understood. The team leader should help members to voice their views, and to achieve consensus (or commonality of views) about their purpose and priorities.

3.   **Norming**
      In this stage, members are beginning to share a common commitment to the purpose of the group, including to its overall goals and how each of the goals can be achieved. The team leader should focus on continuing to clarify the roles of each member, and a clear and workable structure and process for the group to achieve its goals.

4.   **Performing**
      In this stage, the team is working effectively and efficiently toward achieving its goals. During this stage, the style of leadership becomes more indirect as members take on stronger participation and involvement in the group process. Ideally, the style includes helping members to reflect on their experiences and to learn from them.

5.   **Closing and Celebration**
      At this stage, it is clear to members and their organization that the team has achieved its goals (or a major milestone along the way toward the goal). It is critical to acknowledge this point in the life of the team, lest members feel unfulfilled and skeptical about future team efforts.

How to Build Highly Effective Teams

Too often, teams are formed merely by gathering some people together and then hoping that those people somehow find a way to work together. Teams are most effective when carefully designed. To design, develop and support a highly effective team, use the following guidelines:

1.   **Set clear goals for the results to be produced by the team.**
      The goals should be designed to be "SMART." This is an acronym for specific, measurable, achievable, relevant and time-bound. As much as possible, include input from other members of the organization when designing and wording these goals. Goals might be, for example, "to produce a project report that includes a project plan, schedule and budget to develop and test a complete employee performance management system within the next year." Write these goals down for eventual communication to and discussion with all team members.

2.   **Set clear objectives for measuring the ongoing effectiveness of the team.**
      The objectives, that together achieve the overall goals, should also be designed to be "SMART." Goals might be, for example, to a) to produce a draft of a project report during the first four weeks of team activities, and b) achieve Board-approval of the proposed performance management system during the next four weeks. Also, write these goals down for eventual communication to and discussion with all team members.

3. **Define a mechanism for clear and consistent communications among team members.**
New leaders often assume that all group members know what the leaders know. Consistent communications is the most important trait of a successful group. Without communications, none of the other traits can occur. Successful groups even over-communicate, such that:

   a. All members regularly receive and understand similar information about the group, for example, about the group's purpose, membership, status, accomplishments, etc.

   b. These communications are via, for example, regular newsletters, status reports, meetings, emails, etc.

4. **Define a procedure for members to make decisions and solve problems.**
Successful groups regularly encounter situations where they must make decisions and solve problems in a highly effective manner. Too often, the group resorts to extended discussion until members become tired and frustrated and eventually just opt for any action at all, or they count on the same person who seems to voice the strongest opinions. Instead, successful groups:

   a. Document a procedure whereby the group can make decisions and ensure that all members are aware of the procedure.

   b. The procedure might specify that decisions are made, first by aiming for consensus within a certain time frame and if consensus is not achieved, then the group resorts to a majority vote.

5. **Develop staffing procedures (recruiting, training, organizing, replacing).**
Too often, group members are asked to join the group and somehow to "chip in." Unfortunately, that approach creates "chips," rather than valuable group members. Instead, if group members go through a somewhat organized, systematic process, then new members often believe that the group is well organized and that their role is very valuable in the group. Successful groups:

   a. Identify what roles and expertise are needed on the group in order to achieve the group's purpose and plans – they staff according to plans, not personalities.

   b. New group members go through a systematic process to join the group, for example, they understand the group's purpose, their role, their next steps and where to get help.

6. **Determine the membership of the group.**
Consider the extent of expertise needed to achieve the goals, including areas of knowledge and skills. Include at least one person who has skills in facilitation and meeting management. Attempt to include sufficient diversity of values and perspectives to ensure robust ideas and discussion. A critical consideration is availability – members should have the time to attend every meeting and perform required tasks between meetings.

7. **Determine time frames for starting and terminating the team, if applicable.**
Now consider the expertise needed to achieve the goals of the team, and how long it might take to recruit and organize those resources. Write these times down for eventual communication to and discussion with all team members.

8.   **Determine the membership of the team.**
     What expertise might the team need to achieve the goals of the group? For example, an official authority to gather and allocate resources, or an expert in a certain technology. Always consider if the members can have the time and energy to actively participate in the team.

9.   **Assign the role of leader – to ensure systems and practices are followed.**
     The leader focuses on the systems and practices in the team, not on personalities of its members. For example, the leader makes sure that that all team members: a) are successfully staffed, b) understand the purpose of their group and their role, c) are active toward meeting that purpose and role, and d) utilize procedures for making decisions and solving problems. (Note that the leader does not always have to be a strong, charismatic personality – while that type of personality can often be very successful at developing teams, it often can create passivity or frustration in other members over time, thereby crippling the group.)

10. **Assign role of communicator. (Communications is life's blood of teams.)**
     Communication is the most important trait of a successful team. It cannot be left to chance. Someone should be designated to ensure that all members receive regular communications about purpose, membership, roles and status. Communications should also be with people outside the team, especially those who make decisions or determine if the team is successful or not.

11. **Identify needs for resources (training, materials, supplies, etc.).**
     Start from analysis of the purpose and goals. What is needed to achieve them? For example, members might benefit from a training that provides a brief overview of the typical stages of team development and includes packets of materials about the team's goals, structure and process to make decisions. Consider costs, such as reimbursing volunteers to attend the meeting, trainers, consultants, room rental and office supplies. How will those funds be obtained and maintained?

12. **Identify the costs to provide necessary resources for the team.**
     Consider costs, such as paying employees to attend the meeting, trainers, consultants, room rental and office supplies. Develop a budget that itemizes the costs associated with obtaining and supporting each of the resources. Get management approval of the budget.

13. **Contact each team member.**
     Before the first meeting, invite each potential team member to be a part of the team. First, send him or her a memo, and then meet with each person individually. Communicate the goals of the project, why the person was selected, the benefit of the goals to the organization, the time frame for the team effort, and who will lead the team (at least initially). Invite the team member to the first meeting.

14. **Early on, plan team building activities to support trust and working relationships.**
     Team building activities can include, for example, a retreat in which members introduce themselves, exercises in which members help each other solve a short problem or meet a specific and achievable goal, or an extended period in which members can voice their concerns and frustrations about their team assignments.

15.   **Carefully plan the first team meeting.**
        In the first meeting, review the goals of the team, why each member was selected, the benefit
        of the goals to the organization, the time frame for the team effort, who will lead the team (at
        least, initially), when the team might meet and where, and any changes that have occurred
        since the individual meetings. Have this information written down to hand out to each
        member. At the end of the meeting, ask each person to make a public commitment to the
        team effort.

16.   **Regularly monitor and report on status of team members toward achieving the goal.**
        It is amazing how often a team starts out with a carefully designed plan, but then abandons
        the plan once the initial implementation of the plan is underway. Sometimes if the plan is
        behind schedule, team members conclude that the project is not successful. Plans can
        change – just change them systematically with new dates and approval of the changes.

17.   **Support team meetings and the members' processes in the team.**
        At this point, it is critical that supervisors of team members remain available to provide
        support and resources as needed. The supervisor should regularly monitor team members'
        progress on achieving their goals. Provide ongoing encouragement and visibility to
        members. One of the most important forms of support a supervisor can provide is
        coordination with other supervisors to ensure that team members are freed up enough to
        attend meetings.

18.   **Regularly celebrate team members' accomplishments!**
        One of the best ways to avoid burnout is to regularly celebrate accomplishments. Otherwise,
        members can feel as if they are on treadmill that has no end. Keep your eye on small and
        recurring successes, not just the gold at the end of the rainbow.

How to Lead Highly Effective Teams

How to Design Highly Effective Meetings

Meeting design and management tends to be a set of skills often overlooked by leaders. The following guidelines ensure that meetings are highly focused and results-oriented.

1. **Always first identify the purpose or intended outcome from the meeting.**
    One of the most frustrating experiences for people in the workplace is to attend meetings that seem to have no clear purpose. Always know what you want from a meeting and how to measure whether that result was attained or not. Communicate that to participants.

2. **Design the agenda with the topics, decisions and/or assignments to achieve the purpose.**
    Consider the meeting to be a strategy, a tool, to achieve the intended outcome, for example, to get consensus among participants or to make necessary assignments. Do not consider the meeting to occur for the sake of having a meeting.

3. **If possible, design the agenda with some of the people who will be attending.**
    The person who designs the meeting might not be aware of what is needed to achieve its purpose and who should participate in the meeting. It is useful to involve others in the design of the agenda – those other participants might end up helping to facilitate.

4. **Include introductions or some type of "check in" for members early in the meeting.**
    If members do not have an opportunity to speak up early in the meeting, they tend to detach from its proceedings. Therefore, always include some brief activity in which each member can speak up briefly, for example, to introduce themselves or report on status of tasks.

5. **Dedicate time to reviewing the status of actions assigned in previous meetings.**
    If the status of previously assigned actions is not reviewed, then members might feel that it is not really important to make any assignments of new actions either if those new actions are not going to be monitored and reviewed either.

6. **Allow time for brief evaluations, or "satisfaction checks," among the members.**
    If the meeting will be more than 1.5 hours, be sure to include a few minutes to ask members what they think of the meeting so far. Otherwise, if the meeting is not useful to them, they might show it by not speaking up or by not doing tasks assigned to them in the meeting.

7. **Next to each agenda topic, specify the action needed and by when in the meeting.**
    For example, the agenda might include a topic to "Decide team schedule" and allocate 10 minutes in the meeting to decide that schedule. If the decision is not made within that time, then decide whether to extend the time or delegate the decision to a few members to recommend to the entire set of members in the next meeting.

8. **Review the agenda, including the meeting's purpose, at the beginning of each meeting.**
    Always make sure that participants clearly understand the purpose of that particular meeting and the reason for the topics and timing on the agenda. Otherwise, members might not feel strong understanding, ownership and commitment to the activities of the meeting.

9. **Ask participants if they will commit to the agenda.**
This simple gesture often results in the strong participation needed from each member in order to ensure a highly successful meeting. It also provides brief time for members to assert their questions or concerns about the agenda.

10. **Keep the agenda visible to all members during the meeting.**
As you address each topic on the agenda, check off that topic on the posted agenda so all members clearly understand where the meeting is at on the agenda and so members feel a sense of progress during the meeting.

11. **Identify someone to document the decisions and actions assigned from the meeting.**
activities during the meeting and actions to be conducted after the meeting. This person should issue meeting minutes shortly after the meeting (although meeting minutes may seem the most perfunctory duty from a meeting, the minutes can end up being the most useful part of the meeting by helping people remember all of the actions to be completed).

12. **Always issue the minutes (documentation of the meeting) shortly after the meeting.**
This is one of the most important activities to ensuring ongoing, successful meetings. The minutes remind members of the strong value of the meeting and its many accomplishments. It also reminds members that others will monitor their assignments in the meeting.

How to Facilitate for Highly Effective Meetings

How to Prepare to Facilitate Meetings

As a leader of the meeting, it is always important for you to be personally prepared for facilitating the meeting. Depending on the goals of your meeting and the nature of its participants, the experience of facilitation can range from fun and fulfilling to challenging and lonely. The following guidelines will help you to personally prepare for facilitation in any situation.

1. **Always know the goals, structures and membership of the group.**
This is probably the most important activity to successfully prepare for the meeting. Know the purpose of the meeting, the roles of its participants, the methods used to make decisions and solve problems, and the proposed agenda for the meeting.

 Consider "How to Build Highly Effective Teams" on page 184.

2. **Know what "centers" you – what calms you down before a meeting.**
Different people "get centered" by different means. For example, do you meditate, take a walk, or memorize an opening to the meeting? Think about successful meetings that you have facilitated in the past. What worked to keep you centered?

3. **Remember how you successfully deal with feedback and conflict.**
Remember your typical reactions to feedback and conflict and how you have learned to successfully manage those reactions.

Consider "Understand Your Natural Responses to Feedback and Conflict" on page 95.

4.   **Use your emotional intelligence (EI).**
Remember how you recognize and name uncomfortable feelings and how you have learned to successfully manage those emotions.

Consider "What is Your Emotional Intelligence?" on page 96.

5.   **Have an opening – something to say when you start the group meeting.**
Always know what you are going to say for the first minute of the meeting. Your sense of purpose and direction will be contagious to group members. For example, memorize a certain opening to the meeting or tell a joke.

How to Open Meetings

1.   **Start the meeting on time.**
This approach shows strong respect for those who bothered to show up on time and it reminds any latecomers that the meeting and its scheduling are serious. Also, meetings that start late are meetings that usually are rushed to end on time.

2.   **Ask if anyone is missing who should be present.**
If there is anyone who should be there and is not, visit the reason for the absence and address how to get him or her involved. Decide how those not present will be updated about the highlights and actions from the meeting.

3.   **Ask if introductions would be useful.**
Do not assume that everyone knows everyone else in the meeting. Even though members of the group might all be from the same organization, some members still might not know each other. Introductions are a very useful opportunity for members to begin speaking at the beginning of the meeting and to quickly feel involved.

4.   **Review the agenda, including the topics and timing of each topic for the meeting.**
This ensures that all members fully understand the agenda and the timing with each topic. When you have finished reviewing the agenda, always ask the group if they will work according to the agenda. This gets their implied commitment to focus during the meeting.

5.   **Model the kind of energy and focus needed by the meeting's participants.**
One of the most powerful means to ensure that all members actively participate and focus on the current topic in the meeting is for the facilitator to show the same kinds of energy and focus. A seemingly detached and disinterested facilitator can be toxic to a meeting.

6.   **Clarify your roles for that meeting – when you will be facilitating, training or directing.**
It is very important for participants to understand how they should be participating in a meeting, for example, whether they should be very participative (in which case you might be facilitating), listening to expert information (you are a trainer) or capturing actions to do (you are the supervisor directing your workers).

How to Establish Ground Rules for Meetings

The ground rules establish the overall "personality" of the meeting, so they are important to establish early on when working with a group. Ground rules can be identified before the group meeting and then proposed to the group members for their review, modification and/or approval. Or, members of the group in a meeting can develop the ground rules. Common ground rules are:

1. Meetings start and stop on time.

2. Focus on priorities, not on personalities.

3. Everyone participates.

4. All opinions are honored.

5. No interruptions.

6. No sidebars (or conversations not involving the main group).

7. Celebrate accomplishments.

How to Manage Time in Meetings

One of the most difficult facilitation tasks is time management. In a highly energized meeting, time seems to run out before tasks are finished. Therefore, the biggest challenge is keeping the process moving.

1. **Start the meeting on time.**
    As mentioned above, it is very important to start meetings on time in order to respect the effort of those who bothered to come on time. If you do not start on time, then you are sending the strong message that timing is not really that important in the meeting.

2. **Be sure the agenda allocates certain times to address each topic on the agenda.**
    This is one of the most powerful means to ensure strong time management. If the time allotted for a topic has expired, then ask the group if they want to allocate more time, make a decision about the topic now, or assign an action to a subgroup to get more information in order to make a more timely decision the next time that you meet.

3. **Ask the group for a volunteer to help monitor and remind the group about the time.**
    If you will be leading the group as a facilitator, trainer or work director, then it is very useful to ask someone to help you manage the time. That if perhaps the most useful form of help to you in a meeting. It affords you to completely focus on leading the meeting.

4. **Adjourn a meeting when scheduled – rarely deter from this guideline.**
    It is far better to adjourn a meeting even if members feel work is incomplete than to drag a meeting on and on with the illusion that everyone should leave the meeting with a strong sense of closure. Adjourning a meeting on time ensures that all members feel their time is respected and they can continue to count on sound meeting management.

How to Guide Members to Evaluate the Meeting

Leave 5-10 minutes (depending on the number of participants in the meeting) near the end of the meeting in order to evaluate the quality of the meeting. This is one of the most powerful means to ensure that future meetings will be high quality. The following technique not only assesses the quality of the meeting, but also ensures that all participants take strong ownership in this and future meetings. Have each member privately write down a rating of the overall quality of the meeting, with 1 representing "very poor" and 5 "very good." Then, one at a time, out loud, each member:

1.   Shows other members the rating that he/she wrote down.

2.   Very briefly explains why he/she gave that rating.

3.   Says what he/she could have done *during that meeting* to earn a rating of 5 now for the meeting.

Have the members of senior management provide their evaluation last.

How to Capture Learning During and From Meetings

1.   **Ask to hear from a few participants about what they have learned during the meeting.**
      Remind them that learning is enhanced knowledge, skills and perceptions.

2.   **Ask them about what spawned that learning during the meeting.**
      Was it a comment someone said? Was it an insight that came to them? New knowledge?

3.   **Share your own learning, as well.**
      Show your learning after others have had an opportunity to speak up.

4.   **Document participants' learnings in the minutes of the meeting.**
      Ask each participant if his/her learning can be documented in the minutes.

How to Close Meetings

1.   **Review decisions, assignments and actions from the meeting.**
      The value of meetings usually is in the decisions, assignments and actions from a meeting. Therefore, it is very important to review them at the end of the meeting to be sure that everyone is aware of, and understands, them.

2.   **Ensure that someone will be distributing minutes from the meeting.**
      This is extremely important. Regardless of how useful a meeting was, if the decisions, assignments and actions are not documented and distributed to all those who will be interested, then the meeting's participants tend to forget these highlights altogether.

3.   **Establish the time and location for the next meeting, if necessary.**
      The scheduling of meetings is often the most challenging and frustrating aspect of having meetings. Therefore, use the opportunity when all participants are together now with their calendars to schedule the next meeting.

4. **Ask who should be at the next meeting and ensure that someone invites them.**
Now, when the important topics have been discussed and addressed, is a very useful time to consider who else plays an important role with those topics and, therefore, should be in attendance at future meetings.

5. **Ask for agenda items for the next meeting.**
Attendees to a meeting are much more likely to participate in the meeting if they had strong involvement in the designing the agenda for that meeting. Now is a useful time for them to make suggestions for the agenda.

How to Manage Conflict and Come to Decisions

If there seems to be prolonged conflict among several members of a group, then consider the following guidelines:

1. **First, verify if members indeed are in conflict. Ask the members. Listen for 3 minutes.**
They might not be in destructive conflict, at all. Name or describe what behaviors you are seeing that might indicate destructive conflict. Do not try to "diagnose" causes of those behaviors, just name what you are seeing or hearing. Acknowledge that conflict is natural in healthy groups, but why you conclude that conflict has become destructive.

2. **If members are in destructive conflict, then select approaches to resolve conflict.**
Take a 5-minute break. Ask one or two other members (a subgroup) to step aside with you. Ask them to suggest the best approach(es) to address the conflict, and then read the ideas listed immediately below. Ask them to suggest which approach(es) would be most likely to move things along.

3. **Use the approaches, selected by the subgroup, with the Board.**
Explain that the approaches were selected by several of you, not by just one person. Ask that members set aside 10-15 minutes on the agenda to try them out. The more the members are in destructive conflict, the more likely they will be willing to try out the approaches.

Possible approaches that members can use to resolve destructive conflict:

- Focus on what members agree on, for instance by posting the mission, vision and/or values statements to remind people of why they are there.

- Ask members, "If this disagreement continues, where will we be? How will it hurt our organization?"

- Have members restate their position. If it will take longer than three minutes, allow opportunities for others to confirm or question for understanding (not disagreement).

- Shift to prioritizing alternatives, rather than excluding all alternatives but one.

- Take a 10-minute break in which each member quietly reflects on what he/she can do to move the group forward.

- Take 5-10 minutes and in pairs of two, each person shares with the other what he/she is confused or irritated about. One person in the pair helps the other to articulate his/her views to the larger group. Then switch roles and repeat the process.

193

- Propose an "agree to disagree" disposition.

- If disagreement or lack of consensus persists around an issue, have a subgroup select options and then report back to the full group.

- Tell stories of successes and failures in how group members operate, including how members got past their differences and reached agreement.

- Call for a vote on a stated question or decision.

How to Get Your Group Members Unstuck

Sometimes, even if there is a lot of participation from members and no prolonged conflict, a group might not seem to be making any progress on group activities. Members may simply be stuck, for example, during planning or when needing to make a major decision. Consider a similar general process as when a group seems in prolonged conflict (listed above). You could:

1. **First, verify if members indeed are stuck. Ask the members. Listen for 3 minutes.** They might not be stuck, at all. Name or describe what behaviors you are seeing that might indicate they are stuck. Do not try to "diagnose" causes of those behaviors, just name what you are seeing or hearing.

2. **If members are stuck, then select approaches to move the group forward.** Take a 5-minute break. Ask two other members to step aside with you. Ask them to suggest the best approach(es) to move things along, and then read the ideas listed immediately below. Ask them to suggest which approach(es) would be most likely to move things along.

3. **Use the approaches, selected by the subgroup, with the entire group.** Explain that the approaches were selected by several of you, not by just one person. Ask that members set aside 10-15 minutes on the agenda to try them out. The more the members are stuck, the more likely they will be willing to try out the approaches.

Possible approaches that members can use to become un-stuck:

- Ask the group, "If we continue to be stuck, where will we be? How will we be hurting our organization?"

- Take a five-minute break to let members do whatever they want.

- Resort to some movement and stretching.

- Ask for five examples of "out of the box" thinking.

- Resort to thinking and talking about activities in which resources do not matter.

- Play a quick game that stimulates creative thinking.

- Use metaphors, such as stories, myths or archetypal images. For example, ask each person to take five minutes to draw or write a metaphor that describes his/her opinions and position in the meeting.

- Have each or some of the planners tell a story and include some humor.

- Use visualization techniques, for example, visualize reading an article about the organization's success some years into the future. What does the article say about how the success came about?

- Play reflective or energizing music (depending on the situation).

- Restructure the group to smaller groups or move members around in the large group.

- Have a period of asking question after question after question (without answering necessarily). Repetition of questions, "why?" in particular, can help to move planners into deeper levels of reflection and analysis, particularly if they do not have to carefully respond to each question.

- Establish a "parking lot" for outstanding or unresolved issues, and then move on to something else. Later, go back to the stuck issue.

- Turn the problem around by reframing the topic and/or issue. Usually, questions help this reframing happen.

- Ask key questions, for example, "How can we make it happen? How can we avoid it happening?"

- Focus on what the group agrees on, for instance by posting the mission, vision and/or values statements to remind people of why they are there.

PART VI:

HOW TO LEAD

EMPLOYEES AND

VOLUNTEERS

How to Ensure Fair and Equitable Treatment of Your Employees and Volunteers

As mentioned near the beginning of this guide, the practices of leadership and supervision must be in close accordance with the Board-approved personnel policies and procedures of the organization. Previous sections in this Field Guide were primarily about non-personnel practices, for example, leading and managing yourself, leading and changing the organization, and leading teams. This PART VI is primarily about leading and supervising employees and volunteers. Consequently, guidelines about personnel policies are provided early in this PART VI.

How to Develop and Update Your Personnel Policies

Role and Need for Personnel Policies

Numerous laws and regulations regulate the nature of the relationship between an employee or volunteer and his or her organization. They are intended primarily to ensure that everyone is treated fairly and equitably regardless of their race, creed, color or sexual orientation. They are intended to ensure that the treatment of employees and volunteers is based primarily on their job performance. Common types of activities guided by the laws and regulations are, for example, hiring and firing, benefits and compensation, affirmative action, rights of privacy, discrimination and harassment, and wrongful termination.

One of the fastest growing types of lawsuits brought by employees against their organizations is wrongful termination of employment. Other common types of lawsuits are in regard to allegations of discrimination and harassment. It is far better for organizations first to ensure that these types of improper types of behaviors do not occur, than to have to defend themselves later in courts of law. The best way to ensure occurrence of proper behaviors is to enact comprehensive guidelines regarding how employees and volunteers should be treated in the workplace. These general guidelines are called personnel policies. Specific sequences of activities resulting from the guidelines are often called procedures.

Note the difference between operational policies and personnel policies. Operational policies are to guide how employees conduct the ongoing activities of the organization, ranging from how a client joins a program to making sure the coffee maker is unplugged at the end of the day. Operational policies are not about the nature of the relationship between the employee or volunteer and the organization.

Developing Personnel Policies

Each organization should carefully consider what policies it requires and how they should be worded. When developing policies, always consult an expert who is very knowledgeable about federal, state/provincial and local laws regarding employment practices. For example, in the USA, consider the Civil Rights Act of 1964, Americans with Disabilities Act of 1992, and Occupational Safety and Health Acts. In Canada, some major employment laws are Employment Insurance Act, Canada Pension Plan, Old Age Security Act, Canada Labour Code, etc. Personnel policies might also be governed by union rules or other contractual agreements.

Many organizations develop their policies first by closely reviewing policies of organizations with similar programs and services. While that practice is a good start, you still should have an authority on employment practices review your policies. Finally, the Board should formally approve the policies and the approval should be documented in Board meeting minutes.

> The Minnesota Council of Nonprofits provides a suitable starting point for developing your policies. Go to http://www.mncn.org/info/basic_hr.htm#Personnel%20Policies . You should modify them by having an authority on employment law review and update them to suit the nonprofit.

Training on Policies

If employees' or volunteers' behaviors do not conform to the written personnel policies for your organization, and if an employee or volunteer sues your organization, then courts will consider your written policies to be superseded (or replaced) by your employees' or volunteers' actual behaviors that you appeared to be permitting to occur. For example, if policies specified that employees should not discriminate on the basis of race, creed or color, yet there was a history of your employees clearly discriminating against other employees on that basis, then courts will conclude that your policies are to permit discrimination. Therefore, it is critical that employees and volunteers have clear understanding of each personnel policy and that their behaviors conform to those policies. The best way to accomplish that understanding is for employees and volunteers to be trained on the policies and for their supervisors to always be sure that policies are followed. Training about policies can be carried out by ensuring that:

- All employees and volunteers receive an orientation that includes overview of the policies and procedures.

- All employees and volunteers sign a document that indicates that they have reviewed the policies and will act in accordance with them.

- Supervisors regularly issue reminders to employees and volunteers about key policies.

- All supervisors themselves act in accordance with the policies.

- Any violation of terms of the policies is immediately addressed with reprimand or termination of the employee or volunteer, depending on the nature of the violation.

Recommended Personnel Policies

Table VI:1 on the following page lists many examples of types of personnel policies.

Table VI:1 – Sample List of Personnel Policies

Work Schedule

Work day hours
Lunch periods and break times
Holidays
Vacation
Sick Time
Personal Leave
Leave of Absence
Severe Weather
Jury Duty

Hiring Procedures

Interviewing job candidates
Conducting background checks
Offering employment

New Employee and Internal Orientation

New employee orientation – general information
Intern orientation
New employee and internal orientation checklist

Compensation

Paydays
Overtime and compensation time
Classifying employees as exempt or non-exempt
Salary ranges
Positioning pay within a salary range
Maintaining competitive salary information
Reclassifying positions
Salary review policy
Promotional increases
Withholding salary increase due to performance
Withholding salary increase due to leave of
  absence

Payroll Information & Timekeeping Procedures

Payroll information – General
Payroll information – Direct deposit procedures
Payroll information – Required and voluntary
  payroll deductions
Timekeeping – salaried and hourly employee
  classifications
Supervisor's signature

Benefits

Eligibility and general information
Types of available benefits
Medical insurance
Dental insurance
Disability insurance
Supervisory communication of benefits
Life insurance
Confidentiality note
Retirement plan
Social security (in USA)
Employee advisory resource

Workers' Compensation Information & Procedures

When there is an injury or accident on the job
What is covered under Workers Compensation
Type of injury covered by Worker's
  Compensation Insurance
Medical expenses resulting from a work-related
  injury
Resources available

Employee Performance Management

Performance assessment cycle
Performance assessment process
Dealing with performance issues
Discipline: when the positive approach does not
  work
Separation from employment checklist
Communications by the supervisor regarding
  personnel issues
COBRA (in USA)
Leave-taking procedures

Data Practices

Policy
Procedures
Definitions
Security of Records
External releases
Internal releases
Use of data
Legal procedures
Destruction of records
Employee access

How to Use an Employee Manual

All personnel policies and procedures should be organized into a manual commonly referred to as an employee manual (although it is used for volunteers, as well), employee handbook or personnel handbook, which each employee and volunteer retains. As mentioned in the above paragraphs, all employees and volunteers should be oriented to the policies in the manual and have signed an agreement that they will follow the policies.

Each manual should have a cover page which specifies that the Board has authorized the policies to be followed in the workplace, that policies can be changed at any time, that notice of changes will be communicated to employees and volunteers, and that the policies do not constitute a contract between the organization and the employee or volunteer. The following suggested language is not to be interpreted as legal advice. Consider the following wording on the cover of your policies manual:

> "Nothing contained in or implied by this manual creates or shall be deemed to create or constitute a contractual obligation to employees or volunteers on the part (of the organization). The policies, procedures and guidelines contained in this manual are subject to change at any time, do not confer any obligation (on the part of the organization) and do not create any right to employment on the part (of the organization)."

How to Ensure Fair Compensation of Your Employees

Basics of Benefits and Compensation

Benefits

Benefits are forms of value, other than payment, that are provided to employees in return for their contribution to the organization, that is, for doing their jobs. Some benefits, such as Workers Compensation in the USA and Canada, are required by law for certain sized organizations. (Some people see Worker's Compensation as a worker's right, rather than a benefit.)

Prominent examples of benefits are insurance (medical, life, dental, disability, worker's compensation, etc.), vacation pay, holiday pay, maternity leave, contribution to retirement (pension pay), profit sharing, stock options and bonuses. Some people would consider profit sharing, stock options and bonuses as forms of payment or compensation.

You might think of benefits as being tangible or intangible. The benefits listed previously are tangible benefits. Intangible benefits are less direct, for example, appreciation from a boss, likelihood for promotion and a nice office. People sometimes talk about fringe benefits, usually referring to tangible benefits, but sometimes meaning both kinds of benefits.

You might also think of benefits as company-paid and employee-paid. While the company usually pays for most types of benefits (holiday pay, vacation pay, etc.), some benefits, such as medical insurance, are often paid, at least in part, by employees because of the high costs of medical insurance.

For the purposes of estimating personnel costs, you might consider the cost of fringe benefits to be about 40% of the cost of the wages or salaries, although this percentage continues to increase. Note that fringe benefits are usually higher for salaried personnel than for personnel who are paid hourly wages.

Compensation

Compensation is payment to employees in return for their contributions to the organization, that is, for doing their jobs. The most common forms of compensation are wages, salaries and tips.

Compensation is usually provided as base pay and/or variable pay. Base pay is usually based on the role in the organization and the market value for the expertise required to conduct that role. Variable pay is based on the performance of the person in that role, for example, for how well that person achieved his or her goals for the year. Incentive plans, for example, bonus plans, are a form of variable pay. (Some people might consider bonuses as a benefit, rather than a form of compensation.)

Organizations usually associate compensation/pay ranges with job descriptions in the organization and on salary surveys about similar jobs in similar organizations. The ranges include the minimum and the maximum amount of money that can be earned per year in that role.

Employers have to pay various payroll-related payments. For example, in the USA, employers pay Workers Compensation and FICA (social security). In Canada, employers pay Workers Compensation and Employee Health Tax.

Employees have certain monies withheld from their payroll checks. For example, in the USA, employees have deductions taken from their paychecks for state and federal income taxes, FICA (social security) and optionally, employee contributions to the costs of certain benefits, such as supplementary life, medical insurance and retirement. In Canada, employees have deductions from their paychecks for various provincial and federal taxes, Canada Pension Plan, employment insurance and optionally, employee contributions to the costs of certain benefits, such as supplementary life and medical insurance.

Salaried and Hourly Job Roles

In various countries, job roles in organizations often have two primary classifications based on the approach to computing compensation. These classifications include "salaried" and "hourly" jobs. The compensation of salaried jobs is usually based on a bi-weekly (once every two weeks) or monthly, fixed amount. The compensation of hourly jobs is usually based on an hourly rate. In the USA, salaried jobs are referred to as "exempt" jobs and hourly jobs are referred to as "non-exempt" jobs, meaning whether they are exempt or not exempt from certain requirements of the Taft-Hartley Act.

- Unskilled or entry-level jobs are usually referred to as hourly jobs (non-exempt in the USA). Hourly jobs also usually get paid over-time (at least, in the USA and Canada), that is, extra pay for hours worked over 40 hours a week or on certain days of the week or on holidays.

- Professional, management and other types of skilled jobs are usually referred to as salaried jobs (or exempt in the USA). It is not uncommon for salaried positions to receive higher compensation rates and benefits than hourly jobs, although hourly (non-exempt) workers sometimes can make more money than salaried (exempt) workers overall simply by working more hours.

Each job must have the same pay range for anyone performing that job, that is, one person cannot be eligible for a higher maximum pay in that job than someone else doing that same job.

How to Establish Benefits and Compensation Programs

Nature of Programs Vary

The various forms of benefits and compensation that an organization chooses to provide and how it chooses to provide them are often referred to as the organization's benefits and compensation program. The nature of the program depends very much on the size of the organization (usually its headcount), where it is located and the nature of its mission. For example, a small nonprofit that is helping the elderly in a small, rural area would usually have a smaller, less complex program than a nonprofit with many people that is helping low-income families in a large, urban area.

The nature of the program often changes as the organization grows. For example, the program might offer a wider range of benefits to meet the increasingly diverse needs of its increasing number of employees. An organization that has very limited financial resources might offer a very attractive set of benefits to offset its limited ability to provide high compensation. Likewise, an organization that has strong financial resources might offer rather high compensation, yet rather limited benefits.

Developing Benefits and Compensation Programs

A new nonprofit often develops its program by getting help from local expertise, example, assistance from the local United Way, from an association of nonprofits having similar programs, or from specialists in benefits and compensation. The benefits and compensation program must be clearly described in the nonprofit's personnel policies. The Board must approve the policies; thus, the Board must approve the forms of benefits and compensations and how they are delivered to employees.

- A new nonprofit usually starts by offering a base-pay compensation program and a rather limited list of benefits, including standard forms of paid leave, including vacation pay (usually two weeks per year for new employees), holiday pay (usually the major holidays), funeral leave and maternity/paternity leave.

- Salary ranges for a position are often established by doing some basic research, including contacting other nonprofits in the area to see what they pay their people. Another useful approach is to reference various salary surveys.

Idealist.org has a list of nonprofit salary surveys at
http://www.idealist.org/en/career/salarysurvey.html .

- Nonprofits must be sensitive about their compensation programs in order to ensure that there is not any appearance of exorbitant pay, that is, of pay that is much more than reasonable for a particular role in the organization.

- Nonprofits, by definition, cannot provide profit sharing or stock options.

- Considering the rising cost of medical insurance, many employees would rather have medical insurance than life insurance as their only insurance benefit.

How to Hire the Best Employees

How to Identify the Best Candidates

It is very important that your activities of hiring an employee are based, as much as possible, on the person's match to the specifications and requirements in a written job description, rather than on your subjective impression of the person's personality or nature. The latter approach leaves you open to losing a lawsuit that alleged that you discriminated against (that you did not hire) a potential employee because you did not like the person's race, creed, color or orientation.

 Consider "How to Develop and Update Your Personnel Policies" on page 199.

1. **Encourage current employees to apply for the job.**
    Whether internal candidates would be leaving another job in the organization that is critical or not, all internal candidates deserve equal opportunity to apply for new jobs in the organization.

2. **Advertise the position. The ad should be based on content of the job description.**

    a. Post ads in classified sections of local major and neighborhood newspapers. In the ads, include the job title, general responsibilities, minimum skills and/or education required, whom they should send a resume to if they are interested and by when. Consider having a closing date after which you will not accept resumes.

    b. Mention the open position to customers.

    c. Send cover letters and job descriptions to professional organizations.

    d. Be sure to mention the open position to all employees to see if they can recommend any favorite candidates.

    e. Ask candidates to send a resume to your organization (to whomever is designated to collect the resumes).

3. **Screen resumes.**

    a. When screening resumes, notice the candidate's career objective – or the lack of it. If an objective is not specified, then the candidate may not have considered what he/she really wants to do in the future, which may impact the candidate's commitment to your new role.

    b. Notice if the candidate stayed at jobs long or left quickly. Are there unaccounted for period in the work history? If so, are there acceptable explanations for that period?

    c. Notice the candidate's education and training. Is it appropriate for the new role?

d. Consider what capabilities and skills might be evidenced in the person's past and current work activities.

e. If you have many resumes, then create one document on which to summarize and compare the "highlights" and "concerns" about each of the candidates; otherwise, after about 10 resumes, they will all seem to read the same.

How to Interview Candidates

The thoroughness and professionalism you use to interview candidates can make a strong, positive impression on candidates. It also conveys to them that you expect the same thoroughness and professionalism from them if they are hired by your organization.

Preparation

1. **Schedule interviews with all candidates that meet the minimum qualifications.**
   Those qualifications were specified in the job description. This practice helps to make sure that you are not excluding candidates because of any unfair biases on your part.

2. **When inviting them for an interview, also send them the job description.**
   That ensures they have reasonable preparation for the interview. Also mention who will interview them.

Use Multiple Interviewers Per Interview

1. **Consider having multiple people at the interview.**
   Although this can be intimidating to the interviewee, this practice can ensure them a more objective and fair consideration for the job because several perspectives (among the interviewers) will be considered, rather than only one. Have the same interviewers in all of the interviews, if possible, to ensure that each candidate received equal treatment.

Questions to Pose During Interviews

When posing the following types of questions, always be courteous and respectful to the candidates. Do not share reactions between interviewers until after all interviews are complete.

1. **Do not rely on your memory – ask permission from the candidate for you to take notes.**
   Be sure that you document the name of the candidate and the date on the notes.

2. **While interviewing candidates, always apply the same questions to all candidates.**
   That approach ensures the fair treatment and comparison of all candidates.

3. **All questions should be primarily in regard to performing the duties of the job.**
   Do not ask questions about the candidate's race, nationality, age, gender, disabilities (current or previous), marital status, spouses, children and their care, criminal records or credit records. Asking those types of questions leaves you open to losing lawsuits that allege discrimination.

4.   **Ask open-ended questions and try to avoid questions answered with "yes" or "no."**
      Open-ended questions tend to generate more useful information and provide the opportunity
      for the interviewer to observe how well the candidate articulates answers to questions.

5.   **Consider asking some rather thought-provoking and challenging questions.**
      Ask "What skills do you bring to this job?", "What concerns do you have about filling this
      role?" and "What was your biggest challenge in a past job and how did you meet it?"

6.   **Talk for at most 25% of the time – listen for the rest.**
      This often is a challenge for new interviewers who feel that silence is somehow to always be
      avoided. The more time that the interviewer talks, the less time to learn about the candidate.

7.   **If it is clear that the candidate is not suitable for the job, then "sell" the organization.**
      If he/she does not meet the minimum qualifications, after all, or there are other stronger
      candidates, then use the time in the interview to enlighten the candidate about the positive
      attributes of the organization in case the candidate chooses to spread the word to others.

Administrative / Human Resource Questions

1.   **Ask the candidate about what he/she expects for compensation and benefits.**
      Even though the job description might specify the pay ranges and benefits, the candidate
      might have strong preference for other provisions that suit his/her nature.

2.   **Find out when the candidate can start work, if offered the job.**
      Allow him/her at least two weeks to get his/her affairs in order. Expecting a candidate to
      start sooner might convey to the candidate that the organization operates in a crisis mode,
      which can be very unattractive to good candidates.

3.   **Explain to the candidate when you will be getting back to the person.**
      Then always do get back to each person soon regarding whether he/she got the job. If your
      first choice for candidate does not work out, you might have to resort to choosing the
      second-best candidate. He/she might not accept the job if offended that you did not get back
      to him/her.

4.   **Ask if you can get, and check, any references from the candidate's previous jobs.**
      Always contact at least three references that the candidate offers from his/her past work
      history. Share the results of these activities with the interviewers. If your programs involve
      direct services to children, adults and the elderly, then seriously consider conducting
      background checks on the most preferred candidates for the job.

5.   **Be sure to tell candidates of any relevant conditions from your personnel policies.**
      For example, tell the candidate whether there is a probationary period for the job. (The best
      way to deal with a poor performer is not to hire him or her in the first place. It is often wise
      to have a probationary period of, for example, six months, wherein if the employee does not
      meet the responsibilities of the position, you can quickly terminate the employee.)

How to Choose the Best Candidate

At this point, usually one or two candidates clearly stand out as the most qualified for the job. However, it is surprising how much interviewers' impressions can change once they all have an opportunity to carefully discuss and consider all of the candidates. Be sure your approach to selecting the best candidate is a comprehensive and consistent approach.

1. **Soon after interviews are completed, interviewers together select the best candidate.**
   Within one or at most two weeks after all interviews have been completed, convene the interviewers. Consider a consistent method to select the best candidate from among the interviewers. For example, mention the name of a candidate, and allow 15 minutes total for all interviewers to share their impressions of that candidate. Also share results of any comments from references and/or background checks. Repeat the process for each candidate. After all candidates have been discussed, then list the candidates again, this time having interviewers vote for the best candidate from the list.

2. **If there does not seem to be suitable candidate, then consider the following:**

   a. Are the job requirements too stringent or an odd mix? For example, the job might require someone with strong technical skills and also someone with strong clerical skills. Those two types of skills are sometimes unusual to expect to mix together.

   b. Reconfigure the job so that the nature of the required skills and training are somewhat similar and so that the overall nature of the job becomes more common.

   c. Hire the candidate who most closely matched the requirements of the job and then plan for dedicated training to bring that person's skills up to needed levels.

   d. Re-advertise the position.

   e. Get advice from a human resources professional. At this point, your need for their advice is probably quite specific, so they might provide services on a pro bono basis.

   f. Hire a consultant for the position on a short-term basis, but only as a last resort as this may be quite expensive.

How to Hire the New Employee

You send a strong message to the candidate in the way that you provide the job offer to them. It is best to be both business-like and personal in your approach.

1. **Provide a written job offer to the most qualified candidate.**
   The letter should come from the person who will be supervising the new employee. In the letter:

   a. Convey that you are pleased to offer the job to the candidate.

   b. Specify the exact amount of compensation offered to him/her.

   c. Specify the benefits offered to him/her.

d.   Specify the date on which to start the job.

e.   Include a signature line that the candidate can sign.

f.   Ask him/her to sign a copy of the offer letter and return it to you by a certain date. Give them at least one week to consider the job offer.

g.   Mention if there is a probationary period and the length of the period.

h.   Mention who he/she can contact if there are any questions.

i.   Attach a copy of the job description to be sure that the offer is associated with the correct job.

2.   **If everyone declines the job offer, then consider the following:**

a.   Ask the best candidates why they declined the offer. Usually, you will hear the same concerns, for example, the pay is too low, the benefits incomplete, the organization seems confused about what it wants from the role, or the interview process seemed hostile or contentious.

b.   Reconvene the interviewers and consider what you heard from the candidates. Recognize what went wrong and correct the problem. Contact your favorite candidate, admit the mistake and what you did to correct it, and why you would like to make an offer to him/her again.

c.   Go to the second choice. Sometimes the process of re-examining the candidates can bring a second-choice candidate to the front.

d.   Re-advertise the position.

3.   **Otherwise, start a personnel file for the new employee.**
The personnel file with contain all of the job-related information and material, for example, the employee's resume, job description, job offer, signed offer letter, completed tax withholding forms, signed forms for benefits, etc.

4.   **Do not forget to send letters to the candidates who did not get the job.**
They deserve a sincere letter from you that thanks them for their consideration and for interviewing for the job. Clearly explain that another candidate most closely matched the qualifications specified in the job description. If you plan to retain their job applications, then mention that to them so they are aware that they still might be considered for other jobs that arise in the organization.

How to Train Your Employees and Volunteers

Most workplace training is on-the-job training, which, many times, is inadequate. Also, it is common for leaders and supervisors to not really understand how to design and conduct effective employee training – even though a primary role of supervisors is to ensure effective training and development of employees and volunteers. This section gives useful, overall perspective on training, and includes guidelines to help you to fully train your employees and volunteers to do their jobs.

Many Forms of Job Training You Can Use

Reasons for Job Training

Employee or volunteer job training can be initiated for a variety of reasons, for example:

- To equip the employee or volunteer who is new to the job or task.

- As part of an overall professional development program.

- To "benchmark" the status of improvement so far in a performance improvement effort.

- When a performance appraisal indicates performance improvement is needed.

- As part of succession planning to help an employee be eligible for a planned change in role in the organization.

- To "pilot," or test, the operation of a new performance management system.

Major Types of Training

When planning the training for your employees or volunteers, it helps to understand some basics about training and development. There are four major types of training:

1. **Self-Directed Versus Other-Directed Learning**
    Self-directed learning is where the learner decides what he or she will learn and how. Other-directed learning is where other people decide what the learner will learn and how.

2. **Informal Training Versus Formal Training**
    Informal training has no predetermined form. Examples are reading books to learn about a subject, talking to friends about the subject, attending a presentation, etc. Formal training has a predetermined form. The form usually includes specification of learning results, learning objectives and activities that will achieve the results, and how the training will be evaluated. Examples might be college courses, workshops, seminars, etc. Note that because formal training has a form, it does not necessarily mean that formal training is better than other forms. Informal training is probably the most common type of training and includes: on-the-job training, coaching from supervisors, using manuals and procedures, advice from peers, etc.

Other-directed, formal training is typically more expensive than other approaches, but is often the most reliable to use for the learner to achieve the desired knowledge and skills in a timely fashion.

Self-directed, informal learning can be very low-cost; however the learner should have the capability and motivation to pursue his/her own training. Training may take longer than other-directed forms.

Highly specific and routine tasks can often be trained without complete, formal approaches. On the other hand, highly complex and changing roles often require more complete and formal means of development, which can be very expensive as a result.

If training is needed right away, then other-directed training is often very useful, for example, to sign up for a training course at a local university, college or training center. Or, training professional can be brought in. Again, other-directed training is usually faster and more reliable, but more expensive.

Self-directed forms of training require that the learner be highly motivated and able to conceptualize his/her approach to training, particularly in formal training.

Common Forms of Training

Training methods are either on-the-job, implemented outside the organization or a combination of both. The following is a brief overview of rather typical methods of development (in alphabetical order). Knowledge of the forms can be very useful when designing training programs for employees and volunteers.

1.   **Apprenticeships**
      For centuries, apprenticeships were the major approach to learning a craft. The apprentice worked with a recognized master craftsperson. Particularly during times of low unemployment, businesses are eager to get any kind of help they can find. Seeking an apprenticeship may be a very useful and effective way to eventually develop a new skill.

2.   **Career counseling**
      Hopefully, learners have the opportunity to work with their supervisors to develop career plans that identify areas for improvement or advancement, how those areas can be addressed and when.

3.   **Coaching**
      Coaching is becoming a very popular means of development, and often includes working one-on-one with the learner to conduct a needs assessment, set major goals to accomplish, develop an action plan, and support the learner to accomplish the plan. The learner drives these activities and the coach provides continuing feedback and support.

4.   **Continuing professional development**
      Many professions require verification of ongoing training to retain certification, for example, social workers, some fields of law, nurses, etc. Professionals must stay up-to-date in the views and practices necessary to lead and manage in today's organizations. There seems to be an increasing number of universities, colleges and training centers associating continuing education units (CEUs) with their courses and workshops.

5.   **Courses**
      Universities, colleges and training centers often have a large number of courses in management, professional and personal development. If the learner is looking to build a skill, then he or she must actually apply new information from these courses – otherwise, the learner is collecting information (hopefully, knowledge), rather than building skills.

6. **Distance learning**

   This typically includes learning by getting information and / or guidance from people who are not face-to-face with the learner, for example, learning via satellite broadcast, broadcast over the Internet, e-mail or postal mail correspondence, etc. Some people consider online learning (for example, information, tutorials, etc., available on diskette, CD-ROM, over the Internet, etc.) to be distance learning, as well.

7. **Internships**

   Internships are offered usually by organizations to college students wanting to find work experience during the summer months. The internships offer precious, real-life job experience and the organizations often get skilled, highly dedicated service. Many times, interns go on to be hired by the organizations, as well.

8. **Job assignments**

   Job assignments are wonderful opportunities from which to learn. We just are not used to thinking of them that way. To cultivate learning, consider having employees write short reports, including an overview of what they did, why they did it, what areas of knowledge and skills were used, how the job might have been done better, and what areas of knowledge and skills would be needed to improve the job.

9. **Job rotations**

   This can be one of the most powerful forms of development, allowing learners to experience a broad range of managerial settings, cultures and challenges.

10. **Lectures**

    Lectures, or focused presentations by experts on subject matter, are held in a wide variety of locations, not just in classrooms. Professional associations often bring in speakers. Guest lectures are often sponsored by local universities, colleges and training centers, and announced to the public. Many times, the lectures are repeated over local radio and television.

11. **Management development programs**

    Local universities, colleges and training centers usually offer these programs. Carefully review their program content and design to ensure that training includes real-life learning activities during which learners can develop skills for the workplace.

12. **Mentoring**

    Hopefully, learners find experienced managers in the workplace who are willing to take learners "under their wing" and provide ongoing coaching and mentoring.

13. **Online training**

    There are now numerous sources of online training (learning information from computer diskette, CD-ROM, the Internet, etc.). This form of learning is sometimes called Web-based-training. Various forms of distance learning involve learning over the Internet as well.

14. **On-the-job training**

    This form helps particularly to develop the occupational skills necessary to manage an organization, for example, to fully understand the organization's products and services and how they are developed and carried out.

15. **Other-directed learning**
    This includes having someone other than the learner identify the training goal, methods to achieve the goal, and approaches to evaluating the training and progress toward achieving the training goal.

16. **Orientation to new jobs or roles**
    A carefully developed procedure for orienting new employees is very helpful for getting employees "off on the right foot" when starting their jobs.

17. **Peer-based methods**
    This includes formats where peers focus on helping each other learn, for example, by exchanging ongoing feedback, questions, supportive challenges, materials, etc. Perhaps the best example is the action learning process, originated by Reginald Revans.

18. **Professional organizations**
    A wide variety of professional organizations often offer courses, seminars, workshops and sessions from conventions.

19. **Self-directed learning**
    Highly motivated learners can usually gain a great deal of knowledge and skills by identifying their own learning objectives, how to meet those objectives and how to verify they have met the objectives, as well.

20. **Television**
    Various television networks often have a wide variety of very enlightening shows about basic job skills, such as computer basics, business writing, etc.

21. **Tutorials**
    Tutorials include guidance to proceed through learning some technique or procedure, for example, a tutorial on using a computer software package. There are an increasing number of online tutorials (tutorials available on diskette, CD-ROM, over the Internet, etc.).

22. **Training courses and seminars**
    Courses, seminars, convention sessions, etc., are useful for highly focused overviews of a particular subject or training about specific procedures.

23. **University and college programs**
    It seems there is an exponential number of management development programs in universities and colleges.

24. **Workshops**
    Workshops typically include some hands-on practice by the learner, and can be very practical means to learn a certain technique or procedure.

Most Basic Form of Training – Tell, Try, Adjust, Repeat

Probably the most common form of informal training is a form of on-the-job-training. The approach is rather straightforward and includes:

1.   The supervisor, or some other expert at the subject matter or skill, tells the employee or volunteer how to do something.

2.   The employee or volunteer does what he/she was told to do.

3.   The expert watches and promptly shares feedback.

4.   The employee or volunteer tries it again until he/she does it right.

The above approach works best in straightforward tasks. However, as jobs become more complex, employees often require more formal training.

How to Orient Your New Employee or Volunteer

Employee or volunteer orientation is a form of training. Develop an orientation checklist and consider the following activities for inclusion on the list. The employee's or volunteer's supervisor should conduct the following activities.

1.   **When the employee or volunteer starts in the organization, meet with him/her.**
      Explain how he/she will be trained, introduce him/her to other staff members, give keys to facilities, get him/her to sign any needed benefit and tax forms, explain the time-recording system (if applicable), and provide copies of important documents (an organization chart, last year's final report, the strategic plan, this year's budget, and the personnel policies and procedures manual).

2.   **Show him/her the facilities.**
      Describe the layout of offices, bathrooms, storage areas, kitchen use, copy and fax systems, computer configuration and procedures, telephone usage, and any special billing procedures for use of office systems.

3.   **Schedule any needed computer training.**
      Include use of passwords, overview of software and documentation, location and use of peripherals, and where to go to get questions answered.

4.   **Review any policies and/or procedures about use of facilities.**
      Be sure to explain procedures to minimize damage to themselves or facilities, for example, what to unplug from electrical connections, where to go in case of fire, etc.

5.   **Assign an employee or volunteer as a "buddy" who is available to answer questions.**
      This simple practice goes a long way toward making new employee or volunteer feel much more comfortable in his/her new surroundings.

6.   **Take him/her to lunch on the first day and invite others along.**
      Similar to assigning a buddy, this simple practice also really helps to make the new employee or volunteer feel much more accepted and welcome in their new role.

7. **Meet with him/her at the end of the day to hear any questions or comments.**
   Ask him/her is there is anything else you can do to help him/her feel comfortable and more equipped to do the job. Be sure to follow up on any requests that you hear.

8. **Meet with the new employee or volunteer during the first few days of work.**
   Review the job description again. Remind them to review the employee manual and to sign a form indicating they have reviewed the manual and that they will comply with its contents. Review any specific goals for the position, for example, goals from the strategic plan. In the same meeting, explain the performance review procedure and provide them a copy of the performance review document.

9. **Hold one-on-one meetings on a weekly basis for the first six weeks.**
   Discuss the new employee's or volunteer's transition into the organization, get status on work activities, hear any pending issues or needs, and establish a working relationship with the supervisor.

How to Carefully Design and Implement Training Plans

The guidelines in this section are to help leaders and supervisors to design and implement focused and systematic training plans for their employees and volunteers.

A. Determine the Overall Goals for Your Training Plan

When getting started with your training plan for your employee or volunteer, first think about answers to the following questions:

1. What knowledge, skills and abilities (competencies) are needed by your employee or volunteer to best do the job?

2. Are there others in the organization who can suggest what competencies the employee or volunteer should learn for the job?

3. Should you have the employee or volunteer conduct some form of self-assessment, for example, a questionnaire or interview to discern what competencies that he/she still needs for the job?

4. Write down your training goals as what competencies that the employee or volunteer should achieve.

5. Are you providing training and development for your employee or volunteer in order to address:

   a. A performance gap where he/she seems to have the capability, but somehow is not fully using it?

   b. A growth gap where he/she needs to learn more in order to progress in his/her career?

   c. An opportunity gap where he/she needs to gain certain learning to take advantage of an opportunity?

Consider "How to Set Relevant and Realistic Goals With Your Employees and Volunteers" on page 219.

6. Think about what kind of gap that employee or volunteer has and then about when the employee or volunteer should achieve the competencies? A performance gap might be filled in time for the next performance review. A growth gap might be filled in time for him/her to evolve to the next stage in his/her career. An opportunity gap might be filled in time to take advantage of the opportunity.

B. Identify Learning Objectives for Your Employee or Volunteer

7. Learning objectives are the necessary accomplishments that the person must achieve in new knowledge, skills and abilities. For example, you might want the person to learn certain information about a software application (new knowledge), and then how to use that application (skills) to generate useful financial statements (capabilities). There might be several learning objectives each for new knowledge, skills and abilities.

8. In what sequence should the learning objectives be attained? Usually people must learn new knowledge before they can develop new skills to accomplish overall capabilities. Therefore, objectives should probably be organized in that order.

C. Identify Learning Strategies for Your Employee or Volunteer

9. What are the best learning activities (methods) for the person to use to achieve each of his/her learning objectives, for example, reading a book, working with a mentor or using an online tutorial? Do the learning activities include ongoing reflections about what the person is learning?

D. Identify What Resources Are Needed to Implement Strategies

10. Now that you know what learning activities will be conducted, think about what resources will be needed, for example, tutorial software, tuition in courses or self-study books. Think about what funding will be needed to obtain those resources.

E. Identify What Tangible Results Can Be Evaluated

11. What observable results, or evidence of learning, will the person produce from the learning activities that can be reviewed for verification of achieving the learning objective, for example, will the person show his/her supervisor that he/she can do the job?

12. Who will verify that each of the learning objectives was reached, for example, will the supervisor evaluate the person's progress? If an evaluator will be needed from outside of the organization, think about what funding will be needed to pay that evaluator.

F. Budget Funds for Resources and Services for Training Program

13. Consider costs of trainers, consultants, room rental, books, tuition, travel expenses and labor to pay the employee while attending training. Also consider the cost for any materials that need to be developed, as listed below.

G. Develop Any Training Materials They May Need

14.   Consider if the learner needs to obtain, or start:

     a.   Enrolling in courses.

     b.   Buying books.

     c.   Scheduling time with experts.

     d.   Getting a mentor.

     e.   Scheduling time with the supervisor, etc.

H. Implement Their Training Plan and Evaluate During Implementation

15.   During the training, how will you be sure that the employee or volunteer understands the new information and materials?

16.   Will the learning be engaging and enjoyable? This is important for sustaining your investment in the employee's or volunteer's training.

17.   Are you sure that the employee or volunteer will receive the necessary ongoing feedback, coaching, mentoring, etc., during training and development activities? Identify resources you can call on for this and check in with the employee or volunteer throughout the implementation of the plan.

18.   Where will the employee or volunteer get the necessary administrative support and materials?

19.   Regularly collect the learner's impressions of the training experiences and any evidence how he/she is doing in the program. Does your employee or volunteer understand the learning methods as they are being applied? Is he/she regularly providing feedback about how well he/she understands the materials?

I. Evaluate Their Learning When the Plan Has Been Implemented

20.   Was the employee or volunteer able to sufficiently display the competencies necessary for the tasks, job or role?

21.   Are there any plans for follow-up evaluation, including assessing results several months after the employee or volunteer has completed the training plan?

How to Ensure Maximum Performance From Your Employees and Volunteers

The term "supervisor" is referred to throughout this section. Remember that supervisors exist throughout the ranks of management. A supervisor is someone who has at least one person reporting to him/her and, therefore, is responsible for the progress and productivity of that person. For example, a CEO supervises middle managers who supervise entry-level supervisors who supervise individual contributors.

How to Set Relevant and Realistic Goals With Your Employees and Volunteers

Supervisors Often Lack Understanding of Performance

Performance is when an employee or volunteer is achieving a goal in a highly effective and efficient manner and when that goal is closely aligned with achieving the overall goals of the organization. A common problem for new supervisors is having no clear, strong sense of whether their employees or volunteers are high performing or not.

Employees and volunteers can be very busy in their roles, but that does not mean they are high-performing if their roles are not directly contributing toward achieving the overall goals of the organization. The first step toward solving this problem is to establish clear performance goals. Some people have a strong negative reaction toward setting goals because they fear goals as "the law" that must be maintained and never broken. Some people fear they will never achieve the goals. Others have disdain for goals because goals seem to take the "heart" out their work.

Advantages of Using Goals in the Workplace

Despite the negative views that one can have about goals, they hold certain strong advantages in the workplace. They:

1.   Provide clear direction to supervisors, employees and volunteers.

2.   Form a common frame of reference around which they can effectively communicate.

3.   Clearly indicate success, and can cultivate a strong sense of fulfillment for those working toward achieving the goals.

4.   Help clarify the specific expectations of the supervisor, employee and volunteer.

Performance Gaps, Growth Gaps, Opportunity Gaps and Training Gaps

Goals can be useful for specifying expectations and for setting measurements of progress in working to fill four types of gaps:

1.   **Performance gaps**
         These gaps are identified during the employee or volunteer performance management process. Ideally, performance gaps are addressed by performance improvement plans.

Performance improvement plans are sometimes a last-ditch effort at helping a person to improve his/her performance. Ideally, the performance problem is addressed through ongoing feedback and adjustments during regular one-on-one meetings. In these plans, goals are established to improve performance, and may include, for example, increased effort on the part of the employee or volunteer, support from his/her supervisor, and certain training and resources to assist the person in his/her development. Dedicated employees and volunteers can greatly appreciate having specific performance goals for them to achieve in order to keep their jobs, verify their competence to their supervisor and accomplish overall professional development.

2. **Growth gaps**

These gaps are identified during career planning. Employees perceive certain areas of knowledge and skills that they would like to accomplish in order to qualify for certain future roles and positions. Employees often appreciate having clear-cut goals that mark what they need to do to advance in their careers. Career development usually is not associated with the use of volunteers in an organization, although progressive organizations might do so.

3. **Opportunity gaps**

These gaps are identified when a sudden opportunity arises for the employee or volunteer. If the person is highly interested in taking advantage of the opportunity, then he or she will appreciate knowing exactly what goals must be achieved to take advantages of the opportunity. Growth gaps and opportunity gaps are very similar.

4. **Training gaps**

These gaps are identified when hiring a new employee or recruiting a new volunteer, during performance management planning or career planning. Gaps are usually in terms of areas of knowledge, skills or abilities (competencies). Training plans can be designed with clear-cut training goals to give direction to the employee, volunteer or trainer.

Whatever the type of goal, it is critical that the employee or volunteer have strong ownership and commitment to achieving the goal.

Goals Should Be SMARTER

You can help ensure that goals are agreeable to supervisor, employee and volunteer by ensuring that they are highly involved in identifying the goals. When setting goals with others, strive to describe them to be "SMARTER." This acronym stands for goals that are:

1. **Specific**

For example, a goal to generate three types of financial statements, including cash flow, budget-versus-actual and income statement.

2. **Measurable**

For example, to be able to assess if the three types of statements were generated or not.

3. **Achievable**

For example, the goal would be irrelevant if the person had no access to the financial information from which to generate the statements.

4. **Relevant**

    For example, the goal would not be useful if the organization has no plans to ever make decisions based on the financial statements.

5. **Timely**

    The statements should be generated by a certain deadline, for example, in time for the Board to review and approve the statements.

6. **Extending capabilities**

    Ideally, the goal involves the person's learning more than they already knew about generating statements.

7. **Rewarding**

    Ideally, the activities of generating the financial statements would be fulfilling for the person to accomplish.

If goals seem insurmountable to the employee, then break goals down into smaller goals, or sub-goals or objectives until they are SMARTER.

How to Delegate For Growth and Performance of Your Employees and Volunteers

Delegation is when supervisors give responsibility and authority to their subordinates to complete a task by a certain date, and generally let the subordinates figure out how the task can be accomplished. Effective delegation develops people who not only are more productive in the workplace, but also who are more fulfilled. Supervisors become more fulfilled and productive themselves as they learn to rely more on their employees and volunteers and, thus, are freed up to attend to more strategic matters in their own jobs.

Delegation is often difficult for new supervisors, particularly if they have had to scramble to start the organization or a major new program by themselves. Many supervisors want to remain comfortable, making the same decisions the same way that they have always made decisions – doing the same jobs the same way they have always done those jobs. These supervisors believe they can do the jobs better than anyone else so why ask anyone else to do them. New supervisors often do not want to risk losing any of their new power and stature by sharing them with others (ironically, those supervisors do lose these if they do not soon learn to delegate effectively). Sometimes, supervisors do not want to risk giving authority to subordinates in case the subordinates fail and somehow impair the organization.

However, supervisors do not progress in their careers and do not develop their people if they do not learn how to effectively delegate to others. There are basic approaches to delegation that, with practice, become the backbone of effective supervision and development. Thomas R. Horton, in *Delegation and Team Building: No Solo Acts Please* (Management Review, September 1992, pp. 58-61) suggests the following general steps to accomplish delegation:

1. **Delegate the whole task to one person.**

    This gives the person complete responsibility for doing the task and increases the person's motivation to do the task, as well. It also provides more focus for the supervisor when working with the person to understand that the desired results should look like.

2.   **Select the right person to delegate to.**
Assess the skills and capabilities of the person to be sure that the person can actually accomplish the task. Does he/she have the knowledge, skills and abilities to do the task? If not, the person might need training. Or, perhaps the task should be delegated to someone else.

3.   **Clearly specify your preferred results.**
Provide information on what the results should look like, why those results are desired, when the results should be accomplished, who else might help the person, and what resources the person has to work with. You might leave the "how to accomplish the task" to be decided by the person. It is often best to write this information down.

4.   **Delegate responsibility and authority – assign the task, not the method to accomplish it.**
Let the person complete the task in the manner that he/she chooses, as long as the desired results are like to be what the supervisor specifies. Let the person have strong input as to the completion date of the project. Note that you may not even know how to complete the task yourself – this is often the case with higher levels of management. Make sure that others in the organization understand that this person has both the responsibility and the authority to complete the task.

5.   **Ask the person to summarize back to you, a description of the results you prefer.**
Explain that you are requesting the summary to be sure you effectively described the results to the person, not necessarily to be sure that the person heard you. That explanation helps the person to not feel as if he/she is somehow being treated as if he/she is untrustworthy.

6.   **Get ongoing non-intrusive feedback about progress on the project.**
This is a good reason to continue to get weekly, written status reports from the person. Reports should describe what he/she did last week, plans to do next week, and any potential issues that might arise. Regular meetings with the person provide feedback, as well.

7.   **Maintain open lines of communication.**
Do not hover over the person to monitor his/her performance, but do sense what he/she is doing and do support the person's checking in with you while doing the task.

8.   **If you are not satisfied with the progress, do not do the task yourself!**
Continue to work with the person to ensure that he/she perceives that the task is his/her responsibility. Look for the cause of your dissatisfaction. For example, is it lack of communication, training, resources, commitment of the person, etc?

9.   **Evaluate and reward the person's performance.**
Evaluate achievement of desired results more than the methods used by the person. Address insufficient performance and reward successes. (Upcoming topics in this section will help you to evaluate the performance, including addressing performance problems and rewarding performance.)

How to Support Your Employee's and Volunteer's Self-Motivation

Clearing Up Some Common Myths About Motivation

The topic of motivating employees is extremely important to supervisors. Despite the importance of the topic, several myths persist – especially among new supervisors. Before looking at what management can do to support the motivation of employees, it is important first to clear up these common myths.

Myth #1 – "I can motivate people."
Not really – they have to motivate themselves. You cannot motivate people anymore than you can empower them. Employees have to motivate and empower themselves. However, you can set up an environment where they best motivate and empower themselves. The key is knowing what environment will work for each of your employees.

Myth #2 – "Money is a good motivator."
Not necessarily. Certain things like money, a nice office and job security can help people from becoming less motivated, but they do not always help people to become more motivated. A key goal is to understand the motivations of each of your employees.

Myth #3 – "Fear is a damn good motivator."
Fear is a great motivator – for a very short time. That is why a lot of yelling from the boss will might seem to "light a spark" under employees and volunteers, but not for very long.

Myth #4 – "I know what motivates me, so I know what motivates others."
Different things motivate different people. I may be greatly motivated by earning time away from my job in order to spend more time my family. You might be motivated much more by recognition of a job well done. Again, a key goal is to understand what motivates each of your employees and volunteers.

Myth #5 – "Increased job satisfaction means increased job performance."
Research shows increased job satisfaction does not necessarily mean increased job performance. Employees might be very satisfied just sitting at their desks and playing games on their computers. However, that does not produce high-performing employees and volunteers.

Myth #6 – "Motivation is a complex social science. I cannot understand it."
Not true. There are some very basic steps you can take that will go a long way toward supporting your employees and volunteers to motivate themselves toward increased performance in their jobs. (More about these steps is provided later on in this section.)

Basic Principles to Remember

1. **Motivating employees and volunteers starts with motivating yourself.**
   It is amazing how, if you hate your job, it seems like everyone else does, too. If you are very stressed out, it seems like everyone else is, too. Enthusiasm also is contagious. If you are enthusiastic about your job, it is much easier for others to be, too. Also, if you are doing a good job of taking care of yourself and your own job, then you will have much clearer perspective on how well others are taking care of themselves and their jobs, too.

2. **Key to supporting motivation of others is understanding what motivates each of them.**
    Different things motivate each person. Whatever steps you take to support the motivation of your employees and volunteers, be sure to start with finding out what it is that really motivates each of them.

3. **Recognize that supporting other's motivation is a process, not a task.**
    Organizations change all the time, as do people. Indeed, it is an ongoing process to sustain an environment where people can strongly motivate themselves. If you look at sustaining other's motivation as an ongoing process, then you will be much more fulfilled and motivated yourself.

4. **Support motivation by using organizational systems – not just good intentions.**
    Do not just count on cultivating strong interpersonal relationships with others in order to help them to motivate themselves. The nature of these relationships can change greatly, for example, during times of stress. Instead, use reliable and comprehensive systems in the workplace to help motivate employees. For example, establish fair and equitable personnel policies about employee performance management, and about benefits and compensation.

5. **Always work to align goals of the organization with goals of employees and volunteers.**
    As mentioned above, people can be all excited about their work and be working very hard. However, if the results of their work do not directly contribute to the goals of the organization, then the organization is not any better off than if they were just sitting on their hands – maybe even worse off because you are paying them to not be productive! Therefore, it is critical that supervisors know what they want from their employees and volunteers. These preferences should be worded in terms of SMARTER goals. Whatever steps you take to support the motivation of others, ensure that they have strong input to identifying their goals and that these goals are aligned with the goals of the organization.

Steps You Can Take

The following specific steps can help you go a long way toward supporting your employees and volunteers to motivate themselves in your organization.

1. **Do more than read this Field Guide – actually apply what you are reading here.**
    This maxim is true when reading any management publication.

2. **Write down motivational factors that sustain you and how to keep them.**
    This little bit of "motivational planning" not only helps your motivation, but also can give you strong perspective on how to think about supporting the motivations of others.

3. **Make of list of three to five things that motivate each of your employees and volunteers.**
    Have each of your employees and volunteers complete the checklist on page 227. Then meet with each of them to discuss what he/she thinks are the most important motivational factors to him/her. Lastly, take some time alone to write down how you will modify your approaches with each of them to ensure that his/her motivational factors are being met.

4. **Work with each person to include his/her motivations in how he/she is rewarded.**
    For example, the employee's or volunteer's job might be redesigned to be more fulfilling. You might find more means to provide recognition, if that is important to the person. You might develop a personnel policy that rewards the person with more family time.

5. **Use one-on-one meetings with each person to build a relationship with him/her.**
In the workplace, people often are more motivated by your care and concern for them than by your attention to their work. Get to know each of your employees and volunteers, and a bit about their families, their favorite foods, names of their children, etc. This can sound manipulative – and it will be if not done sincerely.

6. **Cultivate strong skills in delegation.**
Delegation includes conveying responsibility and authority to your employees so they can carry out certain tasks. However, you usually should leave it up to your employees to decide *how* they will carry out the tasks. This also allows employees to take a stronger role in their jobs, which usually means more fulfillment and motivation in their jobs, as well.

 Consider "How to Delegate for Growth and Performance of Your Employees" on page 221.

7. **Implement at least the basic principles of performance management.**
Good performance management includes identifying goals and measures to indicate if the goals are being met or not, providing ongoing attention and feedback about measures toward the goals, and suggesting corrective actions to redirect activities back toward achieving the desired goals when necessary. Good performance management techniques provide strong motivation for employees and volunteers because they clearly understand what is expected of them, feel that they are being treated fairly and equitably, and rewarded for when they have done a good job.

8. **Establish goals that are SMARTER.**
SMARTER goals are: specific, measurable, achievable, relevant, timely, extending of capabilities, and rewarding to those involved.

 See "How to Set Relevant and Realistic Goals With Your Employees and Volunteers" on page 220.

9. **Clearly convey how your desired results contribute to organizational results.**
Employees and volunteers often feel strong fulfillment from realizing that they are actually making a difference in the organization when they achieve your desired results. This realization requires clear communications from you about organizational goals and how the desired results are directly aligned with those goals.

10. **As much as possible, reward desired behaviors when you *see* the behaviors.**
A critical lesson for new supervisors is to learn to focus on employees' and volunteers' behaviors, not on their personalities. One of the best ways to ensure that you maintain focus on behaviors, rather than on personalities, is to use your eyes more than your feelings when assessing performance. You can get in a great deal of trouble (legally, morally and interpersonally) by focusing only on how you *feel* about others' performance, rather than primarily on what you are actually *seeing* or reading regarding their performance.

11. **Or, reward the desired behaviors soon after you see them.**
    This helps to reinforce the notion that you highly prefer the behaviors that you are currently seeing from your employees and volunteers. Often, the shorter the time between an employee's or volunteer's action and your reward for that action, the clearer it is to the employee or volunteer that you indeed highly prefer that action.

12. **Celebrate achievements!**
    This critical step is often forgotten. Celebration of achievements is not direct means of motivating employees, rather it cultivates an environment where employees and volunteers can more readily feel a sense of accomplishment, and thus, fulfillment, in their jobs. New supervisors are often focused on getting "a lot done." This usually means identifying and solving problems. Experienced supervisors have come to understand that acknowledging and celebrating a solution to a problem can be every bit as important as finding the solution itself. Without ongoing acknowledgement of success, employees and volunteers can become very frustrated, skeptical and even cynical about their efforts in the organization.

13. **Let employees and volunteers hear from their customers (internal or external).**
    Let them hear how they have benefited the nonprofit's clients or other employees or volunteers in the nonprofit. For example, if the employee or volunteer is working to keep internal computer systems operating well, then have other employees or volunteers express their gratitude for how well the computers are operating. Similarly, if an employee or volunteer is helping to provide a program to a client, then bring in the client to express his/her appreciation to the employee or volunteer.

14. **Admit to yourself (or to someone else) if you do not like an employee or volunteer.**
    Supervisors are people. You may find that you just do not like someone who works for you. That someone could, for example, look like an uncle you do not like. In that case, admit to yourself that you do not like the person. Then talk about your dislike confidentially with a confidant (someone else who is appropriate to talk to, for example, a peer, your boss, your mentor, etc.). Indicate to the confidant that you want to explore what it is that you do not like about the person who works for you and that you would like to come to a clearer perception of how you can accomplish a positive working relationship with that person. It often helps a great deal just to talk out loud about how you feel and to get someone else's opinion about the situation. As noted above, if you continue to focus on what you *see* about the person's performance, you will go a long way toward ensuring that your treatment of person remains fair and equitable.

Table VI:2 – Checklist of Categories of Typical Motivators

To help you identify what motivates you, consider from among the following categories of typical motivators. Rank the categories, starting with "1" as the highest. You might have several categories that rank a "1". Do not worry about getting your ranking to be "perfect." The point is to go through the process of thinking about what motivates you. Consider discussing the results with your supervisor, friends, etc.

__ Career Development / Success

__ Comfort / Relaxation

__ Health / Balance / Energy

__ Influence / Leadership

__ Learning / Knowledge / Discovery

__ Materials / Possessions

__ Recognition / Praise (It is OK to seek this.)

__ Security / Money / House

__ Social / Affiliation / Popularity / Acceptance

__ Status / Prestige / Stand Out / Reputation (It is OK to seek this.)

__ Task Accomplishment / Problem Solving / Achievement

__ Teaching / Guiding Others

__ Vitality / Energy

__ Others? _____

Are there other comments you could make that would help you (and maybe others) to more clearly understand what motivates you? Take a moment to consider this question and write down your answers.

How to Know What Role to Play – Facilitate, Coach, Direct or Train?

As a nonprofit leader, you might perform a variety of roles when leading others, primarily the roles of facilitator, coach, expert or trainer. There are no specific indicators as to when you should fill a certain role. However, there are general guidelines from which you can get an indication as to which roles you might fill based on current conditions in the organization or in a project.

When You Might Fill the Facilitator Role

Facilitating is helping a person or group of people to decide what results they want to achieve, how they want to achieve them and then helping them to achieve the results. Facilitation styles range from directive to indirectly suggestive. Conditions when a leader might want to act as a facilitator include:

1. **When a project needs strong, ongoing trust, commitment and participation of others.**
   Ongoing ownership and commitment from others usually do not come from others during trainings or when receiving expert advice. Instead, the buy-in of others comes from knowing that their beliefs and opinions are being solicited and valued. The essence of facilitation is to bring out those beliefs and opinions and to help others decide what they want to do and how they want to do it.

2. **When working to address complex problems or major goals with others.**
   The most accurate understanding of a situation often comes from considering the open and honest perspectives of everyone involved. Facilitation often is the most approach to make it safe for, and to solicit, the perspectives from others.

When You Might Fill the Coaching Role

You might choose to fill the coaching role when the following conditions exist:

1. **An individual seems stalled or troubled.**
   Coaching can be a powerful means to guide and support an individual to clarify current challenges or priorities, identify suitable strategies to address the challenges, and then to actually implement the strategies.

2. **To maximize an individual's learning from experience.**
   Individuals learn differently. Coaching can be a powerful means to guide and support individuals to reflect on their experiences and then use that learning to improve effectiveness in life and work.

Consider "How to Coach for Deep Problem-Solving and Learning" on page 230.

When You Might Fill the Expert Role

You might choose to fill the expert role when the following conditions exist:

1. **The situation requires knowledge that would likely be used the same in any context.**
   There are certain types of general knowledge that would probably be used the same in any organization or project, for example, setting up and operating financial systems, and many of the practices in management.

2. **The project needs knowledge that is highly specialized and proceduralized.**
   For example, installing computers, conducting market research, conforming to laws and regulations, designing and providing certain program services, financial processes and procedures, or use of specific tools for problem solving and decision-making.

When You Might Fill the Trainer Role

Training includes activities to help a learner or learners to develop or enhance knowledge, skills and attitudes to improve performance on current or future task or job. You might choose to fill the trainer role when the following conditions exist.

1. **Expert knowledge needs to be conveyed in a concise and timely manner.**
   There may be times where employees and volunteers need to learn certain expert-based knowledge in a highly focused and efficient manner. The knowledge might be any form of expert-based knowledge as listed in the above topic about playing the expert role.

2. **Knowledge needs to be conveyed to a group of people.**
   Training is often most useful when a group of people need to learn expert-based knowledge. This can be quite common in projects, for example, when training project members about the nature of organizational change or the project's change plans or methods of data collection.

Guidelines for Switching Roles Between Facilitator and Expert

1. **Be clear which "hat" you are wearing to your employee or volunteer.**
   You might even refer to your various roles as your wearing various "hats." Otherwise, your employee or volunteer can become confused about your current priorities, how you are addressing them and how they should interact with you.

2. **Be clear about the source of your advice.**
   Be clear as to whether your advice is based on your expertise (your expert role), general knowledge in the field (other experts) or the learners' own wisdom. Facilitators often count on the wisdom of the participants in their groups.

3. **Know your own expertise and the limits of that expertise.**
   When you realize that you do not have sufficient skills to address a current issue or goal with another, then you are often more effective to adopt a facilitator role. That role more advantageously recruits the skills of others, in addition to your own.

4. **Do not fall in love with one role.**
   Leaders who value their own expertise and prefer to exhibit that expertise often resort primarily to the expert role. Similarly, leaders who have strong people skills often resort

primarily to the facilitator role. Highly effective leaders can switch between roles depending on the needs of the current situation, rather than on their personal comfort levels.

How to Coach for Deep Problem-Solving and Learning

One of the primary goals of a leader is to help his/her employees and volunteers to learn to be more effective at solving problems and learning. One of the most powerful approaches to do that is through the use of coaching to help others: a) closely examine their own perceptions, assumptions and conclusions about their current problem or goal; b) take relevant and realistic actions; and c) learn by continuing to reflect on those actions and experiences. You can use coaching at almost any time when your employees or volunteers seem to be struggling to address an issue or achieve a goal. Coaching is powerful means to delegate to employees and volunteers.

What Is Coaching? How Is It Useful in Leadership?

There are a variety of different perspectives on coaching due to the dramatic increase in popularity of the field of personal and professional coaching. For the context of leading others in the workplace, coaching could be described as using skills in listening, questioning and support to help another to:

1. **Take a complete look at his/her current situation.**
   This includes asking the person useful questions to clarify his/her assumptions and perceptions about the current situation.

2. **Set relevant and realistic goals for themselves.**
   Based on insights from answering the questions, the person sets relevant, realistic and specific goals based on his/her own nature, needs, capabilities and timelines.

3. **Take relevant and realistic actions toward reaching the goals.**
   A hallmark of good coaching is supporting others to take ongoing actions toward his/her goals, rather than only to reflect and think about the situation.

4. **Learn by continuing to reflect on useful questions and results of actions.**
   The person who gets coached often learns a great deal from reflecting on the questions posed to him/her and on the results of the actions that he/she is taking.

Coaching is highly adaptable to the nature of the person being coached because it works from the person's answers to the coach's questions, rather than working at the person by asserting directives to him/her. It helps the person to closely examine his/her own style, thinking and approaches to problem solving.

Guidelines for Designing a Coaching Session

The nature of a coaching conversation can be distinctly different from a typical workplace conversation. A typical conversation is usually a spontaneous exchange of information that almost seems to "ping pong" casually back and forth among the participants. The focus of the conversation can move with whatever comments are offered by participants. In contrast, coaching is usually a much more focused conversation in which the nature of exchange is based, in large part, on asking powerful questions to another, while using effective listening and feedback skills, as you support the person in thoughtfully answering the questions.

You need to intentionally prepare yourself and your employee or volunteer for a coaching session. Consider the following guidelines:

1. **Briefly describe the nature of coaching and its benefits to your employee or volunteer.**
    Mention that one of the most powerful ways to help someone solve a problem or clarify plans to achieve a goal is through use of a coaching session. Explain how coaching helps the person closely examine the situation, carefully think about action plans, and learn at the same time. Explain the role of questions during coaching.

2. **Ask the employee or volunteer if he/she would like you to coach him/her.**
    You should always get the person's permission to be coached. Otherwise, the person may feel uncomfortable, manipulated and distrusting during questioning.

3. **Consider any culturally specific conventions.**
    Depending on the conventions in the particular culture of your organization and on the personality of the person you plan to coach, the person might not appreciate getting questioned by you. In some cultures, questions might be perceived as disrespectful.

    Consider "How to Lead in Multicultural Organizations" on page 106.

4. **Focus on organizational issues, not just on the individual's issues.**
    Your role is to facilitate organizational change, not only to facilitate change in one individual. Thus, you should maintain focus on the desired results for the organization in addition to the current challenges of the person whom you are coaching.

5. **Use the guidelines for effective listening.**
    For example, be sure that you can hear the person, listen more than talk, and acknowledge the person's responses.

    Consider "How to Really Listen to Others" on page 103.

6. **Respectfully and supportively offer probing questions.**
    Questions are the heart of the coaching session. The rest of this section on coaching provides numerous guidelines about traits of useful and not so useful questions, along with examples of powerful questions.

7. **Limit advice during the questioning.**
    Sometimes, you might feel an urge to answer a question that the person seems to be struggling to answer. The person might be struggling because he/she is searching for the best answer. That search can yield a great deal of learning for the person.

8. **Limit general discussion during the questioning.**
    A general discussion can diffuse the focus on the questioning. Instead, keep focused on asking questions. Each question might be based on answers to the previous question. There can be other times in the project for general discussion.

9. **Avoid lecturing your employee or volunteer.**
    This guideline is relevant to probably any supportive and respectful communication with another. Lecturing can be detected by regular use of phrases, such as "you should" or "you have to." Lecturing often leaves others feeling judged and angry.

10. **Use questions to help the person develop action plans.**
    Often, it is useful to help your employee or volunteer come to conclusions by helping him/her to decide whether to take action and what those actions should be. Often, actions "shake loose" solutions and generate learning.

11. **Use questions to help your employee or volunteer learn from the coaching session.**
    Your employee or volunteer can generate valuable insights from thinking about and responding to useful questions from you. It is important for you to help the person to identify and take ownership for that learning.

12. **Close the coaching session.**
    Always use some means for specifically ending the coaching session. For example, thank the person, ask what they have learned, mention the value of the coaching session to you, or physically move to a different location. Ask the person to summarize his/her learning and ask him/her about next steps.

Why Questions Are So Important in Coaching

The primary tool in coaching is your respectfully and supportively posing powerful questions to your employee or volunteer. There are several advantages to questioning when coaching a person.

1. **It helps the person to recognize his/her own perceptions and assumptions.**
    Usually, a coaching session starts with the person describing some issue or goal that is important to him/her. For example, the person might explain to you that he or she believes that he/she has a significant problem with time management. The person might add that he/she has tried hard to address the problem, but does not seem to be getting anywhere. The person might suggest that he/she needs to take a time management course.

2. **It helps the person to clarify his/her own assumptions.**
    As the person continues to think about the questions posed by you, he/she usually provides more information about the reasoning that led to the conclusion that there's a time management problem, for example, the person might mention that other leaders seem to get more done, and feel much less frustrated.

3. **It helps the person to verify his/her own assumptions.**

   As you pose more questions (for example, about whether others really do get much more done and really do not feel frustrated), the person might question him/herself about whether the person is being realistic about the amount of tasks to get done in a day, and ultimately, whether the time management problem might be a symptom of another larger problem.

4. **It helps the person to modify their views on the issues.**

   Many times, finding the right problem is at least as important as finding the right answer. As the coaching session progresses, the person might seem to be talking about another problem or goal. For example, the person might mention that he/she wishes for more guidance from you about setting priorities and providing more resources, but that he/she is reluctant to ask you for help for fear of appearing incompetent.

5. **It helps the person to arrive at realistic conclusions about what to do.**

   Many times, leaders in nonprofit organizations are faced with so many challenges and options for meeting those challenges that they do not know what to do. Other times, leaders of nonprofits are so inspired and driven that they struggle to be realistic. Coaching helps people to move on to action-oriented conclusions that are relevant and realistic.

6. **It helps the person to develop powerful skills in inquiry and reflection.**

   In our example, over several coaching sessions, the person often begins to develop his/her own skills in asking useful questions to others and themselves. Conversations become more focused, particularly on useful actions and learning. The person is learning to solve his/her own problems and identify learning, too.

7. **It allows you to help your employee or volunteer without extensive background.**

   One of the major advantages of using questions during coaching is that often you can help another person without having to know a great deal of history about the particular issue or goal faced by that person. Actually, the more that you know about how the person got stuck on a particular issue, the more that you can sometimes get as stuck as that person during coaching. Many times, people struggle because of strong misperceptions. The more that you closely examine the background and thinking about those misperceptions, the more that you might adopt those misperceptions yourself. You can avoid that trap by asking questions during coaching sessions.

Traits of Destructive Questions

Before suggesting guidelines to conduct supportive questioning, it is important for you to know what types of questions to avoid. Consider these guidelines:

1. **Avoid asking questions that can be answered simply with "yes" or "no."**
    You and your employee or volunteer gain little understanding or direction from such pointed questions that have such short answers. Instead, consider questions that start with "What," "How," "When" and "Where."

2. **Avoid leading questions.**
    Leading questions are questions that are asked to lead another to a certain pre-determined conclusion or insight. Those questions can be perceived by the other as being manipulative and dishonest. Leading questions often can be answered with "yes" or "no," for example, "You did what I suggested, right?"

3. **Avoid frequently asking questions that begin with "Why."**
    Those types of questions can leave others feeling defensive, as if they are to be accountable to you to justify their actions. That feeling of defensiveness can damage feelings of trust and openness between you and your employees and volunteers.

Traits of Useful Questions

Consider these guidelines:

1. **Where possible, use open-ended questions.**
    Open-ended questions are those that are not answered with "yes" or "no." They generate thinking and reflection on the part of the person you are coaching. They also ensure that the person keeps focused in the coaching session.

2. **Focus questions on the here-and-now.**
    The goal of coaching is to help the person to go forward by changing how he/she looks at the problem, identifying realistic actions to take, and learning from those actions.

3. **Ask questions to clarify what the other is saying.**
    Clarifying questions help you and the person you are coaching to understand the key point or "bottom line" of what he/she is saying. They often lead to discovering the root cause of issues.

4. **Ask questions about the person's perspectives, assumptions and actions.**
    Adults can learn a great deal by closely examining their own thinking. Often, they struggle because of inaccurate perceptions or assumptions. Therefore, ask questions about their thinking, assumptions and beliefs about current priorities. Do not ask lots of questions about other people – you cannot coach people who are not with you.

5. **Ask the other person for help.**
    It can be powerful when you show enough trust and confidence in the relationship with your employee or volunteer that you can ask him/her for help with helping them. For example, you might ask, "What question should I ask you?" or "What additional questions should I be asking now?"

Examples of Powerful Questions for Coaching

It is common that a coaching session goes through a certain life cycle. Initially, the person you are coaching will report some major problem, goal, challenge or priority. Your questions can be useful at that time to help the person to report the problem or goal, and then to closely examine and clarify that priority. Next, you can help the person to identify useful actions to take to effectively address the priority. Lastly, you can help the person to learn from the coaching session itself. Consider the questions in the following table when coaching your employee or volunteer. Notice the grouping of the questions into the four stages of a useful coaching session.

Table VI:3 – Useful Questions to Ask When Coaching Others

1. To Help Another Report a Priority:

- What do you want to work on today?
- What is wrong? What is missing?
- What would be exciting to achieve?
- What would you like from me today?
- How would you like to get it?

2. To Help Another Clarify the Priority:

- What is important?
- How is this issue important?
- What do you think the real problem is?
- What is your role in this issue?
- Where do you feel stuck?
- Is what you are doing getting what you want?
- What is the intent of what you are saying?
- Where are those strong feelings coming from?
- What would you like me to ask?

3. To Help Another Move to Action(s):

- Have you experienced anything like this before? What did you do? How did it work out?
- What do you hope for?
- What is preventing you from...?
- What would you be willing to give up for that?
- If you could change one thing, what would it be?
- Imagine a point in the future where your issue is resolved. How did you get there?
- What can you do before the next meeting?
- Who will do that action? By when? What will it look like when done? How will you know it is done?

4. To Help Another Deepen Learning:

- Have you said everything that you want to say?
- How did this coaching session go for you?
- What is the learning in this for you?

How to Share Useful – and Respectful – Feedback

Feedback to employees and volunteers is information regarding their performance and also is information they can act on. Feedback must be shared in a manner that is understandable to them and is perceived by them as being provided in a highly respectful manner. Sharing feedback involves skills in effective listening, verbal and non-verbal communications, and working in multi-cultural environments. Consider the following guidelines, as well.

1. **Be clear about what you want to say before you say it.**
   You might have already sensed what feedback you want to convey. However, you should be clear to yourself about what you want to convey and how you want to convey it.

2. **Share your feedback in a concise and specific manner, then you can embellish.**
   People often lose specificity when they speak because they say far too much, rather than not enough. Or, they speak about general themes and patterns. When giving feedback, first share what you saw or heard, what you want instead, and how the person can achieve it. Then you can add more descriptive information if necessary.

3. **Avoid generalizations.**
   Avoid use of the words "all," "never" and "always." Those words can seem extreme, lack credibility and place arbitrary limits on behavior. Be more precise about quantity or proportion, if you address terms of quantities, at all.

4. **Be descriptive rather than evaluative.**
   Report what you are seeing, hearing or feeling. Attempt to avoid evaluative words, such as "good" or "bad." It may be helpful to quickly share your particular feeling, if appropriate, but do not dwell on it or become emotional.

5. **Own the feedback.**
   The information should be about your own perception of information, not about the other's perceptions, assumptions and motives. Use 'I' statements as much as possible to indicate that your impressions are your own.

6. **Be careful about giving advice.**
   When giving feedback, it is often best to do one thing at a time – share your feedback, get the person's response to your feedback, and then, when he/she is more ready to consider additional information, share your advice with him/her.

How to Understand and Manage Conflict

Clarifying Confusion About Conflict

Conflict occurs with two or more people who, despite their first attempts at agreement, do not yet have agreement on a course of action, usually because their values, perspectives and opinions are contradictory in nature. Conflict can occur:

1.   Within yourself when you are not living according to your values.

2.   When your values and perspectives are threatened.

3.   Discomfort from fear of the unknown or from lack of fulfillment.

Conflict is inevitable and often necessary when forming high-performing teams because they evolve through "form, storm, norm and perform" periods. Getting the most out of diversity often means addressing contradictory values, perspectives and opinions.

Conflict is often needed. It:

- Helps to raise and address problems.

- Energizes work to be focused on the most important priorities.

- Helps people "be real" and motivates them to fully participate.

- Helps people learn how to recognize and benefit from their differences.

Conflict is not the same as discomfort. The conflict is not the problem – poor management of the conflict is the problem. Conflict is a problem when it:

- Hampers productivity.

- Lowers morale.

- Causes more and continued conflicts.

- Causes inappropriate behaviors.

Types of Managerial Actions That Cause Workplace Conflicts

1.   **Poor communications**

a.   Employees and volunteers experience continual surprises, for example, they are not informed of major decisions that affect their workplaces and lives.

b.   Employees and volunteers do not understand the reasons for the decisions – they are not involved in the decision-making.

c.   As a result, they trust the "rumor mill" more than their management.

237

2. **The alignment or the amount of resources is insufficient. There is:**

   a. Disagreement about "who does what."

   b. Stress from working with inadequate resources.

3. **"Personal chemistry," including conflicting values or actions, for example:**

   a. Strong interpersonal natures among workers do not seem to match.

   b. We do not like others because they seem too much like ourselves (we often do not like in others what we do not like in ourselves).

4. **Leadership problems**
   For example, inconsistent, missing, too-strong or uninformed leadership (at any level in the organization), evidenced by:

   a. Avoiding conflict, "passing the buck" with little follow-through on decisions.

   b. Employees and volunteers see the same continued issues in the workplace.

   c. Supervisors do not understand the jobs of their subordinates.

Key Managerial Actions / Structures to Minimize Conflicts

1. **Regularly review job descriptions.**
   Get your employee's input to them. Write down and date job descriptions. Ensure:

   a. Job roles do not conflict.

   b. No tasks "fall in a crack."

2. **Intentionally build relationships with all subordinates.**

   a. Meet at least once a month alone with them in office.

   b. Ask about accomplishments, challenges and issues.

3. **Get regular, written status reports that describe:**

   a. Accomplishments.

   b. Currents issues and needs from management.

   c. Plans for the upcoming period.

4. **Conduct basic training about:**

   a. Interpersonal communications.

   b. Conflict management.

    c.   Delegation.

5.   **Develop procedures for routine tasks and include the employees' input.**

    a.   Have employees and volunteers write procedures when possible and appropriate.

    b.   Get employees and volunteers' review of the procedures.

    c.   Distribute the procedures.

    d.   Train employees and volunteers about the procedures.

6.   **Regularly hold management meetings with all employees.**
For example, every month, communicate new initiatives and status of current programs.

7.   **Consider an anonymous suggestion box in which employees can provide suggestions.**
This can be powerful means to collect honest feedback, especially in very conflicted workplaces.

Ways People Deal With Conflict

There is no one best way to deal with conflict. It depends on the current situation. Here are the major ways that people use to deal with conflict:

1.   **You can avoid it.**
They can pretend it is not there or ignore it. Use this approach only when it simply is not worth the effort to argue. Be aware that this approach tends to worsen the conflict over time.

2.   **You can accommodate it.**
You can give in to others, sometimes to the extent that you compromise yourself. Use this approach very sparingly and infrequently, for example, in situations when you know that you will have another more useful approach in the very near future. Usually this approach tends to worsen the conflict over time, and causes conflicts within yourself.

3.   **You can compete with the others.**
You can work to get your way, rather than clarifying and addressing the issue. Competitors love accommodators. Use this approach when you have a very strong conviction about your position.

4.   **You can compromise.**
You can engage in mutual give-and-take. This approach is used when the goal is to get past the issue and move on together.

5.   **You can collaborate.**
You can focus on working together. Use this approach when the goal is to meet as many current needs as possible by using mutual resources. This approach sometimes raises new mutual needs. Collaboration can also be used when the goal is to cultivate ownership and commitment.

To Manage a Conflict with Another Person

1. **Know what you do not like about yourself, early on in your career.**
   We often do not like in others what we do not want to see in ourselves.

   a. Write down 5 traits that really bug you when see them in others.

   b. Be aware that these traits are your "hot buttons."

2. **Manage yourself.**
   If you and/or another person are getting upset, then manage yourself to stay calm:

   a. Speak to the person as if the other person is not upset – this can be very effective!

   b. Avoid use of the word "you" – this avoids your appearing to be blaming the person.

   c. Nod your head to assure the person that you heard him/her.

   d. Maintain eye contact with the person.

3. **Move the discussion to a private area, if possible.**
   Many times, moving to a new environment invites both of you to see or feel differently.

4. **Give the other person time to vent.**
   Do not interrupt the person or judge what he/she is saying.

5. **Verify that you are accurately hearing each other.**
   When the other person is done speaking:

   a. Ask the person to let you rephrase (uninterrupted) what you are hearing to ensure you are hearing it correctly.

   b. To understand the person more, ask open-ended questions (avoid "why" questions – those questions often make people feel defensive).

6. **Repeat the above step, this time for the other to verify that he/she is really hearing you.**
   When you describe your perspective:

   a. Use "I", not "you."

   b. Talk in terms of the present as much as possible.

   c. Quickly mention your feelings.

7. **Acknowledge where you disagree and where you agree.**
   One of the most powerful means to resolve conflict is to mention where you both agree.

8. **Discuss the matter on which you disagree, not the nature of the other person.**
    When the person is convinced that you understand him/her:

    a. Ask "What can we do fix the problem?" The person might begin to complain again.

    b. Then ask the same question. Focus on actions you both can do, too.

    c. Ask the other person if they will support the action(s).

    d. If the person will not, then ask for a "cooling off period".

9. **Thank the person for working with you.**
    It takes patience for a person to engage in meaningful conversation during conflict.
    Acknowledge and thank the other person for his/her effort.

10. **If the situation remains a conflict, then**:

    a. Conclude if the other person's behavior violates one of the personnel policies and
        procedures in the workplace and if it does, then follow the policy's terms for addressing
        that violation.

    b. Otherwise, consider whether to agree to disagree?

    c. Consider seeking a third party to mediate?

How to Conduct Meaningful Performance Appraisals

Yearly formal performance reviews for each employee and volunteer are extremely important to
ensuring their strong performance and fulfillment in their jobs. Performance appraisals have come
under fire recently as not being effective in improving performance of employees and volunteers.
Appraisals are not effective – if they are not done well.

Well-done performance reviews help supervisors feel more honest in their relationships with their
subordinates and feel better about themselves in their supervisory roles. Subordinates are assured of
clear understanding of what is expected from them, their own personal strengths and areas for
development, and a solid sense of their relationship with their supervisor. Avoiding performance
issues ultimately decreases morale, decreases credibility of management, decreases the organization's
overall effectiveness and wastes more of management's time.

The process used to evaluate the performance of employees and volunteers should be clearly
specified in the personnel policies and procedures, which are approved by the Board. The appraisal
process should be a mere formality with no surprises for the employee or volunteer, if the supervisor
has been doing his/her job all along, including: a) sharing the written job description, performance
goals, and the personnel policy which guides the appraisal process; and b) sharing useful feedback
with the employee or volunteer during the appraisal period. Consider the following, additional
guidelines.

1.   **Design a legally compliant and valid performance review process.**

    a.   Patricia King, in her book, *Performance Planning and Appraisal* (McGraw-Hill, 1984), mentions that the law requires that performance appraisals be: job-related and valid; based on a thorough analysis of the job; standardized for all employees; not biased against any race, color, sex, religion, or nationality; and performed by people who have adequate knowledge of the person or job.

    b.   You can us the suggestions in this section to design your process. Be sure to build in the process a route for recourse if an employee feels he or she has been dealt with unfairly in an appraisal process, for example, that the employee can go to his or her supervisor's supervisor and/or file a written response with the appraisal for the personnel file. The process should be clearly described in a personnel policy.

2.   **Design a standard form on which to document the person's performance. Include:**

    a.   Name of the employee or volunteer.

    b.   Date the form was completed.

    c.   Dates specifying the time over which the person's performance is being evaluated.

    d.   Section to describe the major work roles and activities conducted by the employee or volunteer during the appraisal period.

    e.   Section to write opinions about the employee's or volunteers: major accomplishments during the appraisal period, exhibited strengths and weaknesses according to the dimensions on the appraisal form, and suggested actions and training or development to improve performance. The form should ask for examples of observed behaviors during the appraisal period that substantiate comments about where performance needs to be improved.

    f.   Reference to the duties and responsibilities on the person's job description, any additionally assigned performance goals that were previously provided to the person in writing.

    g.   Rating system (for example: "poor," "average," "good" and "excellent;" or "does not meet," "meets" and "exceeds expectations"). Next to the description of each rating should be brief explanation of that rating.

    h.   Space for the supervisor's commentary next to each rating.

    i.   Final section for overall commentary from the supervisor.

    j.   Final section for specifying action plans for the employee or volunteer to address to improve performance and/or progress in his/her career.

    k.   Lines for signatures of the supervisor and employee/volunteer. You can design the form so that the signatures either indicate that the person accepts the comments on the appraisal, or contests certain comments on the form.

3. **Schedule the first performance review for six months after the employee starts.**
   The timing of the review depends on the terms specified in the Board-approved personnel policies and procedures, and if there is a specific probationary period associated with the employee's or volunteer's job.

4. **Initiate the performance review process with the employee or volunteer.**
   By now, the person should have received his/her written job description, performance goals and procedure for performance appraisals well in advance of the upcoming performance appraisal process. In a one-on-one meeting with the employee or volunteer:

   a. Tell him/her that you are initiating a scheduled performance review process.

   b. Remind the person of what is involved in the process. You might the personnel policy that directs how appraisals are done.

   c. Schedule a meeting to occur with the two of you and about two weeks out.

   d. Share the standard performance appraisal form with the person and ask him/her to provide opinions about his/her performance on the form. Ask to get the opinions 2-3 days before the upcoming meeting. Mention that you will consider the employee's or volunteer's opinions when you write your own on opinions on the form. Mention that you will share your opinions in writing on the form at least three days before the appraisal meeting.

   e. Ask the person to review the job description and to share comments in the upcoming meeting.

5. **Before the upcoming meeting, document your (the supervisor's) input on the form.**

   a. When writing your opinions, do not just rely on your memory. Reference your files to remind you of the person's activities, any major accomplishments and any concerns that you have observed.

   b. Also reference the person's opinions on the appraisal form that the person shared with you several days before the appraisal meeting.

   c. Mark the appraisal form as "draft" to indicate that it is not the final version. (The version becomes final when the supervisor and employee/volunteer have agreed on the information on the form or the employee/volunteer has attached descriptions of his/her disagreements to the form.)

   d. Share the draft with the employee/volunteer several days before the upcoming appraisal meeting.

6.   **Conduct the one-on-one performance appraisal with the employee or volunteer.**

    a. State that the goals of the meeting are to understand each other's perceptions about the person's performance and about his/her priorities during the next appraisal period.

    b. In the meeting, let the employee speak first about his/her reactions to the content of the appraisal. Then respond with your own opinions. Then discuss areas where you disagree. Then discuss where you agree. Strive for balance of praise and constructive feedback.

    c. Avoid becoming defensive – the process should focus on observed behaviors, not on character traits of each other.

    d. Discuss behaviors, not personalities. Avoid final terms such as "always," "never," etc. Encourage participation and be supportive.

    e. Come to terms on actions to enhance performance or evolve the person's career, where possible.

    f. End the meeting on a positive note. Thank the person for his/her participation.

    g. Ask the employee or volunteer to sign the form in a section that indicates his/her agreement to the information on the form, or whether he/she disagrees and will add an attachment explaining his/her disagreement.

    h. Update the form with any information that you both agreed upon or with the employee's or volunteer's attachment about disagreement. Be sure the employee or volunteer has signed the form. Share copies of the form with the employee or volunteer, and with the supervisor's immediate supervisor. If the organization has a Human Resources department, it will need a copy of the signed form, as well.

7.   **In one-on-one meetings with the employee or volunteer, review status of actions.**
One of the most powerful approaches to accomplishing meaningful appraisals is to meet with the employee or volunteer in one-on-one meetings at least once every two or three months to discuss the employee's or volunteer's progress on the actions listed on the appraisal form. That practice makes the appraisal much more relevant and important to all persons involved in the process.

How to Reward and Retain High-Quality Employees and Volunteers

Major Myths About Rewarding Employees and Volunteers

Myth #1: "Money is the best reward."
No. Research shows that money does not constitute a strong, ongoing reward in and of itself. It is like having a nice office; it can give a temporary boost in morale and energy. The key roles for money and nice offices are that they can stop people from feeling worse.

Myth #2: "Employees are professionals. They should just 'suck it up' and do their jobs."
That view is outdated. Times have changed dramatically. Workers can no longer be treated like machines. They come at a high price and can cost as much to replace. Workers expect to be valued as human beings. Today, the rewarding of workers is done as a partnership between the supervisors and their workers.

Myth #3: "If I reward every time they do something useful, I will have reward all the time."
Employees and volunteers are mature adults. They do not need to be, and do not expect to be, rewarded for every useful thing they do in the workplace. One of the most important outcomes from regularly rewarding workers is that they believe that their supervisors fully acknowledge their value to the workplace.

Myth #4: "We're working to address critical problems, not to make our workers happy."
That is like saying, "This is a wood saw. It should be able to saw wood all the time. It should not ever have to be sharpened!"

Guiding Principles of Effective Reward Systems

There are a variety of ways to reward people for the quality of the work they do in the workplace. For example, rewards can be in the form of money, benefits, time off from work, acknowledgement for work well done, affiliation with other workers or a sense of accomplishment from finishing a major task.

1. **Rewards should support behaviors directly aligned with accomplishing strategic goals.**
    This principle may seem so obvious as to sound trite. However, the goal of carefully tying employees' and volunteers' behaviors to strategic goals has become an important goal really only over the past decade or so. Recently, the term "performance" is being used to designate behaviors that really contribute to the "bottom line." An employee can be working as hard as anyone else, but if his/her behaviors are not tied directly to achieving strategic goals, then the employee might be engaged only in busy-work.

2. **Rewards should be tied to passion and purpose, not to pressure and fear.**
    Fear is a powerful motivator, but only for a short time and then it dissipates. For example, if you have initially motivated employees or volunteers by warning them of a major shortage of funds unless they do a better job, then they will likely be very motivated to work even harder. That approach might work once or twice, but workers soon will realize that the cause of the organization's problems is not because they are not working hard enough. They might soon even resent management's resorting to the use of fear. If, instead, management motivates by reminding workers of their passion for the mission, the motivation will be much more sustainable.

3. **Workers should be able to clearly associate the reward to their accomplishments.**
    Imagine if someone told you "Thank you" and did not say what for. One of the purposes of a reward is to reinforce the positive behaviors that earned the reward in the first place. If employees understand what behaviors they are being rewarded for, they are more likely to repeat those behaviors.

4. **Rewards should occur shortly after the behaviors they are intended to reinforce.**
    The closer the occurrence of the reward to the occurrence of the desired behavior in the workplace, the easier it is for the employee or volunteer to realize why he/she is being rewarded. The easier it is for him/her to understand what behaviors are being appreciated.

Importance of Sense of Purpose and Feeling Appreciated

Finding and training new employees and volunteers is a substantial cost, no matter the size of the organization. One of the best ways to retain employees and volunteers is to reward them for their work. One of the primary rewards for working adults is to feel a sense of meaning, or purpose, in their work. If employees and volunteers feel that they are serving a useful purpose, then they are much more likely to stay at their current job.

A common complaint from staff in small- to medium-sized nonprofits is that they feel burned out. A common symptom of burnout is to feel unappreciated. One of the best ways to address burnout, and retain employees and volunteers, is to ensure that they feel appreciated for their work.

Thus, it is critical that organizations give careful consideration as to how they reward their employees and volunteers. Organizations do not need huge sums of money in order to reward them (besides, the belief that money is the major reward is just a myth). Guidelines in this section will help you to think about what might be the best rewards for your employees and volunteers and to take steps to ensure that you are providing those rewards.

Guidelines to Rewarding Employees

There is not a set of standard rewards to be used for employees and volunteers everywhere. Instead, each person has his/her own nature and needs. The following guidelines will help you to determine what might be the best ways to reward your employees and volunteers.

1. Reward employees by letting them hear positive comments from clients about how the employees' activities benefited the client. This guideline is especially true for nonprofit staff that are dedicated to meeting a public need.

2. Occasionally have a Board member come to a staff meeting to thank the staff. This usually means a lot to nonprofit staff, almost as much as having clients provide positive feedback about the employees' activities.

3. Understand what motivates each of your employees. You can do this by applying the "Checklist of Categories of Typical Motivators" in the previous subsection "Supporting Employee Motivation" on page 227. A major benefit of this approach is that each employee is afforded the opportunity to explain what motivates him or her.

4. In each monthly staff meeting, take a few minutes to open the meeting by mentioning major accomplishments of various employees.

5.   Present gift certificates to employees who have made major accomplishments. Guidelines for determining who gets this reward should be clearly explained in your personnel policies in order to ensure all employees perceive the practice as fair and equitable. Allow employees to recommend other employees for awards.

6.   Probably the most fulfilling for employees is to be able to do useful work. Be sure that each employee understands the mission of the nonprofit and how his/her work is contributing to that mission. Post your mission statement on the walls. Discuss the action-planning section of your strategic plan with employees so that they see how their activities tie directly to achieving the strategic goals of the organization.

How to Effectively Address Performance Issues

If your organization's personnel policies about performance management indicate a specific procedure for handling performance issues, that procedure should be followed very carefully. Otherwise, a court may interpret your official personnel policies to be modified by how you actually handled a performance issue rather than as specified in your policies and you may lose protection from your related policies in court. In the absence of a personnel policy about addressing performance issues, the following steps are suggested.

Note that performance issues should always be based on behaviors that you see, not on how you felt about the characteristics of the person's personality.

Note that any person deserves to have clear directions about what constitutes appropriate behavior, for example, clearly specified in a job description, personnel policies or in performance goals. It would be grossly unfair to notify an employee or volunteer that he/she has a performance problem if the individual had no idea of what performance was expected of him/her in the first place.

Consider "How to Focus on Real Causes of Problems, Not Just Symptoms" on page 155.

1.   **Convey performance issues to employees or volunteers when you see first see the issues!** Do not wait until the annual performance review! Worse yet, do not ignore the behaviors in case they "go away."

2.   **When you first convey an issue, say what you noticed and want instead.** Consider this to be a verbal warning.

   a.   Be specific about what you saw that you consider a performance problem.

   b.   Ask the employee or volunteer for feedback.

   c.   Ask the employee or volunteer if there is any special training or resources needed to do the job.

   d.   Explore if the job is configured for success or if most people would probably fail, and so the job needs to be redesigned.

e. Tell him/her that the behavior needs to improve. In most cases, the person will understand your assertion. If he/she reacts strongly, for example, the person says that he/she is quitting the job, then provide a day to think it over. In any case, remind the person that you support him/her in the role.

3. **Consider special circumstances.**
    You can usually fire someone if they committed certain gross acts, such as theft, blatant insubordination, a major impropriety, for example, telling information to competitors or spreading confidential information about customers, etc. However, if there is poor performance or chronic absenteeism because of a physical or mental illness, then it is best to consult an expert to deal with this situation.

4. **If the problem recurs, immediately issue them a written warning.**

    a. In the written warning, clearly specify what you saw that you do not like, refer to the previous meeting and verbal warning and its date, say the behaviors have not improved, warn them that if the behaviors occurs again over some specific time period (for example, over the next month), they will be promptly terminated. Meet with them to provide them the written warning. Attempt to have this meeting on other than on a Friday; otherwise, employees are left to ruminate about the situation without ready access to you during the weekend.

    b. If you are convinced that the employee or volunteer is trying hard, but cannot improve, consider placing him or her elsewhere in the organization.

5. **Consider creating a performance improvement plan.**
    This plan details the necessary areas of improvement with specific actions and timelines for addressing those areas. This type of plan is usually developed by the employee's or volunteer's supervisor and the supervisor's supervisor and presented to the employee in a face-to-face meeting. The employee's or volunteer's feedback on the plan might be used to revise it, depending on the nature of the feedback and the criticality of the issues being addressed. The employee, the supervisor and optionally the supervisor's supervisor should sign and date the plan. The signed copy should be placed in the employee's or volunteer's personnel file. Lack of progress on a performance improvement plan is sometimes considered grounds for firing but this should be made clear in the plan if that is the intention.

6. **Make notes about the first warning, meeting and results, and keep in a file.**
    Continue this for any subsequent meetings and communications. The notes may come in handy later on if the performance problem persists. You might mention the situation to your Board if the person is in a management role. The Board will likely be a precious and objective asset to dealing with this situation, especially if things with the employee or volunteer get worse.

7. **On the third occurrence of seeing problem behaviors, consider firing the employee.**
    (See the next section, "How to Fire an Unsuitable Employee or Volunteer.")

How to Fire an Unsuitable Employee or Volunteer

Prerequisites to the Fair Firing of an Employee or Volunteer

The firing of an employee or volunteer is primarily one official action, rather than a long and drawn out process, if the supervisor has done the following activities before the firing became necessary:

1. **You have clear, provable evidence that you conveyed performance requirements.**
   The requirements came to the employee or volunteer by means of the following, which were provided to the employee or volunteer before you first began warning him/her of any performance issue:

   a. Written job description provided to him or her.

   b. Any written performance goals.

   Ideally, you also have evidence of your attempting to further equip the employee or volunteer with resources to improve his/her performance, for example, with training.

2. **You have evidence that the individual was fully aware of procedures for firing.**
   You have clearly written personnel policies, which specify conditions and directions about firing employees and volunteers, and you can prove that the person was aware of the policy, for example, the person initialized a copy of the policy handbook that contained that policy. Those policies should have been reviewed and updated by an expert on employment laws and also the Board should have approved the policies.

3. **You warned the person in successive stages as specified in personnel policies.**
   For example, the policies might have specified that an employee or volunteer should:

   a. First be warned of a performance issue with a verbal warning that clearly explained the nature of the performance issue, and that referenced what he/she was supposed to be doing, but was inappropriately doing instead.

   b. Then be warned in writing with explanation again of the nature of the same performance issue, including what the person should be doing instead.

   c. Be eligible to be faired if he/she again failed to meet the specified standard of performance.

Note that if the employee and volunteer is being fired within a probationary period that was specified in your personnel policies, then you may not have to meet all of the above prerequisites.

Take a day or so to consider what you are about to do. Consult with members of your Board.

Taking Action and Meeting With Employee or Volunteer

If you still decide to fire the employee or volunteer, then do so promptly in order to maintain your credibility with other employees and volunteers, and so as not to begin procrastinating about this sometimes painful, upcoming event.

1. **Write a letter of termination to give the employee or volunteer in an upcoming meeting.** As with the previous letters of warning, be clear about the observed behaviors, when you saw them, earlier warnings and their consequences, what you did in response, and the consequence that must now be enacted according to your personnel policies. In the letter, specify when the firing is to take effect (hopefully it takes effect immediately). Also mention your proof that the employee or volunteer was aware of the policies.

2. **Meet with the person. Provide him/her the letter. Explain how termination will occur.** Have another person in the meeting, for example, a Board member. Give the person several minutes to read the letter. Answer any questions to help the person understand the content of the letter, but do not begin justifying your actions to fire the person. Ask the employee or volunteer for any keys to facilities. Give the person half an hour or so to remove personal items. You may choose to monitor the person during this removal, depending on the nature of the grounds for dismissal.

3. **As with other meetings, make notes of what was said and exchanged.** Keep the notes in your records.

Follow-Up

1. **Tell the computer system administrator to change the person's password.** Assert that this action should be done promptly and in complete confidence.

2. **Change any locks on facilities.** This action may seem somewhat drastic, but if you do not change the locks, you will never know who can get into your facilities if he/she wishes.

3. **Inform other co-workers as necessary and appropriate.** Usually, you are better off not to explain everything about the situation to the employee's or volunteer's peers and subordinates. Despite the person's poor performance, the person deserves your respect and protection of his/her dignity. Otherwise, you expose yourself to losing a lawsuit that alleges liable or slander.

APPENDICES:

Appendix A: Glossary

Appendix B: Resources for Nonprofits

Appendix C: Useful, Free Organizational Assessments

Appendix D: Founder's Syndrome –
How to Detect It, How to Avoid It

Appendix A: Glossary

Accountability (in nonprofits)

Board members continually making their nonprofits and themselves responsible to meet the expectations of stakeholders, and verifying with those stakeholders that their expectations are indeed being met. Also see **Stakeholders**.

Assessment

Systematic collection of data, followed by analysis to generate findings and conclusions, for example, an organizational assessment to detect the strengths and weaknesses of all of the organization's most important operations.

Best practices

Practices conducted by individuals, groups or organizations that are widely respected for some particular expertise or activity that involves those practices, for example: best practices in Board operations, personnel management and financial management. There can be wide disagreement about what constitutes a best practice, depending on the context of the practices and the values of those in observance of the practices.

Board development

Raising the performance of the Board of Directors up another level, either to resolve major issues on the Board (restoring the Board) or to make sufficient performance even better. Can include a variety of activities to enhance Board operations, for example, a Board self-evaluation, producing a Board development plan, orienting Board members, training Board members, coaching the Board Chair and re-assessing the Board's performance. (Contrast to **Board orientation** and **Board training**.)

Board model

Structure by which Board members organize themselves and work together, including their level of involvement in management functions, if any. The model can be developed in a proactive, planful manner or emerge as Board members work together and with staff. There are a wide variety of models for governing Boards. See **Collective governing Board**, **Policy governing Board** and **Working governing Board**.

Board of Directors

Group of people legally charged to govern the corporation, whether for-profit or nonprofit. In a for-profit, Board members are responsible to ensure the business meets the needs of stockholders. In a nonprofit, members are responsible to ensure the nonprofit meets the needs of the community. Also see **Governance.**

Board orientation

Orienting Board members to the unique features of the organization, for example, to other members on the Board, where the Board meets, and the organization's programs and services. (Contrast to **Board training** and **Board development**.)

Board policies

General guidelines and sometimes specific procedures by which Board members choose to operate amongst themselves and sometimes with staff members, for example, policies to staff the Board, conflict-of-interest, attendance and evaluation of members.

Board training

Training Board members about the roles and responsibilities of a governing Board of Directors. (Contrast to **Board orientation** and **Board development**.)

Business planning

Activities to clarify the need for a product or service in the community, specific groups of people having that need, how the product or service meets each group's particular needs, resources needed to develop and provide the product or service, how the resources will be organized and managed, costs to obtain and support use of the resources, and how communications between the organization and community will be coordinated. (Contrast to **Strategic planning**.)

By-Laws

Board members' comprehensive, primary policy that specifies how the Board chooses to operate themselves and the nonprofit, including, for example: Board structure, roles, committees, meetings, membership and attendance requirements. The contents of the By-Laws are determined by statute in some states.

CEO

See **Chief Executive Officer (CEO, Executive Director)**.

Charity (nonprofit)

See **Nonprofit (informal, formal, tax-exempt and charitable)**.

Chief Executive Officer (CEO, Executive Director)

(Usually) the singular, organization-wide, staff position that is primarily responsible to carry out the strategic plans and policies established by the Board of Directors. The extent of authority and the scope and level of activities depends on the Board model preferred by the nonprofit. Not all nonprofits have staff members, including a CEO. Particularly in small or new nonprofits, the Board members and Executive Director often seem to work in partnership to oversee and manage the nonprofit's operations, even though the Board has the ultimate authority for governance and operations.

Collective governing Board

One model of a governing Board where Board and staff members work closely together in an egalitarian team to perform the functions of governance and management. (Contrast to **Policy governing Board** and **Working governing Board**.)

Corporate Board

Phrase used to refer to a Board of a for-profit corporation. This is a misnomer because the Board of a nonprofit corporation also is a corporate Board. Also see **Board of Directors**.

Corporation (for-profit or nonprofit)

Organization that is chartered (or incorporated) by the appropriate governmental agency in order to exist as a legal entity separate from the members of the organization. Corporations require a Board of Directors to govern the corporation. Nonprofits often are chartered as corporations; thus, they must have a Board of Directors. There are certain advantages to chartering an organization as a corporation, including limited liability of organization members for the operations of the organization. Also, the corporation can own property, hold its own bank account, enter into contracts, and conduct tax-exempt activities. Also see **Governance**.

Culture (of an organization)

The "personality" of an organization as defined by the aggregate of values, assumptions, opinions, behaviors, etc., by which members act in the organization.

Evaluation

Systematic collection and analysis of data to make a decision. Usually includes generation of findings and recommendations to address findings.

Executive Director

See **Chief Executive Officer.**

Financial management

Activities to ensure the organization's finances are effectively accounted for, legally allocated, utilized in an optimum manner and at minimum risk. Includes operating according to fiscal policies and procedures, bookkeeping to monitor and record transactions, generating and analyzing financial statements, and actions to improve financial management.

Founder's Syndrome

Exists when an overall organization operates more to the personality of one person in the organization than to its mission. Could be according to the founder or another prominent person in the organization.

Fundraising

Activities to solicit and report about funds from donors, including from individuals, foundations, corporations and/or government. Includes identifying fundraising targets (total monies to be raised during a certain period), researching prospective donors, soliciting each donor (via grants, events, etc.), recognition to donors, and managing grant documents and requirements.

Governance

Board of Director's activities to ensure that the nonprofit operates effectively and efficiently, according to its mission and strategic priorities, to meet the needs of the community. New perspectives consider governance to include stakeholders affiliated with the nonprofit.

Inputs (program)

Items that are used by the various processes in the program in order to achieve the overall outputs and desires outcomes of the program. Types of inputs are people, money, equipment, facilities, supplies, people's ideas, people's time, etc.

Leader

Person who sets direction and directs or influences other individuals or groups to follow that direction. Person can be a leader by the nature of the authority in their role, their expertise and/or their personality.

Leadership

Nature of activities or the capacity to establish direction and influence another person or group to follow that direction. Can also refer to leadership traits or leadership roles.

Logic model

The overall conceptual "system" of a nonprofit program by depicting the inputs, processes (or activities), outputs and outcomes from a program. Outcomes might be listed as short-term, intermediate or long-term.

Management (in organizations)

Traditionally, refers to the activities involved in the four overall, general practices: planning, organizing, leading and coordinating. The four functions recur throughout the organization and are highly integrated.

Marketing

The wide range of activities involved in making sure that you are continuing to meet the needs of your customers and getting sufficient value in return. These activities include market research to find out, for example, what groups of potential customers exist, what their needs are, which of those needs you can meet, how you should meet them, etc. Marketing also includes analyzing the competition, positioning your new product or service (finding your market niche), pricing your products and services, and promoting them through continued advertising, promotions, public relations and sales.

Minutes (of Board meetings)

The official documentation of the meeting's date of occurrence, attendance, topics and results from discussions (for example, decisions, resolutions, delegations, etc.). Board members approve the minutes, thereby making the document an accurate and official representation of the results of the meeting.

Mission (nonprofit)

The overall purpose of the nonprofit in the community. A mission statement describes that mission, for example: what groups of clients the nonprofit serves, the results that the nonprofit aims to achieve among those clients, and the types of services/programs the nonprofit uses to achieve those results.

Nonprofit (informal, formal, tax-exempt and charitable)

Organization that exists primarily to meet a public need, rather than to make a profit. An informal nonprofit is a group of people who gather to work on usually a short-term need in the community, for example, to clean up the neighborhood streets. A "chartered," or incorporated, nonprofit has filed with the appropriate government agency to be a legal entity separate from the members of the organization. A tax-exempt nonprofit has attained status from the appropriate government agency that allows the nonprofit to refrain from paying certain federal, state (provincial in Canada) and/or local taxes. A tax-deductible (charitable) nonprofit (or charity) has attained status from the appropriate government agency enabling it to receive donations and allowing donors to reduce their tax liabilities based on the amount of their donations.

Outcomes (program)

The changes, or impacts, on the clients who participated in your program. Outcomes are sometimes specified in terms of changed:
a) Knowledge, often called short-term outcomes
b) Behaviors, especially those that comprise useful skills, often called intermediate outcomes
c) Attitudes, values, conditions, etc., often called long-term outcomes

Outputs (program)

The tangible results produced by the organization or any of its various programs. Outputs are often described by using numbers, for example, the number of clients who completed a certain program. Note that outputs (produced by the program) differ from outcomes (produced by program participants).

Policy governing Board

One model of a governing Board where members attend primarily to developing and enforcing top-level plans and policies, usually delegating implementation of those plans and policies to staff. These Boards often use a variety of committees, some with staff members on them. Sometimes referred to as a "traditional" Board. (Contrast to **Collective governing Board** and **Working governing Board**.)

Processes (program)

Series of activities conducted by the program to manipulate the various inputs in order to achieve the overall desired outcomes from the program.

Program evaluation

Systematically collecting and analyzing information regarding a program in order to make a decision about the program. There are many types of program evaluation, for example, process evaluation to assess the quality of the program's processes and outcomes evaluation to assess the extent of achievement of desired outcomes.

Program planning

Activities to carefully identify what community needs are to be met by a new program, what methods (or program activities) will indeed meet those needs, and what group(s) of clients will be served. Can also include identifying program's collaborators, competitors and pricing. Ineffective fundraising, program evaluations and promotions often are the result of ineffective program planning.

Programs (in nonprofits)

Highly integrated set of activities and resources to meet certain needs of a certain group of people (clients). Well-designed programs also include ongoing evaluations about the activities to deliver services (process evaluations) and about the actual results achieved by participants in the program (outcomes evaluations).

Promotions (marketing)

Methods to keep products in the minds of the customers and helps stimulate demand for the products. The ongoing activities of advertising, sales and public relations are often considered aspects of promotions.

Public relations

Ongoing activities to ensure the organization has a strong public image. Public relations activities include helping the public to understand the organization and its products and services. Often, public relations are conducted through the media, that is, newspapers, television, magazines, etc. As noted above, public relations are often considered as one of the primary activities included in promotions.

Publicity

> Mention in the media. Organizations do not control the message in the media, at least not as much as they do in advertising. Reporters and writers decide what will be said, though press releases often influence what is published.

Revenue

> Refers to the money earned (fees) by, or donated to, the program during operation of the program.

Sales

> Involves most or many of the following activities, including cultivating prospective buyers (or leads) in a market segment; helping leads to understand how the features and benefits of a product or service can be beneficial to the lead; and closing the sale (or coming to agreement on pricing and services).

Staff members

> Personnel, other than the Board members, who have responsibility for operations of the nonprofit. Can be paid or volunteer.

Stakeholders

> People or groups of people who "have a stake," or strong, vested interest in the operations of the organization, for example: Board members, staff members, clients, funders, collaborators, community leaders and government agencies.

Strategic planning

> Activities to clarify the overall mission and most important priorities for the nonprofit to address, and how to address those. There are many different ways to conduct strategic planning, ranging from: 1) formal, explicit and systematic, including intentional and comprehensive analyses of external and internal environments, identification of critical priorities, and the goals, objectives, responsibilities and resource needs to address those priorities, to 2) informal, implicit and non-systematic, including ongoing and occasional clarification of priorities, along with what seems most reasonable to address the priorities for now. Also see **Business planning**.

Supervision

> Activities by a supervisor to oversee the progress and productivity of people who report directly to the supervisor. Includes staffing analysis, specification of duties and responsibilities (job description), recruitment and selection of employees, assignment of goals, feedback on achievement of goals, rewarding achievement of goals and addressing performance problems.

Supervisor

> A supervisor is someone who has at least one person reporting to him/her and, therefore, is responsible for the progress and productivity of that person, for example, a CEO supervises middle managers who supervise entry-level supervisors who supervise individual contributors.

Tax-deductible (charitable nonprofit) (charity)

> See **Nonprofit (informal, formal, tax-exempt and charitable)**.

Tax-exempt (nonprofit)

See **Nonprofit (informal, formal, tax-exempt and charitable)**.

Team building

Activities to form and develop a small group of people to effectively work toward a common purpose and achieve specific goals. There are a wide variety of means to build teams, ranging from enhancing members' feelings about each other to improving structures (plans, roles and policies) in the teams.

Transparency (in nonprofits)

Board members always providing full disclosure and explanation of the nonprofit's governance, finances and effects on communities, and also willingly supporting stakeholders' efforts to understand that information.

Work plan (in Board committees or task forces)

Specification of the goals, along with associated objectives, responsibilities and timing to achieve the objectives, in order to achieve the overall goal.

Working governing Board

One model of a governing Board where members attend both to strategic and hands-on matters. Often used early in the life of a nonprofit when it has few or no staff members. (Contrast to **Collective governing Board** and **Policy governing Board**.)

Appendix B: Resources for Nonprofits

Free Management Library^{SM}

The Library includes extensive free materials about personal, professional and organization development. The Library includes over 675 topics that are organized into the following popular categories. The list of topics is located at http://www.managementhelp.org on the Web.

Advertising and Promotion	Benefits and Compensation	Boards of Directors
Career Development	Chief Executive Role	Communications (Interprsnl)
Communications (Writing)	Computers, Internet & Web	Consultants (using)
Coordinating Activities	Creativity and Innovation	Crisis Management
Customer Satisfaction	Customer Service	E-Commerce
Employee Performance	Employee Wellness Programs	Ethics - Practical Toolkit
Evaluations (many kinds)	Facilities Management	Finances (For-Profit)
Finances (Nonprofit)	Fundraising (Nonprofit)	General Resources
Group Performance	Group Skills	Guiding Skills
Human Resources Mgmnt	Insurance (Business)	Interpersonal Skills
Interviewing (all kinds)	Jobs	Leadership (Introduction)
Leadership Development	Legal Information	Management (Introduction)
Management Development	Marketing	Operations Management
Organizational Alliances	Organizational Change	Org'l Communications
Organizational Performance	Organizations (Introduction)	Organizing (many kinds)
Performance Management	Personal Development	Personal Productivity
Personal Wellness	Planning (many kinds)	Policies (Personnel)
Product Selection & Dev.	Program Management	Project Management
Public and Media Relations	Quality Management	Research Methods
Risk Management	Sales	Social Entrepreneurship
Staffing	Starting an Organization	Supervision (Introduction)
Supervisory Development	Systems Thinking	Taxation
Training Basics	Volunteers	----------------

Free Nonprofit Micro-eMBA^{SM} Organization Development Program

This state-of-the-art, online training program includes 12 highly integrated courses that can be taken for free by anyone, anywhere at any time. At the end of the program, each learner will have all of the basic systems and processes needed to start and operate a nonprofit. Learners are encouraged to work with their Boards of Directors while going through the program. Participants going through the program together can share plans, policies and procedures.

Any of the 12 courses in the program can be taken separately. The courses and their learning objectives are located at http://www.managementhelp.org/np_progs/org_dev.htm on the World Wide Web, in the "Course Catalog." (Your organization may also have a wide range of materials around which you could organize courses.) Courses include the following:

1. Preparatory Workshop (skills in reading, studying, getting help, etc.)

2. Starting and Understanding the Nonprofit

3. Overview of Role of Chief Executive

4. Basic Skills in Management and Leadership

5. Building and Maintaining an Effective Board of Directors

6. Developing Your Strategic Plan

7. Designing and Marketing Your Programs

8. Managing Your Finances and Taxes

9. Developing Your Fundraising Plan

10. Staffing and Supervision of Employees and Volunteers

11. Evaluating Your Programs

12. Organizational "Fitness Test"

Organizations Assisting Nonprofits

In the USA

Contact your Secretary of State and/or state's Attorney General's office and ask for a list of resources.

1.   Executive Service Corps (ESC) provides experienced consultation in the areas of technical and management (http://www.escus.org/).

2.   National Council of Nonprofit Associations (NCNA) has chapters in almost all of the states. (http://www.ncna.org).

In Canada

1.   The Voluntary Sector Knowledge Network provides information, assistance and tools regarding a wide range of functions in nonprofits (http://www.vskn.ca/).

2.   United Way Canada provides information, publications and funding to Canada voluntary sector organizations (http://www.unitedway.ca/english/).

3.   The Canadian Centre for Philanthropy provides programs, resources, tools and information for the benefit of Canadian communities (http://www.ccp.ca/).

General Resources

▪   Contact the local volunteer recruitment organization in your community and ask for assistance.

▪   Look in the Yellow Pages of your local telephone directory for professional associations. Look for networks or associations of organization development practitioners, facilitators or trainers.

▪   Look in the Yellow Pages of your local telephone directory under the categories "Consultant" and "Volunteering".

▪   Contact local large corporations. They often have community service programs and can provide a wide range of management and technical expertise. Speak to the head of the Human Resources Department.

▪   Call a local university or college and speak to someone in the college of Human Resources, Training and Development, or Business Administration.

▪   Ask other nonprofits (particularly those that have similar services and number of staff,) or current clients for ideas, contacts and references.

▪   Ask a retired business person (from a for-profit or nonprofit organization). Often, they have facilitated a wide variety of meetings.

Free, Online Newsletters and Forums

About.com Management Newsletter
This is a free weekly email newsletter on management topics from the Management Guide at About.com. To subscribe enter your e-mail address at http://management.about.com/gi/pages/stay.htm .

About.com Nonprofit Charitable Organizations Newsletter
This is a free weekly email newsletter on topics relevant to nonprofit charitable organizations from the Nonprofits Guide at About.com. To subscribe enter your e-mail address at http://nonprofit.about.com/gi/pages/stay.htm .

Board Cafe
This is a free online newsletter for nonprofit Boards of Directors. To subscribe send an e-mail message to "msimpson@supportcenter.org" and in the body of the message type: "SUBSCRIBE BOARD CAFE". You may also call (415)-541-9000.

CharityChannel forums
CharityChannel provides a wide array of forums, including forums on Canada-specific topics. Go to http://www.charitychannel.com/ and scroll down until you see the topic "Forums" on the left-hand side. At the time of this writing, there is an annual fee of $37 to use CharityChannel forums.

Free Management Library
Additional newsletters and forums are listed in the Free Management Library under the topic "General Info," in the subtopics "Periodicals" at http://www.managementhelp.org/gen_rsrc/nwslttrs/nwslttrs.htm or "Online Groups" at http://www.managementhelp.org/gen_rsrc/newsgrps/newsgrps.htm .

Some Mega-Websites About Nonprofits

- Alliance for Nonprofit Management resources at http://www.allianceonline.org/ARC

- Board Glossary at http://www.boardsource.org/Knowledge.asp?ID=1.1016

- BoardSource FAQ's at http://www.boardsource.org/Knowledge.asp?ID=3

- Canada Revenue Agency at http://www.cra-arc.gc.ca/tax/charities/menu-e.html

- CharityChannel Governance Review articles at http://charitychannel.com/enewsletters/nbgr/

- Energize at http://www.energizeinc.com/art.html

- Free Complete Toolkit for Boards at http://www.managementhelp.org/boards/boards.htm

- Help4Nonprofits at http://www.help4nonprofits.com/H4NP.htm

- Idealist at http://www.idealist.org/

- Internal Revenue Service (in USA) http://www.irs.gov/charities/topic/index.html

- Learning Institute for Nonprofit Organizations at http://www.uwex.edu/li/learner/sites_board.htm

- Nathan Garber's resources at http://garberconsulting.com/links.htm

- National Study of Board Governance Practices in the Non-Profit and Voluntary Sector in Canada at http://www.strategicleveragepartners.com/bhg768kjmhgvxxyxzwq/National_Study_of_Board_Governance_Practices_in_the_Non-Profit_and_Voluntary_Sector_in_Canada.PDF

- Nonprofit FAQ on Boards at http://www.nonprofits.org/if/idealist/en/FAQ/CategoryViewer/default?category-eid=3-1&sid=80627634-248-ewO

- Nonprofit Good Resource Guide at http://www.npgoodpractice.org

- Nonprofit Risk Management center at http://nonprofitrisk.org/library/articles/articles.shtml

- Volunteer BC in Canada at http://www.vcn.bc.ca/volbc/tools/governance.html

Appendix C:
Useful, Free Nonprofit Organizational Assessments

Nonprofit leaders are responsible to ensure that their nonprofit provides programs and services that continue to meet the needs of the public in a highly effective manner. This means that leaders should know what is required to operate as a high-performing nonprofit organization. One of the most useful ways in which leaders can learn what is required to be high-performing – and one of the most useful ways to measure if the nonprofit is indeed high-performing – is through use of organizational assessment tools. A wide variety of free, useful tools are available on the Web now. This section lists many of those tools and includes one such tool (the United Way Management Indicators Organizational Assessment) in its entirety, so that leaders can scan the types of questions asked by that comprehensive tool.

How to Select Best Organizational Assessment Tools

Considerations When Selecting

Before you begin reviewing tools to use, be sure that you are aware of the major types of tools, the advantages and disadvantages of using each, and general guidelines for applying each type of tool.

1. **Focus**
   Does the tool focus on a broad range of nonprofit functions, including operations of the Board, strategic planning, programs, Chief Executive Officer, staff, marketing, finances, fundraising or evaluations?

2. **Purpose of the tool**
   For example, does it detect strengths and weaknesses of the organization, and compare them to certain "best practices?"

3. **Values and assumptions**
   For example, does the tool assume a specific Board structure or top-down leadership?

4. **Languages**
   English? Other(s)?

5. **Audiences for the tool**
   To whom will the tool be applied?

6. **Administrator of the tool**
   Who will guide the application of the tool? An outside person? Self-assessment? Will the data collection be participatory?

7. **User guide**
   Are there adequate descriptions of procedures for how to use the tool and analyze the results?

8. **Duration and frequency**
   How long will it take to use the tool? Is the tool to be applied at certain times? More than once?

9.   **Cost**
     What are any costs to obtain the tool? Use the tool?

10. **Availability**
     How soon can the tool be made available?

11. **Technical support for the tool**
     If you have questions or need guidance, can anyone help you?

12. **Modification**
     You might need permission if you seek to modify the tool.

Available, Free Organizational Assessment Tools

The following list includes free, online tools, each of which assesses numerous aspects of a nonprofit organization. However, before selecting an already designed tool, be sure that you have addressed the considerations listed immediately above. Keep in mind that these types of tools include some inherent bias. To the author's knowledge, none of these tools has been tested for reliability or validity.

McKinsey Capacity Assessment Grid

This is a comprehensive grid that suggests seven elements of organizational effectiveness, each with descriptions of four possible levels of performance for each element. Go to http://www.emcf.org/evaluation/mckinsey_assessment_tool.htm .

Minnesota Council of Nonprofits "Principles and Practices"

This is a widely recognized, comprehensive, principles-based assessment tool that suggests principles for effectiveness in many of the major functions in nonprofits. Go to http://www.mncn.org/info_principles.htm .

Maryland Association of Nonprofit Organizations "Standards of Excellence"

This is a widely recognized, principles-based assessment tool that suggests principles for effectiveness in many of the major functions in nonprofits. Go to http://www.marylandnonprofits.org/html/standards/04_02.asp .

Understanding Organizational Success: Self-Assessment Tool for Nonprofit Organizations

This is a comprehensive, well-designed tool that nonprofits can use to assess their organizations. Directions to apply and analyze the tool are included. Go to http://smifoundation.org/NPAssessmentTool.pdf .

Self-Assessment Tool for United Way Agencies

This is a medium-sized, straightforward assessment tool regarding major functions in nonprofits. Go to http://www.uwac.org/uwac/repositories/Download/oat_uw.pdf .

United Way Management Indicators Organizational Assessment (includes best practices)

This is a well-designed, comprehensive, behaviors-based tool that also includes a suggested "best-practices" standard, as well. This tool, in its entirety, is included on the following pages of this Appendix.

Organizational Assessment Tool with Best Practices

Description

The following checklist is a resource developed by staff and volunteers of the Greater Twin Cities United Way for internal use by nonprofit organizations. Management can use the checklist to identify their organization's administrative strengths and weaknesses. It is believed that widespread use of the checklist ultimately results in a more effective and efficient nonprofit community. The checklist is not intended to be used as a tool for external evaluation, or by grantmakers in making funding decisions. This tool will be used to assist nonprofit organizations to gain a better understanding of their management needs and/or make improvements to management operations.

Note that the following checklist, or assessment tool, originally developed by the Greater Twin Cities United Way of Minnesota (USA), has been slightly modified by the author in order to make it relevant to organizations outside the United States.

This checklist includes the following sections:

- How To Use the Tool
- Disclaimers
- Legal Indicators
- Governance (Board) Indicators
- Human Resources Indicators
- Planning Indicators
- Financial Indicators
- Fundraising Indicators

How To Use the Tool

The checklist indicators represent what is needed to have a healthy, well-managed organization. Since it is a self-assessment tool, organizations should evaluate themselves honestly against each issue and use the response to change or strengthen its administrative operations.

Ratings

Each indicator is rated based on its importance to the operation and effectiveness of any nonprofit organization. The ratings are:

E: Indicators with an "E" are essential or basic requirements to the operations of all nonprofit organizations. Organizations, which do not meet the requirements of these indicators, could place their organizations in jeopardy.

R: An "R" rating signifies that these indicators are recommended as standard practice for effective nonprofit organizations.

A: Additional indicators which organizations can implement to enhance and strengthen their management operations and activities are rated with an "A".

Checklist Responses

Organizations can respond in one of three ways to each indicator used:

Needs Work: An indicator that is marked as "Needs Work" implies that work has been done towards achieving this goal. The organization is aware of the need for this indicator, and is working towards attaining it.

Met: All indicators marked as "Met" demonstrate that the organization has fulfilled that essential management need. However, the organization should review these indicators in the future to be sure that its management remains healthy in view of the many internal and external changes that constantly occur in all organizations.

N/A: Indicators marked as "N/A" can mean several things, including:
- the indicator is not applicable to the management operations of this organization
- the organization is not sure of the need to meet the requirements of this indicator
- the organization has not met, nor is working on this indicator presently, but may address it in the future.

All Organizations Should Take Note

All responses to indicators should be reviewed carefully to see if they could improve management operations. Indicators checked "N/A" due to uncertain applicability to the organization must be further reviewed to determine if they should become a part of "doing business." If the assessors simply do not know what the indicator means, further information may be needed to accurately assess the feasibility of its application. Indicators may require immediate attention if they were marked "N/A" because they have not been met but still apply to the organization. Technical assistance, consulting, or training may be required to implement these indicators.

The indicators in this checklist should be informative and thought provoking. The checklist can be used to not only achieve a beginning level of good management, but also improve existing management to provide the organization with greater stability, reliability and success in the nonprofit community. If an organization is experiencing management problems, the checklist can be useful to help pinpoint any weaknesses where action can be taken or assistance sought to improve the organization's health. All organizations should use the checklist to re-assess themselves periodically to ensure compliance with established rules and regulations and to continue improving administrative health through the indicator's helpful suggestions.

Disclaimer

This checklist is designed to provide accurate and authoritative information regarding the topics covered. Legal requirements and non-legal administrative practice standards reflected herein are capable of change due to new legislation, regulatory and judicial pronouncements, and updated and evolving guidelines. The same are utilized with the understanding that the provision of this checklist does not constitute the rendering of legal, tax or other professional services.

If the organization requires professional assistance on these or other nonprofit tax, management, or accounting issues, please contact your own professional advisors.

This tool is available free, online at
http://www.managementhelp.org/aboutfml/diagnostics.htm#anchor421212 .

Rating Best Practices in Legal Activities

Rating *	Indicator	Met	Needs Work	N/A
E	1. All relevant legal filings are current and have been made according to the laws and regulations of the nonprofit's country. (For example, in the USA, requirements might include: Annual Registration, Articles of Incorporation with all amendments, Change of Corporate Name or Address.)			
E	2. The organization is registered with and has filed its annual report with the appropriate governmental agency. (For example, in the USA, the report might be filed with the state's Attorney General's office.)			
E	3. For organizations operating on a tax-exempt basis, the organization has filed the necessary government form to obtain tax-exempt status. (For example, in the USA, IRS form 1023 was filed and the IRS provided a letter of determination. If the Form 1023 was filed after 7/15/87 or was in the nonprofit's possession on this date, it is available for public inspection.)			
E	4. Tax reports are filed on a regular basis. (For tax-exempt organizations in the USA, the IRS form 990 and 990T for unrelated business income, if required, have been filed and copies of the 990 are available to the public.)			
E	5. Federal and state (or provincial) payroll tax withholding payments are current. (This requirement applies to organizations with employees.)			
E	6. Quarterly and annual payroll report filings are current. (This requirement applies to organizations with employees.)			
E	7. If the organization has qualified employee health, welfare and/or retirement benefit plans, they meet with all the federal and state/provincial laws. (For example, in the USA: COBRA; initial IRS registration; plan documents; annuals filings of the 5500 C/R with copies available to employees.) This requirement applies to organizations with employees.			
E	8. Organization acknowledges and discloses to their Board and auditor any lawsuits or pending legislation which may have a significant impact on the organization's finances and/or operating effectiveness.			
E	9. When the Board of Directors makes decisions, a quorum is present and minutes are maintained.			
E	10. If the organization is subject to sales tax(es), then federal, state/provincial and/or city filings and payments are current.			
E	11. Organizations that participate in grassroots or direct lobbying have complied with all necessary filings and government regulations.			
E	12. Organizations that conduct charitable gambling have complied with government regulations.			
E	13. Organizations with employees represented by a union have copies of the union contracts on file.			
E	14. Organizations that operate in a fiscal or host-organization relationship with another organization or group have a written agreement on file.			
Indicators ratings: E=essential; R=recommended; A=additional to strengthen organizational activities				

Rating Best Practices in Governance / Boards Operations

Rating *	Indicator	Met	Needs Work	N/A
E	1. The roles of the Board and the Chief Executive Officer (if applicable) are defined and respected, with the Chief Executive Officer delegated as the manager of the organization's operations and the Board focused on policy and planning.			
R	2. The Chief Executive Officer is recruited, selected, and employed by the Board of Directors. The Board provides clearly written expectations and qualifications for the position, as well as reasonable compensation.			
R	3. The Board of Directors acts as governing trustees of the organization, on behalf of the community at large and as contributors, while carrying out the organization's mission and goals. To fully meet this goal, the Board of Directors must actively participate in the planning process as outlined in planning sections of this checklist.			
R	4. The Board's nominating process ensures that the Board remains appropriately diverse with respect to gender, ethnicity, culture, economic status, disabilities, skills and/or expertise.			
E	5. The Board members receive regular training and information about their responsibilities.			
E	6. New Board members are oriented to the organization: the organization's mission, bylaws, policies and programs, as well as their roles and responsibilities as Board members.			
A	7. Board organization is documented with a description of the Board and Board committee (if applicable) responsibilities.			
A	8. Each Board member has a Board operations manual.			
E	9. If the organization has any related party transactions between Board members or their family, they are disclosed to the Board of Directors (the Internal Revenue Service in the USA) and the auditor.			
E	10. The organization has at least the minimum number of members on the Board of Directors as required by their bylaws, federal statute and/or state/provincial statute.			
R	11. If the organization has adopted bylaws, they conform to federal and/or state/provincial statutes and have been reviewed by legal counsel.			
R	12. The bylaws should describe: a) how and when notices for Board meetings are made; b) how members are elected/appointed by the Board; c) what the terms of office are for officers/members; d) how Board members are rotated; e) how ineffective Board members are removed from the Board; and f) a stated number of Board members to make up a quorum which is required for all policy decisions.			
R	13. The Board of Directors reviews the bylaws annually.			
A	14. The Board has a process for handling urgent matters between meetings.			
E	15. Board members serve without payment unless the agency has a policy identifying reimbursable out-of-pocket expenses.			
Indicators ratings: E=essential; R=recommended; A=additional to strengthen organizational activities				

Rating Best Practices in Governance Operations (Cont.)

Rating *	Indicator	Met	Needs Work	N/A
R	16. The organization maintains a conflict-of-interest policy and all Board members and executive staff review and/or sign to acknowledge and comply with the policy.			
R	17. The Board has an annual calendar of meetings.			
R	18. The Board also has an attendance policy, which requires that a quorum of the organization's Board meets at least quarterly.			
A	19. Each Board meeting has a written agenda and the materials relating to significant decisions are given to the Board members in advance of the meeting.			
A	20. The Board has a written policy prohibiting employees and members of employees' immediate families from serving as Board Chair or treasurer.			
Indicators ratings: E=essential; R=recommended; A=additional to strengthen organizational activities				

Rating Best Practices in Human Resources (Staff and Volunteers)

Staff

Rating *	Indicator	Met	Needs Work	N/A
E	1. The organization has a written personnel handbook/policy that is regularly reviewed, updated and approved by Board: a) to describe the recruitment, hiring, termination and standard work rules for all staff and b) to maintain compliance with government employment laws and regulations. (For example, in the USA, this includes: Fair Labor Standards Act, Equal Employment Opportunity Act, Americans with Disabilities Act, Occupational Health and Safety Act, Family Leave Act, Affirmative Action Plan if required, etc.)			
R	2. The organization follows nondiscriminatory hiring practices.			
R	3. The organization provides a copy of or access to the written personnel policies to all members of the Board, the Chief Executive Officer (if applicable) and all staff members. All staff members acknowledge in writing that they have read and have access to the personnel handbook/policies.			
R	4. The organization has job descriptions including qualifications, duties, reporting relationships and key indicators.			
R	5. The organization's Board of Directors conducts an annual review/evaluation of its Chief Executive Officer in relationship to a previously determined set of expectations.			
R	6. The Chief Executive Officer's salary is set by the Board of Directors in a reasonable process and is in compliance with the organization's compensation plan.			
R	7. The organization requires employee performance appraisals to be conducted and documented at least annually.			
A	8. The organization has a compensation plan and a periodic review of salary ranges and benefits is conducted.			
A	9. The organization has a timely process for filling vacant positions to prevent an interruption of program services or disruption to organization operations.			
A	10. The organization has a process for reviewing and responding to ideas, suggestions, comments and perceptions from all staff members.			
A	11. The organization provides opportunities for employees' professional development and training with their job skill area and also in such areas as cultural sensitivity and personal development.			
A	12. The organization maintains contemporaneous records documenting staff time in program allocations.			
Indicators ratings: E=essential; R=recommended; A=additional to strengthen organizational activities				

Rating Best Practices in Human Resources (Cont.)

Volunteer HR Management

Rating *	Indicator	Met	Needs Work	N/A
E	1. The organization has a clearly defined purpose of the role that volunteers have within the organization.			
E	2. Job descriptions exist for all volunteer positions in the organization.			
R	3. The organization has a well-defined and communicated volunteer management plan that includes a recruitment policy, description of all volunteer jobs, an application and interview process, possible stipend and reimbursement policies, statement of which staff has supervisory responsibilities over what volunteers, and any other volunteer personnel policy information.			
E	4. The organization follows a recruitment policy that does not discriminate, but respects, encourages and represents the diversity of the community.			
E	5. The organization provides appropriate training and orientation to the agency to assist the volunteer in the performance of their volunteer activities. Volunteers are offered training with staff in such areas as cultural sensitivity.			
R	6. The organization is respectful of the volunteer's abilities and time commitment and has various job duties to meet these needs. Jobs should not be given to volunteers simply because the jobs are considered inferior for paid staff.			
R	7. The organization does volunteer performance appraisals periodically and communicates to the volunteers how well they are doing, or where additional attention is needed. At the same time, volunteers are requested to review and evaluate their involvement in the organization and the people they work with and suggest areas for improvement.			
R	8. The organization does some type of volunteer recognition or commendation periodically and staff continuously demonstrates their appreciation towards the volunteers and their efforts.			
A	9. The organization has a process for reviewing and responding to ideas, suggestions, comments and perceptions from volunteers.			
A	10. The organization provides opportunities for program participants to volunteer.			
A	11. The organization maintains contemporaneous records documenting volunteer time in program allocations. Financial records can be maintained for the volunteer time spent on programs and recorded as in-kind contributions.			
Indicators ratings: E=essential; R=recommended; A=additional to strengthen organizational activities				

Rating Best Practices in Planning (Strategic and Programs)

Strategic Planning

Rating*	Indicator	Met	Needs Work	N/A
E	1. The organization's purpose and activities meet community needs.			
R	2. The organization frequently evaluates, by soliciting community input, whether its mission and activities provide benefit to the community.			
R	3. The organization has a value statement that is reflected in the agency's activities and is communicated by its constituents.			
A	4. The value statement includes standards of ethical behavior and respect for other's interests.			
E	5. The organization has a clear, meaningful written mission statement, which reflects its purpose, values and people served.			
R	6. The Board and staff periodically review the mission statement and modify it to reflect changes in the environment.			
E	7. The Board and staff developed and adopted a written strategic plan to achieve its mission.			
A	8. Board, staff, service recipients, volunteers, key constituents and general members of the community participate in the planning process.			
E	9. The plan was developed by researching the internal and external environment.			
R	10. The plan identifies the changing community needs including the agency's strengths, weaknesses, opportunities and threats.			
R	11. The planning process identifies the critical issues facing the organization.			
R	12. The plan sets goals and measurable objectives that address these critical issues.			
E	13. The plan integrates all the organization's activities around a focused mission.			
R	14. The plan prioritizes the agency goals and develops timelines for their accomplishments.			
A	15. The plan establishes an evaluation process and performance indicators to measure the progress toward the achievement of goals and objectives.			
R	16. Through work plans, human and financial resources are allocated to ensure the accomplishment of the goals in a timely fashion.			
A	17. The plan is communicated to all stakeholders of the agency – service recipients, Board, staff, volunteers and the general community.			
Indicators ratings: E=essential; R=recommended; A=additional to strengthen organizational activities				

Rating Best Practices in Planning (Cont.)

Planning Regarding the Organization's Programs

Rating *	Indicator	Met	Needs Work	N/A
E	1. Programs are congruent with the agency's mission and strategic plan.			
A	2. The organization actively informs the public about its programs and services.			
A	3. Clients and potential clients have the opportunity to participate in program development.			
R	4. Sufficient resources are allocated to ensure each program can achieve the established goals and objectives.			
R	5. Staff has sufficient training and skill levels to produce the program.			
A	6. Programs within the organization are integrated to provide more complete services to clients.			
R	7. Each program has performance indicators to ensure that the program meets its goals and objectives.			
R	8. Performance indicators are reviewed annually.			
A	9. The agency networks and/or collaborates with other organizations to produce the most comprehensive and effective services to clients.			
Indicators ratings: E=essential; R=recommended; A=additional to strengthen organizational activities				

Planning Regarding the Organization's Evaluations

Rating *	Indicator	Met	Needs Work	N/A
R	1. Every year, the organization evaluates its activities to determine progress toward goal accomplishment.			
A	2. Stakeholders are involved in the evaluation process.			
R	3. The evaluation includes a review of organizational programs and systems to insure that they comply with the organization's mission, values and goals.			
R	4. The results of the evaluation are reflected in the revised plan.			
A	5. Periodically, the organization conducts a comprehensive evaluation of its programs. This evaluation measures program outcomes (impacts on clients).			
Indicators ratings: E=essential; R=recommended; A=additional to strengthen organizational activities				

Rating Best Practices in Financial Management

Rating *	Indicator	Met	Needs Work	N/A
E	1. The organization follows accounting practices that conform to generally accepted standards.			
E	2. The organization has systems in place to provide the appropriate information needed by staff and Board to make sound financial decisions and to fulfill government requirements (for example, the requirements of the Internal Revenue Service in the USA).			
R	3. The organization prepares timely financial statements including the balance sheet, income statement and cash flow statement, which are clearly stated and useful for the Board and staff. (Note that these statements might be referred to by different names in various countries.)			
R	4. The organization prepares financial statements on a budget versus actual (comparative) basis to achieve a better understanding of their finances.			
E	5. The organization develops an annual comprehensive operating budget that includes costs for all programs, management and fundraising and all sources of funding. This budget is reviewed and approved by the Board.			
R	6. The organization monitors unit costs of programs and services through the documentation of staff time and direct expenses and using a process for allocation of management, general and fundraising expenses.			
E	7. The organization prepares cash flow projections.			
R	8. The organization periodically forecasts year-end revenues and expenses to assist in making sound management decisions during the year.			
E	9. The organization reconciles all cash accounts monthly.			
E	10. The organization has a review process to monitor that they are receiving appropriate and accurate financial information, whether from a contracted service or internal processing.			
E	11. If the organization has billable contracts or other service income, procedures are established for the periodic billing, follow-up and collection of all accounts, with documentation to substantiate all billings.			
E	12. Government contracts, purchase of service agreements and grant agreements are in writing and are reviewed by a staff member of the organization to monitor compliance with all stated conditions.			
E	13. Payroll is prepared following appropriate federal and state/provincial regulations and organizational policy.			
E	14. Persons employed on a contract basis meet all federal and state/provincial requirements for this form of employment. (In the USA, disbursement records are kept so 1099's can be issued at year-end.)			
E	15. Organizations that purchase and sell merchandise take periodic inventories to monitor the inventory against theft, to reconcile general ledger inventory information and to maintain an adequate inventory level.			
R	16. The organization has a written fiscal policy and procedures manual and follows it.			
Indicators ratings: E=essential; R=recommended; A=additional to strengthen organizational activities				

Rating Best Practices in Financial Management (Cont.)

Rating *	Indicator	Met	Needs Work	N/A
E	17. The organization has documented a set of internal controls, including handling of cash and deposits and approval over spending and disbursements.			
E	18. The organization has a policy identifying authorized check signers and the number of signatures required on checks in excess of specified dollar amounts.			
E	19. A designated person approves all expenses of the organization before payment is made.			
R	20. The organization has a written policy related to investments.			
R	21. Capital needs are reviewed annually and priorities established.			
R	22. The organization has established a plan identifying actions to take in the event of a reduction or loss in funding.			
R	23. The organization has established, or is actively trying to develop, a reserve of funds to cover at least three months of operating expenses.			
E	24. The organization has suitable insurance coverage, which is periodically reviewed to ensure the appropriate levels and types of coverage are in place.			
E	25. Employees, Board members and volunteers who handle cash and investments are bonded to help assure the safeguarding of assets.			
E	26. The organization files forms in regard to tax-exempt and/or tax-deductible (charity) status in a timely basis within prescribed time lines.			
R	27. The organization reviews income annually to determine and report unrelated business income to the necessary government agency (for example, to the IRS in the USA).			
R	28. The organization has an annual, independent audit of their financial statements, prepared by a certified public accountant.			
R	29. In addition to the audit, the auditor prepares a management letter containing recommendations for improvements in the financial operations of the organization.			
R	30. The Board of Directors, or an appropriate committee, is responsible for soliciting bids, interviewing auditors and hiring an auditor for the organization.			
R	31. The Board of Directors, or an appropriate committee, reviews and approves the audit report and management letter and with staff input and support, institutes any necessary changes.			
E	32. The audit, or an organization-prepared annual report which includes financial statements, is made available to service recipients, volunteers, contributors, funders and other interested parties.			
A	33. Training is made available for Board and appropriate staff on relevant accounting topics and all appropriate persons are encouraged to participate in various training opportunities.			
Indicators ratings: E=essential; R=recommended; A=additional to strengthen organizational activities				

Rating Best Practices in Fundraising Activities

General Fundraising

Rating *	Indicator	Met	Needs Work	N/A
E	1. Funds are raised in an ethical manner for activities consistent with the organization's mission and plan.			
E	2. The Board of Directors and organization staff are knowledgeable about the fundraising process and the roles in the organization.			
E	3. The organization's Board of Directors has established a committee charged with developing, evaluating and reviewing fundraising policies, practices and goals.			
E	4. The committee is actively involved in the fundraising process and works to involve others in these activities.			
R	5. The Board of Directors, Chief Executive Officer (if applicable) and committees support and participate in the total fundraising process, including project identification, cultivation, solicitation and recognition.			
R	6. The fundraising program is staffed and funded at a level consistent with fundraising expectations.			
A	7. There are direct communications and relationships between information services or marketing, accounting and other administration support functions to assist in the fundraising needs and efforts.			
E	8. The organization is accountable to donors and other key constituencies and demonstrates its stewardship through annual reports.			
Indicators ratings: E=essential; R=recommended; A=additional to strengthen organizational activities				

Rating Best Practices in Fundraising Activities (Cont.)

Using an Outside Fundraiser

Rating *	Indicator	Met	Needs Work	N/A
A	1. The organization meets the nonprofit standards of the state/provincial charities review council, if one exists.			
R	2. If the organization chooses to use outside professional fundraisers, several competitive bids are solicited. Each prospective outside fundraiser's background and references are checked.			
E	3. The organization makes legal, mutually agreed upon, signed agreements with outside professional fundraisers, outlining each parties' responsibilities and duties, specifying how the contributed funds will be physically handled, and guaranteeing that the fees to be paid are reasonable and fair.			
E	4. The organization has verified that the contracted fundraiser is registered as a professional fundraiser with the appropriate government agency and all necessary filings have been made before the work commences.			
E	5. The Fundraising Committee, or other appropriate representatives from the Board of Directors, reviews all prospective proposals with outside professional fundraiser and reviews and accepts all agreements before they are signed.			
R	6. If the outside professional fundraiser plans to contact potential donors directly, the organization must review the fundraising materials (e.g., public service announcements, print or broadcast advertisements, telemarketing scripts, pledge statements, brochures, letters, etc.) to verify their accuracy and to ensure that the public disclosure requirements have been met.			
E	7. The organization properly reports all required information regarding use of outside professional fundraisers, amount of funds raised and the related fundraising expenses as required by federal and state/provincial governments. The gross amount of funds raised by the contracted fundraiser is reported on the organization's financial statement. The fees and costs of the campaign must be reported on the statement of functional expenses.			
	Indicators ratings: E=essential; R=recommended; A=additional to strengthen organizational activities			

Appendix D:
Founder's Syndrome –
How to Detect It, How to Avoid It

What is Founder's Syndrome?

Blindly Following the Leader – Not Mission, Plans and Policies

Often the first major challenges in the "maturing" process for a Board – or for an entire organization – is to move away from always following the nature of certain personalities in the organization and instead work according to its mission, plans and policies. That challenge is common to any type of Board model, whether it is a working Board, policy Board, Policy Governance® Board or collective Board. The maturing process does not mean that members cannot choose any of these models. It means that members must use the model for the betterment of the nonprofit, not for the betterment of the leader.

It is common for members of new Boards to follow the lead of whoever seems to be the most persuasive person in the organization. Often that person is the founder of the organization and the person who goes on to become its first Chief Executive, Board Chair or both. Other times, it can be a variety of people on the Board and/or staff. In any case, the Board is not referencing the mission, policies and plans to guide the organization; rather it is just playing "follow the leader."

The problems inherent in working according to personalities, rather than according to the mission, have become so common, especially in new and small organizations, that some experts refer to the problems collectively as Founder's Syndrome. That phrase can be misleading, though, because the people having undue influence are not always the founders of the organizations. The "founder" can be one person on the Board or staff or, at times, a certain group of people in the organization.

Typical Problem in New and Small Organizations

To continue to reliably meet the needs of their customers (or clients), organizations must evolve through a particular life-cycle change, just like people must do in order to mature. This change is usually from a highly reactive and seat-of-the-pants approach to growth to a well-planned and managed approach. Plans do not have to be constricting plans that are full of unnecessary paperwork – the nonprofit does not have to become highly bureaucratic. However, there should be enough plans and policies to provide a stable and efficient infrastructure from which to continue to grow.

This necessary evolution often requires a change in the nature of the founder's leadership from a highly reactive, individualistic style to a more proactive, consensus-oriented style. Many charismatic and visionary founders cannot make this transition – whether the founder is the CEO, someone on the Board or a group of people on the Board. They might have more confidence in their own grand plans and intuition than in what they often perceive as unnecessary "paperwork." As a result, more detailed plans and policies are not made, if at all.

As these nonprofits continue to grow and the demand for their services continues to grow as well, the need for more efficiency and resources continues to increase. As a result, the founder demands that people work even harder to take on more roles and that Board members get even more money. Yet, the problem is not from lack of effort and money. It is from people's confusion about their purpose, direction and roles. It is from constant pressure from the leader – pressure that does not really seem to be solving any of the problems in the organization. Soon, Board and staff members become so frustrated that they leave – and the organization continues to struggle from one crisis to another.

No one really seems to know what is going on. Those who remain in the organization continue to look to the leader who seems to be doing the same things as before, but now even harder. Things just get worse. As a result, the organization remains managed, not in a manner that reliably provides services to clients, but in a manner that suits the personality of the increasingly frustrated founder.

Eventually, stakeholders confront the founder about the organization's recurring problems. Funders may confront the Chief Executive or Board. Without ongoing coaching and support, it is likely that the founder will be replaced, or even worse, the organization will fold. Founder's Syndrome is no one's fault – no founder sets out to intentionally damage the organization. Besides, the syndrome does not occur without members of the Board and staff blindly following the leader.

Leadership and Founder's Syndrome – the Good and Bad

Troublesome Traits Among Founders and Boards

Whether the founder is the CEO, someone on the Board or a group of people on the Board, founders are dynamic, driven and decisive. They carry clear vision of what their organization can be. They know their client's needs and are passionate about meeting those needs. Often these traits are strong assets for getting the new organization off the ground. However, other traits of founders too often become major liabilities. For example, founders often:

- Are highly skeptical about planning, policies and procedures. They claim "plans and procedures are overhead and just bog me down." They often believe they have found a new way to get things done.

- Make reactive, crisis-driven decisions with little input from others. They react to most problems with the lament "if only I had more money."

- Attend mostly to fundraising and generating new ideas for services.

- Handpick their Board members and staff. See these people as working for the founder as much as working for the organization's mission.

- Attract Board members through the founder's dynamic, often charismatic personality – not through focus on the organization's mission.

- Hold occasional staff meetings to report crises and rally the troops.

- Count on whoever seems most loyal and accessible, and motivate by fear and guilt, often without realizing it.

- See their Boards mostly as a source for fundraising, and work to remove Board members who disagree with the founder.

- Have a very difficult time letting go of the strategies that worked to quickly grow the organization, despite evidence that the organization can no longer absorb this rapid growth without major changes.

Ultimately, Founder's Syndrome sets in because the organization becomes dependent, not on the systems and structures of the organization, but on the unique style of the leader – whether the leader is consistently decisive or consistently indecisive.

Typical Traits of Well-Developed Leaders

The following traits are important for the Board members and Chief Executive to have if they are to effectively lead their nonprofits. They are in sharp contrast to leaders with Founder's Syndrome. Traits include:

- Appreciating plans and budgets as guidelines, and realizing that these ultimately make the nonprofit more responsive to the needs of their customers.

- Making proactive decisions based on mission and affordability.

- Making staffing decisions based on staff's responsibilities, training and capabilities.

- Valuing Board and staff members for their strong expertise and feedback.

- Sustaining strong credibility among clients and service providers.

Basic Principles in Developing Leadership

Eventually, most founders realize they must change the way they operate. Many go on to evolve their leadership style to the next level. First, they realize they must change from within. They:

- Understand that the recurring problems are not their fault – they are doing the best they can.

- Are willing to ask for and accept help.

- Communicate often and honestly (often difficult for crisis-driven, "heroic" leaders).

- Engage in stress management, especially forms not related to their jobs.

- Are patient with themselves, their Boards and staff.

- Regularly take time to reflect and learn, particularly about their value to others.

The following guidelines assume that the founder is the person who founded the organization and is also the Chief Executive, reporting to the Board. The Board model includes use of committees, as well. The CEO has staff reporting to him or her. However, as you read the following guidelines, adapt them to the particular model used by the Board and staff (if the nonprofit has staff) of your organization.

For more information, see the section on restoring nonprofit Boards in the guidebook, *Field Guide to Developing, Operating and Restoring Your Board,* from Authenticity Consulting, LLC. Go to the "Publications" link at http://www.authenticityconsulting.com .

Actions Your Board Members Must Take

If the organization seems stuck in a highly reactive way of doing things, addressing the same problems over and over again, then it may be facing Founder's Syndrome. This requires a major change in the way that the Board and Chief Executive operate together. Making this change in leadership style is usually confusing, lonely and stressful for the founder, whether the founder is the CEO, someone on the Board or a group of people on the Board. The Board can be the founder's greatest source of help if they:

1. **Understand and take full responsibility for the role of Board member.**
    Insist on highly condensed and focused Board training sessions on an annual basis in order to review the roles and responsibilities of a governing Board. Undertake a yearly self-evaluation of the Board to ensure it is operating effectively.

2. **Once a year, conduct a key risk management exercise.**
    Pretend the founder suddenly left the organization. Who will/can quickly step in? Are you sure? What activities is the staff really doing to carry out programs? What grants does the organization have to perform against and when must you report on them? What is the cash flow situation? What stakeholders must be contacted? Where are the files/records?

3. **Know what is going on in the organization or how to quickly come up to speed.**
    Ensure job descriptions are up-to-date. Have staff complete weekly or biweekly written status reports. Ensure yearly written performance reviews are completed. Ensure regular staff meetings are held and actions are written. Is a staff member being cultivated as an assistant Chief Executive? Is this needed?

4. **Strategic planning is one of the best ways to engage the Board and take stock.**
    Conduct regular and realistic strategic planning with the Board and staff. Ensure the planning is carried out according to the nature of the organization, in a realistic and practical fashion. Focus on the top three or four issues facing the organization. Although most organizations scope plans to the coming three years, focus careful planning on the next six to 12 months. Establish clear goals and strategies, and work hard to establish objectives and timelines.

5. **Develop a highly participative Finance Committee or task force.**
    You might need to do the same with a Fundraising Committee or task force, too. Too often, Boards are extremely reluctant to face the founder by getting involved in finances. However, organizational problems are often revealed as financial problems. If a founder struggles or eventually leaves the organization, the finances are usually the first area to show major problems. Therefore, closely review the financial statements, especially cash flow.

6. **Do not be part of the problem!**
    Do not take on the traits of the crisis-driven founder and staff, or worse yet, just "numb out." Meet consistently and make decisions based on mission, planning and affordability, not on urgency. Avoid the notion of any quick fixes, such as hiring an associate director with "people skills." This does not address the problem and may make things even worse.

7. **Help Board members and staff to keep up their hopes.**
Regularly communicate with each other (through appropriate channels). Remind each other that the recurring problems are the result of the organization's success and that current changes are to best serve the needs of its clients. Staff members' morale will improve as they perceive stability, security, and progress.

8. **Support the founder with ongoing coaching and affirmation.**
The founder will change to the extent that he or she feels safe, understands the reasons for change, and accepts help along the way. Consider a Board Personnel Committee or task force to provide ongoing coaching to the founder (but not to replace his or her responsibilities and accountabilities). Include at least one or two experienced organizational leaders on this committee. Note that the founder is not changing roles, but priorities.

9. **Carefully monitor implementation and deviations from plans.**
Do not hold the founder to always be doing what is in the plan or budget – but do hold the founder to be always explaining deviations and how they can be afforded.

10. **Implement development and evaluation plans for the founder.**
Include the founder's input. Focus on the founder's accountability to implementing the plans or explaining deviations from them. Evaluate the founder as to how well he/she met his/her strategic objectives and responsibilities in his/her job description.

11. **Consider policies to carefully solicit feedback from staff to the Board.**
Consider having staff representatives on Board committees or task forces. Consider a 360-degree evaluation process for the Chief Executive, wherein staff provides feedback about the Chief Executive's performance. Establish a grievance procedure where staff can approach the Board about concerns if they can prove they have tried to work with the Chief Executive to resolve these issues.

12. **Closely monitor key indicators of successful change.**
Ensure ongoing communications between Board members and the founder, sound financial management, implementation of plans and policies, and stable turnover of staff. Perhaps the most useful indicator is continued positive feedback from customers.

13. **If problems recur, take action.**
If, after attempting to follow the above suggestions, the same major problems recur over the next six to nine months, then take major actions regarding the founder's position in the organization. The Board should have been highly involved in strategic planning, financial management, fundraising, authorizing policies, reviewing programs, and evaluating the Chief Executive. If the founder's leaving would cause the organization to fold, then the Board has not been doing its job all along.

Actions Your Founder Must Take

The major actions mentioned below are intended to help the organization to retain focus and direction, and become more stable and proactive. Each nonprofit follows the practices according to its own nature and needs. The practices are not developed overnight and are never done perfectly. They should be followed to the extent that they are supportive, not restrictive. Start simple, but start! The following guidelines assume that the founder is the CEO, which, of course, is not always the case.

1. **Accept a mentor outside the organization and an advocate within.**
    Founder's Syndrome comes from doing what is natural for you. Changing your leadership approach may be rather unnatural. Seek and accept help.

2. **Ensure a client-driven organization.**
    Always focus on the needs of clients. Regularly ask clients what they need and how the organization can meet their needs. Establish straightforward and realistic means to evaluate services. Start with basic questionnaires to gather clients' impressions. Interview some clients to get their "story."

3. **Set direction through planning.**
    Support the Board to carry out strategic planning. Ensure staff input as well. Conduct regular staff meetings to hear staff input. Cultivate a strong Finance Committee, Fundraising Committee or task forces and help them to fully understand the organization's finances and fundraising plans.

4. **Organize resources to meet goals.**
    Develop job descriptions with staff input to ensure mutual understanding of responsibilities. Develop staff-driven procedures for routine, but critical tasks.

5. **Motivate leadership and staff to meet goals.**
    Delegate to staff members by helping them understand the purpose of tasks. Get their input as to how the tasks can be completed. Give them the authority to complete the tasks. In regular staff meetings, celebrate successes! Bring in clients to tell staff how the organization helped meet their needs. Conduct regular performance reviews with staff to ensure organizational and staff needs are being met. In regular staff meetings, share status information and conduct day-to-day planning.

6. **Guide resources to meet goals.**
    Share management challenges with the Board and ask for policies to guide management. Work from the strategic plan and develop an associated budget to earmark funds.

7. **Think transition!**
    Help the Board to regularly undertake contingency planning, including thinking about what the organization will do if/when you are gone. Have the Board members pretend that, for some unknown reason, you were suddenly gone. What would they do? How?

Actions Your Staff Members Might Take

If the founder is on the Board or is the CEO, then other staff still might play a major role in helping the organization to recover. However, staff may be in somewhat of a high-risk situation because the founder (who often values loyalty at least as much as effectiveness) may perceive staff actions as hurting the organization, rather than helping it. Therefore, staff are advised to proceed with caution.

The syndrome can be quite stressful for staff. They can lose perspective amidst the continued confusion and anxiety in the workplace. If they have been in the organization long enough, they, too, become part of the problem. Therefore, it is important for staff to get perspective on the nature and extent of the problem.

1. **Work hard to identify an external mentor and an internal staff advocate.**
   Bounce ideas off someone else whose judgment you highly revere.

2. **Get clear perspective by privately writing down a list of problems you perceive.**
   Privately record your concerns. In order to minimize your own biases, record only what you have seen with your eyeballs, not just felt with your heart. Document only those problems that seem to be persistent and/or which various people have tried to resolve.

3. **Match your list with previous section, "Some Troublesome Traits Among Founders."**
   How many of the symptoms match those recorded in your list? Consider sharing your list and results with someone whom you trust. Do they agree with your approach and results? It is up to you to conclude if the organization has the syndrome or not. Whether the organization has the syndrome or not, if there are enough other persistent problems, you may still want to take action.

4. **Assess if you want to stay in the organization and help it recover.**
   This requires that you carefully reflect on why you are in the organization, what you can do to help the organization recover, the likelihood of it recovering and how well you manage your own stress.

5. **If you stay in the organization and help it to recover, use the organization's structure.**
   That is, communicate your suggestions with peers and your immediate supervisor, whether that is the founder or not. Give them a chance to address your concerns. Promptly go to the Board only if symptoms of the problem result in discrimination or harassment of you and if your personnel policies include a grievance procedure for you to go directly contact the Board. You might consider a letter to the Board if you resign, but this may hurt your career.

6. **Give suggestions from "Actions Board Must Take", "Actions Founders Must Take."**
   Do not provide all of the suggestions at once. Always associate your suggestions with a description of how they can constructively advance the mission of the organization. Do not personalize your descriptions of concerns by blaming them on someone. Make your suggestions in writing, for example, in status reports or in memos. Put a date on the suggestions so you can keep perspective on whether the suggestions are acted on or not.

7. **Monitor whether the organization is recovering or not.**
   Have you given the organization time to address concerns? Has the organization made substantial changes and symptoms have decreased? Or, do you see the same symptoms?

8. **Update your resume and consider looking for another job.**
    Keeping your own health and happiness is the best thing you can do for yourself and the community. You will become ill if you stay in the organization. Your leaving may actually contribute to the organization's recovering if other staff members realize why you left. Even if you decide to stay, the knowing that you can leave might shift your attitude enough to approach the situation with fresh energy or perspective.

9. **Do not "burn bridges."**
    It is extremely compelling to write a blistering letter to all members of the Board and various staff members, explaining each and every problem in the organization. This may temporarily relieve you of your frustration, but it may also hurt your credibility with key members of the organization's community. If you communicate your concerns and reasons for leaving, be respectful and tactful.

Bibliography

Various categories of readings are included below. The following readings are by no means all of the important works in each category. However, the listed works will provide you a strong start to understanding information in that particular category. Also the bibliographies of many of the works listed below will help you to find related works from which you can continue to develop your knowledge about the particular category.

Boards of Directors

Building Better Boards, David A. Nadler (Editor), Jossey-Bass, 2005.

This book describes how Boards can become high-performing teams. Lists the influences that have the greatest effects on Board success and principles to improve Boards. Although the book is based on research with organizations that have many resources, the principles still apply to small- and medium-sized nonprofits.

Exploring the Puzzle of Board Design: What's Your Type, David Renz, Nonprofit Quarterly, Winter 2004, Vol 11, Issue 4. (Also at http://www.nonprofitquarterly.org/section/655.html)

The article reminds consultants that there is no one right design for Boards. The article clearly conveys the wide range of types, or personalities, of Board of Directors and how to categorize them. Includes a well-designed graph for discerning the type of any governing Board.

Field Guide to Developing, Operating and Restoring Your Nonprofit Board, Carter McNamara, Authenticity Consulting, LLC, Minneapolis, MN, 2008.

This guidebook explains how to start a Board and nonprofit organization, or to fix a struggling Board. It also explains all of the activities required for effective Board operations, such as staffing, meetings, decisions and self-evaluation. It includes 20 of the most common samples required by Boards of Directors.

Governance Models: What's Right for Your Board?, Nathan Garber, Nathan Garber & Associates.

Describes Board models, including: Advisory, Cooperative, Patron, Management Team and Policy, and includes guidelines for how to pick the best model. Free at http://garberconsulting.com/governance%20models%20what's%20right.htm .

Governing for Results: A Director's Guide to Good Governance, Mel D. Gill, Trafford Publishing, 2005.

Well-researched guide to a practical understanding of the roles of a governing Board and the wide range of different Board structures actually used by Boards (one of the best books for understanding the different structures). Explains the practices and structures to achieve good governance, and suggests the extent of governance versus management for each structure.

Quick Overview of Governance Models/Board Types, Mel Gill, Synergy Associates.

Overviews of Board models, including: Operational, Management, Collective, Constituent Representational, Traditional, Results-Based, Policy Governance, Fundraising and Advisory. Free at http://www.synergyassociates.ca/publications/OverviewGovernanceModels.htm .

The Strategic Board: The Step-by-Step Guide to High-Impact Governance, Mark Light, Wiley, 2001.

Includes broad guidelines for achieving effective governance, such as establishing clear vision and values for strong leadership, effective delegation through clarity of roles and responsibilities, and translating Board decisions throughout the organization via clear management plans and measures.

Capacity Building

Building Capacity in Nonprofit Organizations, edited by Carol J. De Vita, Urban Institute Press, 2001.

Written especially for foundations considering capacity building programs, but relevant to all providers. Depicts overall framework for nonprofit capacity building. Suggests eight aspects of effective capacity building programs and describes continuum of capacity building services. Free at http://www.urban.org/UploadedPDF/building_capacity.PDF .

Building for Impact: The Future of Effectiveness for Nonprofits and Foundations, Grantmakers for Effective Organizations, 2002.

Report on the 2002 National Conference of grantmakers that highlights expected trends in philanthropy, suggesting more priority on nonprofit performance. Offers four possible scenarios that grantmakers might follow in the future. Challenges grantmakers to focus on their own organizational effectiveness for capacity building. Free at http://www.geofunders.org/_uploads/documents/live/conference%20report.pdf .

Building the Capacity of Capacity Builders, Conservation Company, June 2003.

Provides overview of nonprofit capacity builders, suggests four key capacities for effective nonprofit organizations: leadership, adaptive, managerial and technical. Includes recommendations for capacity builders to improve services. Free at http: //www.tccgrp.com/pdfs/buildingthecapacityofcapacitybuilders.pdf

Echoes from the Field: Proven Capacity Building Principles for Nonprofits, Environmental Support Center and Innovation Network, Inc., 2002.

Suggests nine principles of effective capacity building. An excellent read for those who want to understand the broad context of capacity building and the realities of providing capacity building programs. Free at http://www.envsc.org/bestpractices.pdf .

Effective Capacity Building in Nonprofit Organizations, Venture Philanthropy Partners, 2001.

Suggests seven overall elements of nonprofit capacity building. Describes lessons-learned from nonprofits that have engaged in successful capacity building efforts. Provides comprehensive assessment instrument to assess organizational effectiveness according to the seven elements. Free at http://vppartners.org/learning/reports/capacity/capacity.html .

Lessons from the Street: Capacity Building and Replication, Milton S. Eisenhower Foundation.

Based on street-level experience from 1990 to 2000 in offering technical assistance and training for capacity building, especially with grassroots organizations in inner cities. Offers top ten lessons and recommendations for funders regarding assistance and replication of programs. Free at http://www.eisenhowerfoundation.org/aboutus/publications/lessons_intro.html .

Mapping Nonprofit Capacity Builders: A Study by LaSalle University's Nonprofit Center, Kathryn Szabat and Laura Otten (1999?).

> Overview of research to identify "the universe of capacity builders ..." Mentions capacity builders by general characteristics and reports results of research, with percentage of capacity builders in various categories. This is an interesting perusal for those wanting a quick impression of the world of capacity builders. Free at http://www.np-org-dev.com/survey.doc .

Reflections on Capacity Building, The California Wellness Foundation.

> Lists numerous lessons-learned from TCWF's implementation of capacity building services. Reflections and lessons-learned are numerous and meaningful for funders providing capacity building services. Free at http://www.tcwf.org/reflections/2001/april/index.htm .

Results of an Inquiry into Capacity Building Programs for Nonprofits, by Susan Doherty and Stephen Meyer of Communities for Action.

> Describes organizational capacity and why it is important. Explains why capacity building does not happen naturally and offers seven overall elements that work for capacity building efforts. Brief overviews of major areas of capacity building. Free at http://www.effectivecommunities.com/ECP_CapacityBuildingInquiry.pdf .

Strengthening Nonprofit Organizations: A Funder's Guide to Capacity Building, by Carol Lukas, Amherst H. Wilder Foundation.

> Describes types of capacity building services. Provides straightforward explanation of process for funders to consider offering capacity building programs, and adds general strategic process for funders to identify which capacity building services to offer.

Consulting

Consultants Calling, Geoffrey M., Jossey-Bass, 1990.

> Does an excellent job helping readers closely examine why they want to be a consultant. Includes numerous guidelines to set up a practice, understand organizations and clients, maintain balance and boundaries, and more.

Consulting for Dummies, Bob Nelson and Peter Economy, IDG Books, 1997.

> Highly readable resource that touches on the most important aspects of setting up and marketing a consulting business. The *Dummies* series is well-known for being easy to reference and well-designed.

Consulting With Nonprofits: A Practitioners Guide, Carol Lukas, Amherst H. Wilder Foundation, 1998.

> Easy-to-read, general overview of one perspective on stages of consulting to nonprofits, including the "artistry" of working with others and the business and marketing of consulting with nonprofits.

Flawless Consulting: Guide to Getting Your Expertise Used, Second Edition, Peter Block, Jossey-Bass Publishers, 2000.

> Block's break-through book first heralded in the innovative approach of collaborative consulting. His book is probably the most referenced general resource when first training consultants to conduct collaborative and effective consulting projects.

How to Succeed as an Independent Consultant, Herman Holtz, Third Edition, Wiley, 1993.

This well-known resource goes into more depth than most other consulting books about the roles of a consultant, starting a business, writing proposals and contracts and reports, etc.

Jumping the Job Track, Peter C. Brown, Crown, 1994.

Comprehensive guidelines for considering changing jobs to consulting, including conducting a skills inventory, thinking about your markets, setting up shop, etc. Includes many real-life examples.

Financial Management

Bookkeeping Basics: What Every Nonprofit Bookkeeper Needs to Know, Debra L. Ruegg and Lisa M. Venkatrathnam, Amherst H. Wilder Foundation, 2003.

The book explains important practices and procedures in bookkeeping and the overall bookkeeping cycle, generating the most important nonprofit financial statements, and how to establish the most important financial controls in a nonprofit organization.

Streetsmart Financial Basics for Nonprofit Managers, Thomas A. McLaughlin, John Wiley and Sons, 1995.

The book describes how to make management decisions based on financial information. The book includes numerous, easy-to-reference diagrams, along with numerous examples. Includes online copies of useful checklists and worksheets.

Fundraising

Fundraising Basics: A Complete Guide, Second Edition, Barbara L. Ciconte and Jeanne Jacob, Jones and Bartlett, 2001.

This book explains the basics of fundraising, including critical foundations for successful fundraising, types of fundraising, how to plan your fundraising activities, and trends in fundraising. Includes fundraising on the Internet. Includes case studies and real-life examples.

Fundraising for Dummies, Second Edition, John Mutz and Katherine Murray, Jossey-Bass, 2000.

This book describes the most important basic considerations and activities to plan and conduct your fundraising. Includes how to get the Board engaged in fundraising, and how to research major donors and write grants. Similar to other *Dummies* books, this book includes a lot of handy tips and conventional wisdom.

Raise More Money: The Best of the Grassroots Fundraising Journal, Kim Klein and Stephanie Roth, Jossey-Bass, 2001.

This book combines the best advice from Klein's seminal publications on grassroots fundraising. The advice is always specific and easy-to-apply. This is a must-read for anyone working with small- to medium-sized nonprofit organizations. The advice still applies to nonprofits of any size.

Leadership and Supervision (includes staffing and volunteers)

Executive Director's Survival Guide, Mim Carlson and Margaret Donohoe, Jossey-Bass, 2003.

This book was written for the Chief Executive Officer who wants to understand all aspects of the role and develop into a wise and effective leader. Includes guidelines to avoid burnout, identify organizational effectiveness, lead organizational change and work effectively with the Board.

Executive Leadership in Nonprofit Organizations: New Strategies for Shaping Executive-Board Dynamics, Robert D. Herman and Richard D. Heimovics, Jossey-Bass, 1991.

The is one of the first publications to suggest that, although theory and law assert that the Board governs the organization, the quality of the working relationship between the Board and Chief Executive Officer is one of the most important determinants of the effectiveness of the organization.

Marketing (including advertising and promotions)

Field Guide to Nonprofit Program Design, Marketing and Evaluation, Carter McNamara, Authenticity Consulting, LLC, Minneapolis, MN, 2003.

There are few resources about program planning, so this book is unique. It addresses the activities of program design, marketing and evaluation as they should be – as activities that are highly integrated with each other. This guidebook includes complete step-by-step guidelines and online worksheets to successfully conduct activities on an ongoing basis.

Successful Marketing Strategies For Nonprofit Organizations, Barry J. McLeish, Wiley, 1995.

The author argues that marketing is not just an activity, but should be an orientation among all management. Guidelines describe how to develop a strategic marketing plan from analyzing the external and internal environments of the nonprofit and then producing a plan that best fits both environments.

Workbook for Nonprofit Organizations: Volume 1 Develop the Plan, Gary J. Stern, Amherst H. Wilder Foundation, 1990.

This book explains the theory and importance of marketing in nonprofits. It describes a five-step process to develop a marketing plan: establishing goals, positioning the nonprofit, doing a marketing audit, developing the plan, and associating a promotions campaign. Includes worksheets.

Organizational Development and Change

Appreciative Inquiry: Change at the Speed of Imagination, Jane M. Watkins and Bernhard J. Mohr, Jossey-Bass, 2001.

> Appreciative Inquiry (AI) has become a prominent movement in organizational change and development. It offers a truly new paradigm in how we see organizations and its members, and as a result, how we plan and change organizations. There are numerous resources on AI, but this book is one of the most well-organized and understandable, replete with various models to apply AI and how to explain AI to other people.

Changing the Essence, Richard Beckhard and Wendy Pritchard, Jossey-Bass, Inc., 1992.

> This is one of the seminal works on organizational change and written by the "father" of the field of Organization Development. It includes a comprehensive and strategic overview of key considerations in achieving successful organizational change.

Making Sense of Life's Changes, William Bridges, Addison Wesley, 1980.

> Bridge's book provides an excellent overview of the psychological and sociological aspects and considerations for successful organizational change. His book, combined with Block's (in the "Consulting" section in this Appendix) and Beckhard's (above), comprise a comprehensive "toolkit" for conducting successful organizational change.

Organizational Culture and Leadership, 3rd Edition, Edgar H. Schein, Jossey-Bass, 2004.

> Seminal work on the subject. Defines culture, levels and dimensions, key issues to manage during change, relationship between leadership and culture, and how leaders create organizational cultures.

Organization Development and Change, Seventh Edition, Thomas G. Cummings and Christopher G. Worley, South-Western Educational Publishing, 2000.

> This is a classic, up-to-date text on the field and practices of Organization Development (OD). Includes history, movements and major research findings. It is a must-read for the reader serious about becoming a professional in the field of Organization Development.

Power of Appreciative Inquiry: Practical Guide to Positive Change, Diana Whitney and Amanda Trosten-Bloom, Berrett Koehler, 2002.

> This is a comprehensive, yet practical, book about AI. It provides numerous approaches to AI across a wide variety of organizations, and includes case studies for the approaches, as well.

Practicing Organization Development: A Guide for Consultants, William J. Rothwell, Roland Sullivan and Gary N. McLean, Jossey-Bass, 1995.

> This book is focused on guidelines and other advice for the practitioners who seek "how to" resources to conduct successful organizational development projects.

Reframing Organizations, Lee Bolman and Terrence Deal, Jossey-Bass, 1991.

> This book has been a wonderful gift to organizational consultants because it reminds them that different people can have quite different perspectives on the same organization. Those different perspectives can result in widely varying interpretations and suggestions about organizational change.

The 5 Life Stages of Nonprofit Organizations, Judith Sharken Simon, Amherst H. Wilder Foundation, 2001.

Provides a highly understandable and meaningful overview of life stages of nonprofits and includes a comprehensive, yet practical, life-stage assessment tool with examples, analysis and advice.

Program Evaluation

Evaluation of Capacity Building: Lessons from the Field, Deborah Linnell, Alliance for Nonprofit Management, 2003.

Describes results of research among a variety of capacity builders, along with descriptions of the general activities of each builder and what they are doing to evaluate their particular programs. Numerous lessons-learned are conveyed, as well as suggestions for further research.

Field Guide to Nonprofit Program Design, Marketing and Evaluation, Carter McNamara, Authenticity Consulting, LLC, Minneapolis, MN, 2003.

There are few resources about program planning, so this book is unique. It addresses the activities of program design, marketing and evaluation as they should be – as activities that are highly integrated with each other. This guidebook includes complete step-by-step guidelines and online worksheets to successfully conduct activities on an ongoing basis.

Qualitative Evaluation and Research Methods, Michael Quinn Patton, Sage Publications, 1990.

Provides comprehensive overview of qualitative research and data collection methods, many of which can be used in practical approaches to market research and program evaluation.

Program Planning and Design

Field Guide to Nonprofit Program Design, Marketing and Evaluation, Carter McNamara, Authenticity Consulting, LLC, Minneapolis, MN, 2003.

There are few resources about program planning, so this book is unique. It addresses the activities of program design, marketing and evaluation as they should be – as activities that are highly integrated with each other. This guidebook includes complete step-by-step guidelines and online worksheets to successfully conduct activities on an ongoing basis.

Designing and Planning Programs for Nonprofit and Government Organizations, Edward J. Pawlak, Robert D. Vinter, Jossey-Bass, 2004.

Book focuses on nonprofit and government organizations. Suggests step-by-step activities for major phases, including planning, implementation and program operations. Ideally suited to large organizations with complex programs and systems.

Strategic Planning

Field Guide to Nonprofit Strategic Planning and Facilitation, Carter McNamara, Authenticity Consulting, LLC, Minneapolis, Minnesota, 2003.

> Comprehensive, step-by-step guidebook to facilitate a Strategic Plan that is relevant, realistic and flexible. Includes a variety of planning models that can be used and guidelines to select which model is best. Also includes online tools that can be downloaded for each planner.

Five Most Important Questions You Will Ever Ask About Your Nonprofit Organization: Participant's Workbook, Peter F. Drucker Foundation, Jossey-Bass Publishers, 1993.

> Top-level workbook guides organizations through answering five key strategic questions: What is our business (mission)? Who is our customer? What does the customer consider value? What have been our results? What is our Plan?

Strategic Management: Formulation, Implementation, and Control, Fourth Edition, John A. Pearce II and Richard B. Robinson, Jr., Irwin Publishing, 1991.

> Explains the strategic planning process in the overall context of strategic management. Explains complete strategic management cycle, primarily for large for-profit corporations. Much of the information applies to nonprofits, including processes that nonprofits tend not to do, but should.

Strategic Planning for Public and Nonprofit Organizations: A Guide to Strengthening and Sustaining Organizational Achievement, 3rd Edition, John Bryson, Jossey-Bass Publishers, 2004.

> Provides an extensive, well-organized and in-depth explanation of a 10-step strategic planning cycle that can be used in planning with organizations ranging from small to large. This updated version has new information on stakeholder analyses, strategizing, collaborative planning and balanced scorecard.

Strategic Planning Workbook for Nonprofit Organizations, Revised and Updated, Bryan Barry, Wilder Foundation, St. Paul, MN, 1997 (651-642-4022).

> Well-organized and readable, top-level workbook provides guidelines and worksheets to conduct strategic planning for a variety of types, sizes and designs of nonprofit and public organizations.

Index

Additional Titles Specific to Nonprofits

Field Guide to Nonprofit Strategic Planning and Facilitation

The guide provides step-by-step instructions and worksheets to customize and implement a comprehensive nonprofit strategic plan – that is relevant, realistic and flexible for the nonprofit organization. The guide describes the most useful traditional and holistic approaches to strategic planning. It also includes the most important tools and techniques to facilitate strategic planning in an approach that ensures strong participation and ownership among all of the planners. Emphasis is as much on implementation and follow-through of the plan as on developing the plan document. Hardcopy and online worksheets help you to collect and organize all of the results of their planning process.

284 pp, softcover, revised 2007   Item #7120, ISBN 978-1-933719-06-1 / 1-933179-06-0 $32

Field Guide to Developing, Operating and Restoring Your Nonprofit Board

This guide will help your Board to be highly effectively in all of the most important aspects of governance, including strategic planning, programs, marketing, staffing, finances, fundraising, evaluations, transparency, sustainability and lobbying. It includes guidelines to detect and fix broken Boards; select the best Board model for the nonprofit to implement; define how much the Board members should be involved in management, depending on the Board model; decide whether to use committees or not, and if so, which ones; establish specific, appropriate goals for Board committees; conduct comprehensive succession planning of the CEO position; ensure legal compliance to the Sarbanes-Oxley act; and ensure highly ethical behavior of Board members. Comprehensive guidelines and materials are written in an easy-to-implement style, resulting in a highly practical resource that can be referenced at any time during the life of a Board and organization.

296 pp, softcover, revised 2008   Item #7110, ISBN 978-1-933719-05-4 / 1-933719-05-2 $32

Field Guide to Nonprofit Program Design, Marketing and Evaluation

Nonprofits have long needed a clear, concise – and completely practical – guidebook about all aspects of designing, marketing and evaluating nonprofit programs. Now they have such a resource. This guide can be used to evolve strategic goals into well-designed programs that are guaranteed to meet the needs of clients, develop credible nonprofit business plans and fundraising proposals, ensure focused and effective marketing, evaluate the effectiveness and efficiencies of current programs in delivery of services to clients, evaluate program performance against goals and outcomes, and understand how a program really works in order to improve or duplicate the program.

252 pp, softcover, revised 2006   Item #7170, ISBN 978-1-933719-08-5 / 1-933719-08-7 $32

Field Guide to Consulting and Organizational Development With Nonprofits

This highly practical book combines the tools and techniques of the field of Organization Development with the power of systems thinking and principles for successful change in nonprofits. The book also addresses many of the problems with traditional approaches to consulting and leading. The result is a proven, time-tested roadmap for consultants and leaders to accomplish significant change in nonprofits. You can use this book to accomplish change in small or large nonprofit organizations, for instance organizations that 1) have a variety of complex issues, 2) must ensure a strong foundation from which to develop further, 3) must evolve to the next life cycle, 4) need a complete "turnaround," 5) must address Founder's Syndrome or 6) want to achieve an exciting grand goal.

517 pp, softcover, 2005   Item #7180, ISBN 978-1-933719-00-9 / 1-933719-00-1 $58

Additional Titles for Business, Government and General Use

Field Guide to Leadership and Supervision in Business

Top-level executives, middle managers and entry-level supervisors in organizations need the "nuts and bolts" for carrying out effective leadership and supervision, particularly in organizations with limited resources. This guide includes topics often forgotten in trendy publications, including: time and stress management, staffing, organizing, team building, setting goals, giving feedback, and much more.

204 pp, comb-bound, 2002   Item #7430, ISBN 978-1-933719-23-8 / 1-933719-23-0 $25

Field Guide to Consulting and Organizational Development

This highly practical book combines the tools and techniques of the field of Organization Development with the power of systems thinking and principles for successful change in for-profits and government agencies. The book also addresses many of the problems with traditional approaches to consulting and leading. The result is a proven, time-tested roadmap for consultants and leaders to accomplish significant change. You can use this book to accomplish change in small or large organizations, whether the organization is dealing with a variety of complex issues or striving to achieve goals for the future.

499 pp, softcover, 2006   Item #7480, ISBN 978-1-933719-20-7 / 1-933719-20-6 $58

Additional Titles About Action Learning and Peer Coaching Groups

Authenticity Circles Program Developer's Guide

Step-by-step guidelines to design, build, manage and troubleshoot an Action Learning-based, peer coaching group program. The program can be used by consultants or an organization's leaders for training enrichment, problem solving, support and networking among peers.

127 pp, comb-bound, 2002   Item #7730, ISBN 978-1-933719-10-8 / 1-933719-10-9 $25

Authenticity Circles Facilitator's Guide

This guide describes how to organize, facilitate and evaluate peer coaching groups. Groups can be facilitated by an external facilitator or groups can self-facilitate themselves. It can also be used to recruit, develop and support facilitators of peer coaching groups. The guide includes appendices with worksheets for the facilitator's use and a handy Quick Reference tool.

114 pp, comb-bound, 2002   Item #7720, ISBN 978-1-933719-11-5 / 1-933719-11-7 $20

Authenticity Circles Member's Guide and Journal

This guide provides step-by-step guidelines for group members to get the most out of their Action Learning-based, peer coaching groups, including how to select goals to be coached on, how to get coached and how to coach others. The guide includes a journal of worksheets to capture the learning of the group members and a handy Circles Quick Reference tool.

110 pp, comb-bound, 2004   Item #7710, ISBN 978-1-933719-12-2 / 1-933719-12-5 $15

Coming in 2009 – Watch our website for news!

Field Guide to Leadership and Supervision in Business

Enhanced edition in softcover!

Field Guide to Strategic Planning and Facilitation

For business now too!

To order

To get your copies of these and other practical publications, contact us:

Online: http://www.authenticityconsulting.com/pubs.htm

Phone: 800.971.2250 toll-free in North America or +1.763.971.8890 direct

Fax: +1.763.592.1661

Mail: Authenticity Consulting, LLC
4008 Lake Drive Avenue North
Minneapolis, MN   55422-1508
USA